What Customers Value Most

HOW TO ACHIEVE BUSINESS TRANSFORMATION BY FOCUSING ON PROCESSES THAT TOUCH YOUR CUSTOMERS

- Satisfied Customers
- Increased Revenue
- Improved Profitability

Stanley A. Brown

John Wiley & Sons

Toronto • NewYork • Chichester • Brisbane • Singapore

John Wiley & Sons Canada Limited
22 Worcester Road
Etobicoke, Ontario
M9W 1L1

Canadian Cataloguing in Publication Data
Brown, Stanley A., 1946-
    What customers value most
Includes bibliographical references and index.
ISBN 0-471-64123-5

1. Customer service.   2. Organizational effectiveness.
I. Title.
HF5415.5.B76 1995   658.8'12   C95-932687-1

Production Credits
Cover & Text Design: JAQ
Electronic Assembly: Vesna Mayer
Printer: Tri-graphic Printing Ltd.

Printed and bound in Canada
10 9 8 7 6 5 4 3 2 1

Contents

Acknowledgements

Success and the accomplishment of one's goals cannot be achieved without the support, encouragement, and sacrifice of others. I would therefore like to acknowledge and express my deep appreciation to the many people who made this project possible.

To my associates at Coopers & Lybrand, and in particular, Mike Stoneham, David W. Smith, and Hugh Bolton for their encouragement and support.

To the best practices organizations mentioned throughout this book, for their willingness to share their experiences and lessons learned.

To my colleagues, clients, and to my team at the Centre for Excellence in Customer Satisfaction, for their insight and contributions.

To my editor, Karen Milner and her associates at John Wiley & Sons Canada, Ltd. for including me in their family.

To Cynthia Wolff, for her suggestions and critique in the early stages of this book's development.

To the individuals that read this book, for their desire to provide "What Customer's Value Most."

And most of all, to my family, in particular my wife Rhonda and children Lowell, Brian, Cynthia and Neil, for their support during those lost weekends and vacations.

This book is dedicated to A.B. and L.B. who helped to establish its foundation.

Preface

This is not a book on reengineering; it is not a book on customer service, quality, or any of the other buzz-words or latest trends. It is a book on how to achieve success—enhanced revenue and improved profitability.

This book does not deal with classic "slash-and-burn" reengineering, by decreasing costs, cutting the fat out of the organization, downsizing, or outsourcing. This book deals with the positive ways that organizations can reengineer to enhance revenue and improve profitability. It focuses on positive, not negative, activities that can and should be undertaken within your organization. It deals with why and how organizations must reach out and touch the customer and the benefits that can be derived from this course of action.

There are enough books on the market today that reflect the latest tools and techniques, fads, and theoretical thinking. This book, however, is not based on theory but rather on proven practices—practices that I have used and continue to use in my day-to-day dealings with clients around the globe.

This book deals with what customers value most:
- a company that is easy to do business with;
- a company that has devoted time and attention to improving processes that touch the customer (both internal and external customers);
- a company that is not afraid to learn from the best practices of others—not for the purpose of decreasing costs, but increasing revenue and profitability.

It is based on actual results—the best practices of organizations that have been successful in achieving performance improvement. Some have been more successful in the areas of rewards and awards, while others have been successful in coaching or in conducting process benchmarking initiatives. These are just a few of the successes listed in this book. Some of these organizations are mentioned explicitly, while others have preferred anonymous credit.

The book has a solid structure and is based on a unique foundation. The first foundation block is one of the most current and extensive research studies on best practices that have led to performance improvement. This study, the Coopers & Lybrand IDEAS study, surveyed over 1800 organizations across North America. IDEAS is an acronym for "Innovative approaches to Deliver Excellence through improved customer practices And total quality Service." Special tabulations of the data were run to highlight the practices that appeared to be most successful in achieving improved profitability and enhanced revenue. Although this analysis proved to be interesting, it did not reveal enough information. Discussions were subsequently held with a substantial number of these "successful" organizations to gain a deeper understanding of their practices. The objective was simple: to try to uncover a formula for success. The research results and some of the key findings from our interviews are interspersed throughout this book and form the overall framework for its structure, brick by brick.

The second foundation block is actual client experiences. These include not only my own clients' experiences but also those of my colleagues in the Coopers & Lybrand International organization. We have included examples of best practices in organizations with whom we have worked as well as some we have researched.

The third block in our foundation is extensive secondary source research. Anecdotes about organizations that have been successful or stories that can provide additional perspectives on various practices have been included throughout the book.

The fourth and final block that secures the foundation of this book, is a four-phase process. Although research observations and anecdotes on their own may be interesting, they do not help an organization to implement these best practices and achieve performance improvement. They are merely a haphazard pile of blocks without structure. When laying our first three foundation blocks, our ultimate objective was to identify if there was some commonality to these practices or a consistent sequence of activities. In other words, was there a best sequence to assembling the blocks? The fourth block, the keystone, provides this sequence: a four-phased process that is discussed throughout the book and again summarized in the final chapter.

The first two chapters lay the important groundwork to the process itself. They highlight the importance of a focus on "what customers value most," the pitfalls to avoid, and the benefits that can be achieved when one listens to the voice of the customer. The next five chapters deal with the four-phase process and the key issues that must be addressed within each phase. This is followed by two chapters that discuss the tools and techniques that facilitate the process, followed by a summary in the final chapter. Furthermore, at the end of each chapter, you will find a checklist that will help you assess your preparedness to advance to the next stage in the process—the placement of the next block.

Finally, you will find an appendix at the end of the book and a comprehensive glossary of terms. This glossary should be used to ensure that management and the rest of the organization share the same vision and vocabulary.

Although this book will not guarantee success, it will, provide you with a blueprint to success. It is written for those who want to be the builders. Pick up the blocks and read the assembly instructions. May your structure be strong and long-lasting.

How to Read This Book

Like most conventional books this one is divided into chapters that discuss key points and issues. Within each chapter, I have also provided editorial comments. In some cases, these comments may be key thoughts or noteworthy quotations. At other times they may be core principles that must be contained in any customer satisfaction initiative or experiences of best practices organizations.

Most chapters also include brief case studies of organizations that further highlight best practices and warrant further consideration. These corporate case studies follow a common format: a brief description of the organization; what led to the company taking action; and the steps the organization took and, where available, the results achieved. Enjoy!

1

It's Time to Change More Than Bandwagons

The Voice of the Customer: Lessons Learned from the Tortoise

WHY THE TORTOISE? We all know that the tortoise is a slow, plodding animal—yet it always ends up where it is headed. Companies can learn a lesson from the tortoise in terms of their customer satisfaction initiatives. The process of improving customer satisfaction often involves complex changes in a company's philosophy and practices—changes that require determination, patience, and time—but, in the end, a quality outcome can be achieved.

Behold the Tortoise, Which Makes No Progress Unless It Sticks its Neck Out

We can learn other things from this animal. The tortoise can only move forward when it "sticks its neck out." That is, it must come out of its shell, and look around and beyond itself to progress. Companies must follow this same principle to improve customer satisfaction. They must look outside the organization, talk to their customers (both internal and external), and learn from the best practices of other organizations.

How Will Learning From the Tortoise Help?

Like the tortoise, high-performance organizations have learned to stick their necks out in order to succeed. These organizations look outside themselves and take direction from their customers.

In contrast, poor-performing organizations stay within their shell, absorbed with improving internal processes but without taking direction from their customers and the changing marketplace. In an effort to find an easy way to achieve performance improvement, many organizations eagerly jump on the latest bandwagon, hoping that the solution is just around the corner in the form of a new methodology or practice. The result, however, is not the ultimate solution, but rather a mixed success. Perhaps the bandwagon itself does not need to change, but rather the direction in which it is being steered, or perhaps it requires a new team and driver.

Let's first briefly examine the events that led up to the present situation. The first bandwagon arrived during the Industrial Age, when we were told that the solution to increased profitability could be found through increased productivity. Through the teachings of Taylor, Hertzberg, and McGregor, we learned how to be more productive and, consequently, more profitable.

Over time, increased competition brought new challenges. A commodity marketplace emerged. At once, the customer entered the equation and played a new role in the long-term viability of the organization. Increased profitability could then only be achieved through differentiation. To accomplish this, companies needed to better understand customer needs and wants. Addressing customer needs and differentiation in the marketplace became the drivers of success. The teachings of marketing gurus such as Kotler et al predominated this period.

But these concepts soon proved to be insufficient. And so, led by a recycled concept from the Industrial Age, internal operating efficiency regained popularity, known this time as reengineering. According to management guru, Michael Hammer, reengineering is "the fundamental rethinking and radical redesign of business processes to achieve dramatic improvements in critical, contemporary measures of performance, such as cost, quality, service, and speed." By definition, reengineering involved a radical change, with no middle ground. With it, the concept of "processes" and breaking down operational silos became part of the business landscape.

The goal of reengineering was to drive down costs, not by five or 10 per cent, but by at least 40 to 50 per cent, by eliminating non-value-added activities or by reinventing the company. Many organizations embraced this concept—some more successfully than others. In most cases, however, reengineering was viewed as a solution in itself, not simply as one of the tools that could be used to effect change and increase profitability. So, with many organizations, the customer was again forgotten. Companies were driven by change for the sake of change, not by customer intimacy or improved service delivery. Process improvement meant cost improvement. The voice and needs of the customer were ultimately lost and customer alienation resulted.

That important deficiency did not go unnoticed by a number of enlightened organizations. In an effort to achieve performance improvement, some organizations aggressively sought and listened to the voice of the customer (we will discuss this further in Chapter 5).

These improvements did not require big "R" radical-change reengineering, but rather little "r" soft reengineering—what some would call tinkering. Although this type of change may have been less dramatic, it was more acceptable to the customer base. The change nurtured increased loyalty, positive word-of-mouth, and customer retention, which were far more valuable and profitable than simple cost reduction. In effect, these organizations did not change the basic design of the wagon but instead the driver and the team, and achieved some exciting results.

Looking Out of the Shell

Let's return to the tortoise and again consider the benefits of "sticking one's neck out" in order to improve. We will first take a brief overview of a landmark research study that I initiated. The study is entitled "Innovative approaches to Deliver Excellence through improved customer practices And total quality Service," which is more commonly known by its acronym, IDEAS.

Over 1800 organizations across North America participated in this study. Respondents were evenly divided between Canada and the United States, and represented a wide range of industry sectors. One-third of respondents were within the manufacturing sector, one-third within the business services sector, and the rest comprised transportation and communication, health care, retail, the public sector, hospitality, and financial services.

Topics in the IDEAS survey covered two major themes:

i) issues relating to internal and external customer practices; and

ii) results related to these practices; that is, what was most effective and least effective.

The survey also identified tools used to improve customer satisfaction and their relative effectiveness. Many of these tools, such as process benchmarking, performance measurement, customer research, and complaint and suggestion systems, will be discussed further in later chapters.

The survey results revealed some fundamental differences between companies that have achieved improved customer satisfaction and those that have been less than successful in this area. One of the most significant findings was that "successful organizations"—those that have improved their customer satisfaction levels (for reasons that will become self-evident later)—were more likely to have started their performance improvement initiatives with customer-focused processes (CFPs). These processes include any that touch the external customer directly, including customer order fulfilment, billing, complaint systems, account management, and sales force management. Another important finding was that companies made a significant investment to actively pursue this customer input and advice, in the range of 2.5 per cent of their annual operating budget. These companies recognized that customers wanted to be part of the process. They had ideas for improvement in these customer-focused processes and had seen these best practices at work in other organizations. Their advice to organizations was twofold. First, embrace the best practices of others, not just within, but also outside your industry. Second, adopt a dual focus that involves processes that affect both external and internal customers—processes that can drive improved profitability and revenue enhancement.

The following figure shows some of the differences between organizations that have been successful in achieving improved customer satisfaction and those that have been less than successful.

The IDEAS study clearly shows that organizations that have succeeded in achieving improved customer satisfaction are more likely to have initiated performance improvement by focusing on customer-related processes.

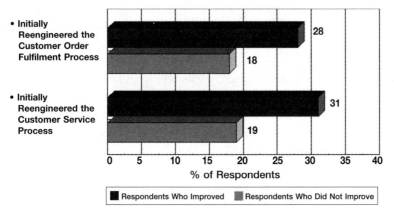

Organizations that are Successful are more Likely to Initially Focus on Customer-Related Processes

• Initially Reengineered the Customer Order Fulfilment Process — 28 / 18

• Initially Reengineered the Customer Service Process — 31 / 19

% of Respondents

■ Respondents Who Improved   ▨ Respondents Who Did Not Improve

Source: 1994 C&L I.D.E.A.S. Study

Our subsequent research and interviews with other best practices organizations indicate that these high-performing companies focused on improving these CFPs and consequently obtained positive results in terms of both improved revenue growth and customer satisfaction. In contrast, poorer-performing, less-than-successful companies tended to focus on systems that particularly affected cost or reduced labour—strategies that could effect only a temporary advantage in the market-place.

Successful companies have also focused their energies on the customer complaints process. These companies practise the philosophy that "what gets measured gets done." That is, they believe that by monitoring performance, employees will focus more on providing improved service. To assist in this monitoring, companies establish elaborate and sophisticated customer feedback systems. Their goal is not to eliminate customer complaints but rather to actively encourage customer feedback. Management is continuously apprised of the types and number of customer complaints in all departments. They also carefully monitor general trends in the quantity of complaints and the corrective action being taken. In many companies, this tracking of information is not just for management—the entire organization needs to be aware of complaint trends (customer complaints will be discussed further in Chapter 8).

Knowing where to begin a process improvement initiative requires an understanding of the company's strengths and weaknesses, particularly relative to its closest competition. This is sometimes known as competitive benchmarking. Companies that are achieving improved customer satisfaction know that a good rating from customers must be measured against the competition's ratings from their customers. For example, if Company A is viewed as an "excellent" service provider, then Company B's "good" rating is obviously not good enough. Company B must understand why Company A is viewed as excellent and, through researching their direct competitors as well as other industry segments, must determine ways to improve. This is called process benchmarking or best practices benchmarking, and it is where less successful companies often drop the ball (we will discuss process benchmarking in Chapter 8).

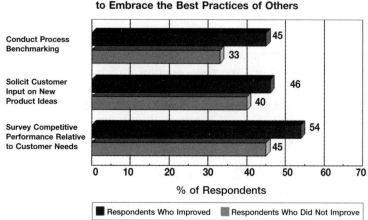

Successful Organizations Show a Greater Willingness to Embrace the Best Practices of Others

Conduct Process Benchmarking: 45 (Respondents Who Improved), 33 (Respondents Who Did Not Improve)

Solicit Customer Input on New Product Ideas: 46 (Respondents Who Improved), 40 (Respondents Who Did Not Improve)

Survey Competitive Performance Relative to Customer Needs: 54 (Respondents Who Improved), 45 (Respondents Who Did Not Improve)

% of Respondents

■ Respondents Who Improved　■ Respondents Who Did Not Improve

Source: 1994 C&L I.D.E.A.S. Study

Customer Satisfaction/Revenue Enhancement Model

Now that we've looked at some new and perhaps familiar concepts—CFPs, competitive benchmarking, and process benchmarking—you might be asking, What should I look at first? and Where do we start?

Our first step is to acknowledge that our primary goal must be increased profitability. At least, that will be the goal of management within the more progressive and proactive organizations. Although you may perceive it to be, increased profitability is not a negative term nor is it a stretch goal. People who merely keep their organization afloat by saying, "All I want is to do as well as we did last year and keep my job," lack the initiative for success. Since "the pursuit of mediocrity is always successful," these organizations will achieve only mediocre performance. People who swim on ahead and push the organization to new heights will be considerably more successful and more profitable. And they will have had more fun striving for these goals.

> The pursuit of mediocrity is always successful.

A word of caution before you forge ahead: as the Cheshire Cat in *The Adventures of Alice in Wonderland* said, "Any road will take you there if you do not know where you are going." Let's first paint the picture of what we should look like when we are finished and work backward from there.

The IDEAS study and our subsequent discussions with a number of best practices organizations led us to some interesting observations about what we should ideally look like. These concepts have been captured in the following figure, entitled "Customer Satisfaction/Revenue Enhancement Model." The way in which you embrace this model and achieve increased revenue and improved profitability are discussed in detail in the following chapters.

Let's look at the model and see how it works to enhance an organization's revenue.

Revenue Enhancement and Improved Profitability

What drives increased sales and revenue? The right products at the right prices? In today's competitive environment, every company can offer this feature. Quality? That's a given—I know of few people who want a poor-quality product.

Instead, people want to deal with organizations that are easy to do business with and, if they find those organizations, they are prepared to tell their friends and associates about them. Positive word-of-mouth is the greatest and least expensive form of advertising. Furthermore, when the organization responds to customer needs, customers are more loyal and willing to give it more of their business. After all, the marketplace offers a wide variety of choices, so when customers are pleased with their choice, they are more likely to stand by that choice—perhaps for life. Why search for something else if you are satisfied?

Consider the following figure, which provides half of the Customer Satisfaction/Revenue Enhancement Model. Revenue enhancement and improved profitability are the by-products of external customer satisfaction. It is not difficult to realize that satisfied customers lead to increased revenue, or in our new terminology, revenue enhancement. But improved customer satisfaction can achieve more than that—it can lead to improved profitability in ways that most organizations do not appreciate.

Customer Satisfaction/Revenue Enhancement Model

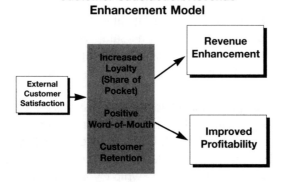

Positive word-of-mouth from your own satisfied customers is essentially free advertising. However, the reverse proves to be very costly. A dissatisfied customer will tell eight to 10 other people about his or her bad customer experience that very same day. Over the next week, possibly 75 more people may become aware of this dissatisfaction, who, in turn, become reluctant to do business with your organization. Remember that if you lose that customer, it costs you five to 12 times more to get a new customer than to keep an existing one. Obviously, customer dissatisfaction represents a significant cost to your organization.

The best way to enhance revenue and increase profitability is to delight your customers and keep them satisfied.

Listen to the Voice of the Customer

By now, I hope I've convinced you that the best way to enhance revenue and improve profitability is through customer satisfaction. But how do you ensure that your organization is aligned to accomplish this? Improve the processes that touch the customer (customer service; account management; sales management, including recruitment and sales targeting; the complaint management system; billing/invoicing) and make it easy for the customer to do business with you. Not surprisingly, your goal should be to become known as "the best customer-focused organization" in your field.

But you cannot do this without input from the person most affected by these processes: the customer. That is, you must listen to the "voice of the customer." By doing this you will pinpoint which activities and which processes affect customer satisfaction and add value in the customer's eyes. Once this is known, you can begin process improvement activities. Without this knowledge, you may be focusing time and effort in the wrong direction.

Where Do Internal Customers (Employees) Fit In?

As we discussed, satisfying external customers is only one-half of the Customer Satisfaction/Revenue Enhancement Model. The other half is satisfying internal customers—your employees. Certainly you will increase revenue and improve profitability by satisfying external customers, but you will not *maximize* either if you neglect your internal customers.

**Customer Satisfaction/Revenue
Enhancement Model**

Internal customer satisfaction results in reduced employee turnover, which means reduced hiring, firing, and retraining costs. That cost saving will also affect profitability in a positive manner. And there's more. Satisfied internal customers treat external customers much better. In turn, those external customers become more satisfied, which feeds back positively to the employees. In fact, the IDEAS study found that organizations that achieve improved customer satisfaction also achieve improved productivity, which positively affects profitability.

The following model shows the impact and importance of the external and internal customer and the role that each plays towards the achievement of improved profitability and enhanced revenue—the Customer Satisfaction/Revenue Enhancement Model.

Customer Satisfaction/Revenue Enhancement Model

But simply reading the model and agreeing with its core principles is not enough. We must capitalize on the key role that the internal customers can play in the Customer Satisfaction/Revenue Enhancement Model. As before, we must listen to the "voice of the customer"—in this case the internal customer—to identify both the barriers and the improvement opportunities in the processes that touch these customers (for example, award and reward systems, suggestion systems, and training systems). These issues will be discussed further in Chapters 6 and 7.

The Role of Management

However, improving processes is not enough. Internal customers must be motivated to use these processes. This is where management plays a vital role. Not just behind the scenes, as coach, mentor, and guiding light, but also through visible involvement. Management must create and encourage a "service culture." They must promote and practise the Golden Rule of Service: "Do unto your internal customers as you would have them do unto your external customers." When this becomes part of the culture of the organization's culture, the organization is aligned and customer satisfaction (internal and external) follows. And, as shown above, revenue enhancement and improved profitability will result.

> The Golden Rule of Service: Do unto your internal customers as you would have them do unto your external customers.

These goals may not necessarily be easy to achieve. In fact, they can be quite difficult to achieve. The following simple analogy helps to explain why. Your organization is like a rubber band. Stretch it or pull it in one direction and then let go—it will snap back to its original shape. Stretch it again, but this time anchor it at both ends, and it will keep its shape. Management becomes the anchors, visible support and encouragement that internal employees require, which must be solid and able to withstand the test of time. Loosen the anchors and the results can be disastrous.

Taking Your Eyes Off the Ball

It is easy to become distracted as you set off on your initiative. One way is to confuse the products or services that customers value with the activities and processes that add value to the customer relationship. In this section, we will show you how to keep focused on your goals.

> People think that customers buy a physical product... They really don't. They buy a total experience. When that total offering satisfies the requirements and expectations of customers, then you have a happy situation. You have achieved quality.
> — David Kearns and David Nadler
> *Prophets in the Dark*

Recently, a financial services organization approached me to assist with an interesting customer satisfaction research initiative. In the past, the organization had conducted various customer satisfaction studies and focus groups and had mailed out surveys. Senior management believed that it had a good understanding of who their customers were, but a poor understanding of what customers value most—in their words, which products or services had perceived value. Through a new research initiative, they hoped to identify which products and services had the greatest perceived value. They believed that by knowing that information, they could obtain valuable input on how and what to sell to various market segments. The logic was simple: they believed that by focusing on the products and services that have perceived value to the customer, sales growth and profits would automatically improve.

Unfortunately, the organization was only half right. When we learn to play baseball, we learn that one of the most important lessons is to keep your eye on the ball. If you do not, you may either miss the ball or hit it in the wrong direction. This same principle applied to this organization as it was setting off on its goal of increased revenue through customer focus. The research requested by the organization was focused in the wrong direction. It had taken its eye off the ball.

The organization did not recognize that the internal processes that deliver these products to market are as important as the products and services themselves. In fact, the processes that touch the customer are the main contributors to what customers value most and, in turn, to customer satisfaction. Rather than strictly concentrating on products and services, the research had to be designed to uncover the activities within the processes that added value and those that irritated, or showed no value to the customer. The focus of the research should have been on those activities and processes that would create increased loyalty and customer retention. By then addressing those activities and eliminating barriers to customer satisfaction, the organization would become easy to do business with, would reap the rewards of positive word-of-mouth, increased loyalty, and improved customer retention.

Now that you have been exposed to the principles underlying the Customer Satisfaction/Revenue Enhancement Model, Chapter 2 will go on to discuss how it works. But first, you may wish to test your readiness with the checklist on the facing page.

> Look at not only the end result but also the activities that lead to this end result. The product or service that the organization delivers is like a service chain...and you are only as good as the weakest link.
>
> Focus your research on finding that weak link and uncover those activities that have the potential to inhibit the organization.

—— CHECKLIST ——

Are you Ready to Start?

This exercise will start you on your way. Answer the following questions about your perception of your organization. You will find a scoring guide and an evaluation of your readiness to proceed at the end of the checklist.

	To a very limited extent				To a very great extent
1. Customer-focused processes are well defined.	1	2	3	4	5
2. The company uses customer satisfaction ratings for driving the improvement effort.	1	2	3	4	5
3. Human resource management practices empower all employees to participate in improvement initiatives.	1	2	3	4	5
4. Employees at all levels receive the education and training they need to participate effectively in customer satisfaction initiatives.	1	2	3	4	5
5. Senior executives are personally and visibly involved in demonstrating that improved customer satisfaction is a high-priority strategic goal.	1	2	3	4	5
6. Customer-service performance measures exist at the organizational, departmental, and individual job levels, and are widely publicized and acted upon.	1	2	3	4	5
7. Hundreds of customer-related improvements are implemented each year.	1	2	3	4	5

—— CHECKLIST ——

8. All employees are aware of their internal customers and suppliers.
    1   2   3   4   5

9. The working environment is conducive to the well-being and morale of all employees.
    1   2   3   4   5

10. The organizational hierarchy does not inhibit effective and constructive two-way communication over process improvement issues.
    1   2   3   4   5

11. The company's values are clearly articulated and understood by all employees. They are constantly and consistently reinforced by the actions of all managers.
    1   2   3   4   5

12. Goals for customer satisfaction make us stretch but are attainable.
    1   2   3   4   5

13. The company encourages close collaboration and teamwork with its suppliers.
    1   2   3   4   5

14. The employee performance appraisal, recognition, and reward processes strongly promote involvement in delivering customer satisfaction.
    1   2   3   4   5

15. Business processes are regularly reviewed to eliminate non-value-adding activities and improve customer satisfaction.
    1   2   3   4   5

—— C H E C K L I S T ——

16. Relationships with customers are managed effectively and involve obtaining information from them to improve products and services.

1 2 3 4 5

17. The management system would be capable of achieving ISO 9000 third-party certification or equivalent.

1 2 3 4 5

18. Customer complaints are welcomed and resolved quickly and positively.

1 2 3 4 5

19. Effective processes for determining current and future customer requirements and expectations are applied both systematically and rigorously.

1 2 3 4 5

20. The strategic and business planning processes have a strong focus on customer service and produce clear objectives for improvement.

1 2 3 4 5

Scoring:

Add up your scores on all 20 questions.

Score: Less than 40   This book will provide you with a strong foundation as you start to build an organization dedicated to continuous improvement.

Score: 40 to 74   You are only halfway there. A stronger focus on customer processes is necessary.

Score: Greater than 75   You are well on the road. The book offers best practices of others to learn from as well as other advanced techniques.

2

Are the Rewards Worth the Battle?

> It must be remembered that there is nothing more difficult to plan, more doubtful to succeed, nor more dangerous to manage than the creation of a new system. For the initiator has the enmity of all who would profit by the preservation of the old institution and merely lukewarm defenders in those who would gain by the new one.
>
> — Machiavelli

Can a Focus on Quality and Customer Satisfaction Lead to Profitable Results?

As you will read, great challenges lie ahead, but are the results worth the battle? We must address this important issue before we examine how to become an organization that customers value most.

First, let's examine some of the bad press that this topic receives. Until now, I have only outlined all the benefits of embarking upon an initiative that will lead to performance improvement. However, many skeptics will argue that this is not easy to accomplish. Furthermore, read any book or news article describing organizations undertaking various initiatives such as TQM, reengineering, or other alphabetical descriptions such as ISO, CQI, ABC, and you will find a common message: seven out of every 10 initiatives fail. This statistic alone is enough to scare many organizations away from becoming more customer focused.

These arguments led me on a search for two things: to determine the validity of those statements on failure, and to learn what other common lessons could be learned from organizations that had succeeded. In the following section, I will use the the term TQM (Total Quality Management), although it is synonymous with TQS (Total Quality Service) and CQI (Continuous Quality Improvement). All three terms lead to the ulitmate same result—customer satisfaction. My findings revealed the information contained in the following chapters. First, contrary to popular belief, most quality initiatives currently in place are successful. A recent study I conducted prior to IDEAS found that over 80 per cent of these initiatives were successful to some degree. How they became successful can be attributed more to logic and common sense than to a unique, proprietary methodology. But as Voltaire so appropriately stated, "If common sense were very common, more people would have more of it."

But the true questions are, Is it worth the effort? Are you prepared to commit? and Will you be just another statistic? The following section describes what it takes to be successful. In later chapters, I will also describe the steps that should be taken to ensure that you are not a fatality.

Committing to a Performance Improvement Initiative: A Cost Justification

"How much is this really going to cost and how will I justify this expenditure?"

Of all the questions my clients ask regarding their involvement in a performance improvement initiative, this one is by far the most frequent and also perhaps the simplest to answer. For those of you about to embark on your initiative, be prepared for senior management to ask you this question.

The answer requires some investigation, number crunching, and soul searching. Both hard and soft costs are involved. Most of the hard costs can be justified and really are only a reallocation of your existing expense budget. The soft costs are somewhat less tangible and more difficult to attach a number to.

Customer-focused process improvement initiatives will undoubtedly cost money, but you can justify the cost of implementing them by calculating the cost to your company of *not* implementing the program.

The results of a recent survey completed by the research organization TARP for a major consumer goods company highlight the importance of customer satisfaction to the bottom line. This study found that of those customers who were dissatisfied with a recent customer service experience, only 17 per cent intended to continue doing business with the company. Of those customers who found customer service to be simply acceptable, only 45 per cent reported brand loyalty. However, brand loyalty increased to 73 per cent among customers who were very satisfied with the company's service. In this instance, poor customer service caused a 56 per cent drop in customer loyalty for this company.

This study also found a similar drop in loyalty for other products within the same category produced by the same company, sometimes referred to as line loyalty. Only 17 per cent of customers who were unhappy with the customer service they received would buy other products or services from that company. Line loyalty increased to 50 per cent when customer service was acceptable and rose to 80 per cent among customers completely satisfied with customer service.

Finally, the study measured the extent to which negative word-of-mouth resulted from customer-service problems. Among consumers who had experienced problems, those whose problems had not been corrected satisfactorily told twice as many people about their negative experience than customers whose problems had been resolved. One organization that researched this phenomenon found that over a one-week period, each disgruntled customer had affected at least 75 other individuals with dissatisfaction. This domino effect occurs when each dissatisfied customer tells eight people, who then tell six people, etc.

By ignoring the Customer Satisfaction/Revenue Enhancement Model, your company is currently losing significant revenue while also incurring huge costs in recruitment, hiring, and training expenses, and in correcting errors.

Here's how to derive the hard costs of *not* implementing customer-focused process improvement in your organization. You need only calculate three numbers:

1. Lost revenue.
2. The high cost of employee turnover.
3. The cost of not doing it right the first time.

Review the following points and consider these issues as they apply to your organization. There is space for you to include your answers at the end of this section.

1. Dissatisfied External Customers: Lost Revenue

Most organizations turn away customers, causing them to "quit" the organization. A recent research study conducted by Sandy Research estimated that lost sales from dissatisfied customers "quitting" an organization averaged 10 per cent of current gross sales levels. This number varied depending on the size of the organization and on the sophistication of its technological interface with its customers. On average, however, these organizations were achieving only 90 per cent of their sales potential with current customers.

Sixty-eight per cent of customers "quit" because of an attitude of indifference toward the customer by the owner, manager, or employee. In other words, these losses are preventable.

For the purpose of this exercise, take 10 per cent of your current sales revenue as the potential increased revenue that could be achieved through improved customer satisfaction. Then estimate the percentage that would fall to the bottom line. For companies that are already close to break-even, this number may be quite significant in improving your company's profitability.

2. Dissatisfied Internal Customers: The High Cost of Employee Turnover

Let's start with the assumption that most of your employees want to do a good job. They want to serve their customers (internal as well as external) but either they do not have the tools or management does not create the environment in which they feel comfortable to work. The organization may not be practising the Golden Rule of Service, "Do unto your internal customers as you would have them do unto your external customers."

In this type of confusing environment, employees (internal customers) are frustrated and high turnover results. Organizations that have created a customer focus (embodied by the Golden Rule of Service) have seen labour turnover reduced by 50 to 75 per cent. This reduction has some significant implications. Recruitment costs decline and nonproductive interviewing time is reduced. The costs of training, reduced productivity during training periods, dehiring, etc., are also dramatically decreased.

How would a 50 per cent reduction in labour turnover affect your training, hiring, and dehiring costs?

3. The Cost of Not Doing It Right the First Time

Have you established a customer service department or quality assurance program? Do you have to reship orders because of errors? Do you frequently have to re-invoice clients because of incorrect billings or spend time on the phone explaining your invoices to customers?

Many organizations have found that they are spending too much time correcting errors. What do you believe you could save if more attention were paid to doing things right, the first time, every time? How could employees be spending their time more productively? How could they be more customer focused?

Here's an example of an actual calculation that was prepared for Company X, which is in the financial services business. Annual sales revenue were $300 million. Its annual operating budget was approximately $285 million, 50 per cent of which was for staffing. Labour turnover, prior to embarking on its process improvement initiative was conservatively 30 per cent per year. The organization estimated that its non-value-added activities surrounding quality assurance and rework were $2 million. The following chart shows their calculations and provides a space for your company's calculations.

	Company X ($)	Your Company ($)
Annual sales revenue	300,000,000	_____
1. Profit impact of a 10% revenue improvement	3,000,000	_____
2. Impact of a 50% reduction in labour turnover ($ Savings)	500,000	_____
3. Potential for a reduction in the cost of quality	1,000,000	_____
Total	**4,500,000**	_____

Now it's your turn. Add up items 1, 2, and 3; these are your potential savings (or rather, your current cost burdens). Your organization should be prepared to spend at least 20 per cent of those hard costs in your first year and at least 10 per cent for each subsequent year. Senior management must be committed to this investment.

These newly claimed funds should be spent on various programs, including customer research, communication programs (internal and external), training, and reward and suggestion systems. You may find that much of these funds are already budgeted and spent on these items, but possibly are directed to the wrong audience or are sending the wrong message.

> Customer research should not just deal with customer satisfaction, but with what drives customer retention, loyalty and positive word-of-mouth. Attention should also be paid to what may potentially drive them to the competition.

Is it Worth the Investment?

This type of budgetary and philosophical commitment reaps significant rewards. Research conducted by the U.S. Department of Commerce and The Strategic Planning Institute made the following conclusions:

1. Return on sales

Companies that provide good service and achieve high levels of customer satisfaction achieve a 12 per cent return on sales, compared to a one per cent return on sales for companies that provide poor service.

2. Share growth

Companies with higher levels of customer satisfaction than their competition generally achieve a higher market share, attain a stronger perception of quality by their customers, and demand and receive a premium price on comparable products or services.

3. Success breeds success

Companies focused on internal customer satisfaction not only reduced turnover, but also had little or no problem attracting new employees, without incurring the expenses of advertising job vacancies.

4. Positive word-of-mouth

Organizations that give good customer service are known in their communities as companies with which to do business. Customer loyalty is strong and repeat business is the rule rather than the exception.

Is there a cost to develop a customer-focused initiative? Sure there is! But companies that have made the investment have profited from it—and profited well.

> A focus on improved customer satisfaction does not cost… it pays—and pays well!

Case Study: Van Kampen American Capital—The Impact of Improved Customer Satisfaction

The Company

Van Kampen American Capital (VKAC) is one of the oldest and largest mutual fund companies in the United States. The company has two distinct customer groups: brokers and other investment professionals who sell its funds; and individual mutual fund investors.

The Challenge: A Call to Action

In 1987, a new chairman was appointed to VKAC. One of his primary goals was to transform the company into an organization that provided "premier services to achieve the highest level of customer satisfaction." This transformation required a "service renaissance,"— a continuous effort to instil a service orientation throughout the company and improve the quality of service that customers receive.

Action Taken

Early in the process, the company identified that listening to the voice of the customer was an essential part of its initiative. It established standards based upon customer requirements (collected through surveys and focus groups), industry benchmarks, and operational capabilities.

Standards were then communicated through training for new employees, refresher training for existing employees, job aid for all associates, and an on-line reference system. It instituted a proprietary system for measuring against both these internal and external standards which had at its core the following three themes: accuracy, timeliness, and courtesy.

Two sets of measures were established to track the voice of the internal and external customer against these themes. They include the following:

Internal Measures

Call Response—Video display boards are prominently displayed in the Customer Service area. These boards measure critical call components such as the number of phone calls waiting and the department's response rate.

Courtesy Measures—Randomly selected calls in the Customer Service department are analyzed and rated in terms of accommodation, knowledge, courtesy, and adherence to the call path.

Quality Assurance—At the organization's transfer agent, American Capital Companies Shareholder Services (ACCESS), correspondence and transactions are statistically sampled for accuracy and tracked for timeliness of response.

Internal Surveys—To ensure that all internal functions are functioning effectively, internal customer surveys are used frequently throughout the organization.

External Measures

Customer Surveys—Over the past four years, approximately 35,000 surveys have been distributed to customers—both shareholders and investment professionals.

Large-Trade Calls—Associates call all investment professionals who place a large trade to thank them for the business and to ask whether VKAC's service met all their requirements. Associates make about 3,800 such calls annually.

Complaint Processing—Customer requests or complaints are logged into the computer system by the associate who receives the call. The computer system tracks the item through completion and notifies the associate who entered the request and management if the item is not completed within three days.

Follow-up Calls—After any customer request or problem, customer service generates a follow-up call or letter to confirm the request and to determine whether the shareholder is satisfied. This follow-up is one source of new ideas for service enhancements.

The Result of the Company's Six-Year Focus on "Premier Service"

The result of Van Kampen American Capital's (VKAC) six-year focus on "premier service" has been a significant improvement in meeting the needs of both its customer audiences.

VKAC had the following goals: to answer more than 90 per cent of calls within 20 seconds; to keep the abandonment rate below one percent; and to resolve 98 per cent of customer concerns within three days or less. Currently more than 95 per cent of customer calls are answered within 20 seconds, its abandonment rate is .06 per cent, and the company resolves more than 99 per cent of investor complaints within three days or less. Even though this performance has made VKAC the industry leader in customer service, the company believes that there is always room for improvement.

Furthermore, VKAC has implemented more than 3,000 team recommendations to date. Customer Service has implemented 70 per cent of these team-generated ideas, which has further enhanced the quality of customer service at VKAC while saving the company more than $1.5 million.

As a result, customers receive faster, more accurate responses to both telephone and mail inquiries; their fund transactions are processed more rapidly; and shareholders receive redemptions more quickly. Not surprisingly, this attention to customer service has resulted in fewer redemptions to process. Even in today's difficult economy, satisfied customers are leaving their investments intact with VKAC. At the same time, sales have risen dramatically.

For brokers, VKAC's service commitment makes it easier for them to do their jobs well; for investors, it makes managing their investments a more hassle-free process; for associates, it promotes a results-oriented and pleasant work environment where turnover continues to decline. It's the ultimate win-win situation.

Research on the Positive Impact of Quality/Customer Satisfaction Initiatives

" The whole thing takes time. You don't do this if you want to hit a home run. You hit some singles. You hit a few doubles. You bunt a bit. But most of us have been accustomed to being told to hit home runs."— Charles E. Clough, CEO and President, Nashua Corporation

As I mentioned earlier, there is no scarcity of skeptics who will quote you statistics or recount third-party stories about why a focus on "What Customers Value Most" will not work. I believe that these stories have become more embellished over time. That's why now it's time to set the record straight.

During my research for this book, I reviewed a report from the U.S.-based Conference Board, entitled, "Does Quality Work? A Review of Relevant Studies," which effectively addresses the concerns and arguments of those who believe that these initiatives will never work. This report analyzed the results of 20 quality/performance improvement studies and identified a number of interesting best practices. This report could be presented at your next executive committee meeting or given to the cynics who will quote the statistcs that seven out of every 10 initiatives fail.

The Conference Board's analysis revealed a number of common themes that are highlighted below.

i)   Quality/performance improvement initiatives are on the rise. Customer-focused performance improvement efforts are increasing. These are driven by a desire to listen to the "voice of the customer" and are achieved through techniques such as continuous process improvement, just-in-time manufacturing, teamwork, benchmarking, statistical process control, and employee participation. Notably, the IDEAS research results also found that U.S.-based companies were more likely to use these techniques than Canadian-based organizations, particularly in areas such as process benchmarking and process mapping. These topics will be discussed further in Chapter 8.

ii) A long and variable list of changes in management practices and corporate culture is associated with these efforts. Firms that have adopted customer-focused practices or initiated performance improvement processes have often made significant investments in training, reorganization, and work-flow redesign. This generally results in reduced management layers, increased decision-making for front-line employees, increased usage of team-based work methods, and increased emphasis on continuous cost reductions and quality improvements.

iii) A renewed focus on quality/customer process improvement is not a short-term fad or waste of money. Instead, it appears to represent a long-term effort on the part of many mid-sized and large companies to make significant changes in the way they operate. In fact, as the IDEAS research also suggests, a long-term commitment is necessary. Improved customer satisfaction is not a short-term fix.

iv) Customer satisfaction initiatives are often considered by executives to have a beneficial effect on their firm's performance. Most of the studies reviewed suggest that customer-focused process improvement can improve company performance on measures including market share, customer satisfaction, employee performance, process costs, cycle times, profits, and return on investments (ROIs).

v) The specific combination of techniques defined as customer-focused/quality performance improvement varies from study to study and company to company, and these variations in approaches appear to be related to the success of the efforts. While variations in approach affect the success of a performance improvement effort, there is not widespread agreement among studies on an optimal approach. That is, there is no single best approach. No single textbook approach works for all organizations. It must be tailored to fit the organizations culture and goals.

vi) None of the studies reviewed provides any substantial evidence that this dedication to customer satisfaction negatively affects company performance. Instead the studies revealed the following:

- most managers report significant benefits in a range of performance measures,
- a smaller but significant number of companies report resulting profit improvements.

Why Companies Adopt Performance Improvement Initiatives

My research also revealed that the benefits achieved as a result of a successful performance improvement initiative typically exceeded the company's initial expectations and produced some unexpected side benefits. In general, these organizations were in serious trouble before embarking on these initiatives because they were not listening to the voice of the customer. The performance improvement initiatives helped to address these deficiencies and to position the organization for the future.

One research study conducted by Alphastat Research Corporation revealed a number of interesting drivers behind expansion of a quality/performance improvement initiative—drivers that may affect most organizations. Major factors include a desire to win back customers, poor customer ratings, and a need for rapid feedback, as shown in the following figure. The implications of this are quite important. Success will not be possible unless we understand our customers' current needs. Their needs are constantly changing and without an active program to reach out and interface with them, the potential for lost customers will increase exponentially.

Pressures to Expand Quality Program

Pressure/Motivation	Percent of Respondents
Product Pride	85%
A commitment from top-level management	78
A need for rapid feedback about out-of-control processes	73
To win back lost customers	60
Poor consumer ratings	60
Cost disadvantage vs. competitors	53
Government regulations	39
To reduce idle time	33
To reduce threat of liability suit	28
Because of competitive advertising	12
Negotiations with unions	2

Another study, by AMA and Ogilvy Adams & Rinehart, helped to define various approaches to the customer-focused process. Respondents were asked to rate the importance of various program components within their performance improvement initiatives. The following figure shows the key components and their importance rating. Not surprisingly, the top two relate to customer satisfaction/relationships.

Importance of Quality Program Components

Component	Importance Ranking (1=unimportant to 7=very important)
Improved Customer Satisfaction	6.6
Strengthen Customer Relationships/Improve Customer Service	6.4
Reduce/Eliminate Defects or Errors	6.3
Improve Support Services	5.5
Reduce Operating Costs	6.0
Develop New/Better Products	5.0
Modernize Plants/Management Systems	4.8

In addition to these findings, it is notable that the studies provide little or no evidence of negative consequences from quality/customer-focused performance improvement for any participants. While some respondents reported more benefit than others, there were no substantial examples of strongly negative consequences. Consequently the weight of evidence from these studies suggests that customer-focused performance improvement initiatives are unlikely to do harm and that the major concern of adopters is whether they will have a neutral or positive effect.

Key Drivers for Success—How to Avoid Failure

Based on a review of the available literature and interviews with organizations with successful customer-focused/quality initiatives, the following broad categories can help to identify why these quality initiatives may fail:

- Lack of visible and actual management commitment
- Insufficient continuous communication
- Reluctance to establish standards of performance (and measure actual performance against these standards)
- Poorly defined co-ordinating and action-oriented structure
- Resistance to change
- Insufficient or unfocused training
- Inadequate allocation of human and financial resources

We will now turn our attention to examining these issues in more detail. Although other publications have addressed them, I offer a unique perspective and in the checklist at the end of the chapter will direct you to later chapters in which the topics are expanded upon further.

Management Commitment

Senior management commitment to the initiative is critical, not only for initially embracing a performance improvement process, but also in sustaining it. Management must drive the initiative and, having established a commitment, must visibly reinforce it throughout the entire organization.

At General Motors, for example, senior managers at the president and vice-president levels actually taught training classes for all levels of staff and regularly took "walkabouts" to hear employees' reactions. Through these efforts, they not only received valuable feedback but also demonstrated their commitment to and belief in the program.

In contrast, the head of a major government body with over 15,000 employees took a more passive approach. Although he initially showed a strong commitment in initiating a quality/customer satisfaction program and establishing a senior management committee, he failed to a large degree to communicate and sustain that commitment. This led to a reduction in overall momentum and ultimate failure.

> Management must drive the initiative and once having established its commitment, they must visibly reinforce it throughout the entire organization.

Communication

Once senior management has committed to the process, this commitment and progress of the initiative must be continuously communicated to the organization's staff and management. That is, everyone must share the vision. Employee buy-in and participation are key binding elements of successful initiatives. To achieve this, all employees must believe that senior management is committed to the program. This commitment can be conveyed through either actions or words, although actions are more powerful.

Let's now look at another example of the power of management's actions in communicating commitment. The Ogden Internal Revenue Service Centre (OIRSC) in Ogden, Utah is a government body that won the Federal Quality Improvement Prototype Award, which recognizes organizations in the federal government that have achieved high quality and customer satisfaction at reduced costs by practising Total Quality Management. This organization demonstrated exemplary performance in its communications program, which included newsletters, announcements, posters, group celebrations, etc. The program proved to be a very effective means of sustaining momentum and commitment. Its success was primarily due to the fact that the organization made customer-focused performance improvement a company-wide commitment. Both senior management and other employees bought into the concept equally. Without the commitment of both groups, the probability of failure is tremendous.

Ongoing communication is a critical part of the initiative. It maintains awareness and supports the process of continuous improvement. By continuing to publish newsletters, holding celebration activities, and generally convey the quality/customer service message, employees will believe that the program is not a fad but is, in fact, an integral part of their everyday activities. Quality has become part of daily work routines at the OIRSC, where quality week, a monthly newsletter, bi-monthly quality award ceremonies, and more, continue to keep quality and customer service at the forefront.

> Ongoing communication is a critical part of the initiative. Awareness must be maintained to ensure that the initiative is viewed as part of the process of continuous improvement and not as a separate or parallel activity.

Measurement and Accountability

Most successful organizations recognize the importance of establishing standards and the need to constantly measure performance against those standards. If this does not occur, all of the rhetoric about customer satisfaction and quality customer care quickly dissipates. Employees and management will view the effort as "just another program" or "flavour-of-the-month." However, when people, including management, find that they are actually accountable for performance improvement in customer satisfaction, there is increased motivation to maintain the improvement initiative. A real sense of the organization's commitment is established, not just through mere words but through actions. Within successful organizations, performance improvement initiatives are designed and implemented to achieve clearly defined goals or objectives.

At Xerox, a recognized leader in quality customer care, measures are incorporated into both individual and group performance evaluations and partly form the basis for rewards and compensation. Goals can be set in two ways: through the bottom-up approach and the top-down approach. Xerox advocates the top-down approach. Top management sets company-wide goals that cascade down the organization. The sum total of the goals of each division is the macro goal initially established by senior management. Each division clearly understands the role it must play in attaining the total corporate goal.

Exxon, however, prefers the bottom-up approach. Within this organization, process teams at lower levels of the organization set their own goals in a co-ordinated and controlled manner. This results in a synergy to improve overall company performance.

> It is essential that performance should be compared against baseline measures or established standards.

Structure and Teams

The company's infrastructure can also be critical to its success. The infrastructure helps to coordinate and implement the performance improvement initiative. Organizations with successful initiatives advocate a structure that complements or is harmonious with the existing organizational structure. Cross-functional teams or councils appear to be the most successful.

At General Motors, natural teams are formed around processes and include diagonal as well as cross-functional membership, involving several disciplines and levels of management.

Culture Change

Previously established paradigms and resistance to change can severely impede an initiative. It is often difficult to change people's beliefs about the way in which work should be conducted.

Organizations with established quality programs frequently cite employee resistance as a problem.

For example, the Legal Aid Board of London, England identified the concept of breaking paradigms to be a particularly difficult problem. Historically, the prevailing attitude toward the legal industry was to view it as a profession, not as a business. Commercial practices and management techniques were not believed to apply to the "legal profession." It was only after establishing an independent governing board composed of non-legal professionals that a quality program was initiated. Similarly, the Georgia Department of Natural Resources, which had operated for 20 years, experienced strong resistance to change by its middle managers. This resistance was based on the fact that many of them had been with the organization since its inception and were very comfortable with the existing processes and culture. By means of a unique approach to first train all the employees and then to implement the program, resistance to the initiative was ultimately overcome.

On the following page is an exercise for those who have trouble breaking paradigms. This classic puzzle illustrates how easy it is to read restrictions that do not even exist in a problem. We unconsciously impose too many imaginary constraints, rules, and boundaries upon our problems and hence fail to reach the optimal solution.

First, join the dots using four straight lines without lifting your pen and without retracing any lines.

Most people have difficulty exceeding the imaginary boundary, although that restriction is not a part of the problem. (Answer at the end of this chapter.) But if that was a breeze, try this. This time connect all dots with only three lines. (By the way, it is possible to use only one line, but you really must think outside the box.)

Training and Education

Inadequate and insufficient training are also common causes of failure or, at best, limited success in quality initiatives. Once people committed to the initiative, they must be given tools and training to implement the program successfully. They must understand their roles and have the skills and knowledge to fill these roles.

A recent North American study reports that of the organizations that have successfully implemented customer-focused quality programs, over 85 per cent have implemented quality/customer service training programs. Of those organizations, over 90 per cent state that the training was an effective part of their initiative.

Resource Allocation

A quality initiative must dedicate adequate resources to it if it is to succeed. These resources include people and their time, financial resources, and technology. Many organizations find it quite difficult to quantify the costs of their program because of the problems associated with measuring people's time and assigning a value to that time. Literature suggests that a quality/customer satisfaction initiative can take up to 15 per cent of an employee's normal working hours plus additional time for supplementary training. This percentage can be even higher in certain areas of management or other specific employees.

A circular problem results when TQM initiatives are intended to improve quality and productivity, but the staff can't find the time to implement the initiative properly. Similarly, adequate financial resources and investment in technology must be provided to support the quality initiative. Many organizations stated that enabling technology is key in meeting customer requirements and in establishing measures....a critical element to be discussed in more detail in Chapter 8.

The Link Between Quality/Customer Satisfaction and Improved Profitability

In August 1994, SPSS Inc. of Chicago conducted a telephone survey in which respondents reported that their quality initiatives had actually saved them money—for some, as much as 14 per cent of total revenue. Furthermore, 69 per cent of respondents reported increased employee morale, which they attributed to their initiatives. Most importantly, these organizations most frequently mentioned improved customer satisfaction as the driving force or goal behind most quality thrusts. The survey report stated, "Quality improvement in this industry is largely customer driven. The benefits are seen in the area of increased customer satisfaction."

To further emphasize this point, consider what would have happened if you had invested $1,000 in each Baldrige Award-winning company, *after* it had won this prestigious award for quality performance. *Business Week* recently reported a hypothetical transaction in which it did just that. The results show that an investment in winners of the Baldrige Award yielded a cumulative 89.2 per cent gain. That compares with a 33.1 per cent return on the Standard & Poor's 500 stock index. An investment in quality paid off for both the company and its investors.

——— CHECKLIST ———

Things to Remember

Earlier in the chapter, I outlined common pitfalls to avoid. These are briefly summarized below to direct you to later chapters where these topics will be discussed in more detail. Feel free to move directly to those chapters that deal with your high-priority issues.

Here's how to use the summary below.

Rate your organization on each of these main success factors. A score of one (1) would mean that your organization exhibits that characteristic to a very limited degree; a score of five (5) shows a high commitment. Once you have completed the checklist, begin with your weakest points, the issues that received the lowest scores, and move directly to the applicable chapters.

Topic	Score/Rating	Chapter Reference
Senior Management Commitment *Management drives the initiative and visibly reinforces its importance throughout the entire organization*	1 2 3 4 5	4
Communication *Communication is a continuous activity throughout the initiative. It maintains awareness and supports the process of continuous improvement.*	1 2 3 4 5	4, 7, and 8
Measurement and Accountability *Performance is continuously compared against baseline measures or established standards*	1 2 3 4 5	4, 5, and 8

── CHECKLIST ──

Structure and Teams *Cross-functional teams or councils are formed as part of the performance improvement initiative*	I 2 3 4 5	6
Culture Change *Culture change is being accomplished easily/effectively*	I 2 3 4 5	7
Training and Education *People have the tools and training to successfully implement required improvement opportunities. They understand their roles and have the skills and knowledge to fill these roles.*	I 2 3 4 5	6
Resource Allocation *Adequate resources are dedicated to the initiative. These resources include people and their time, financial resources, and technology.*	I 2 3 4 5	8

Answers to the Paradigm Puzzle

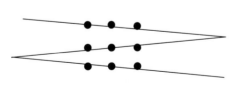 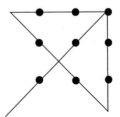

3

Starting Off: A Process for Achieving Business Transformation

In Chapters 1 and 2, we prepared the groundwork for building an organization that "Customers Value Most." By doing so, hopefully we have cleared away any confusion, misinterpretation, or just lack of knowledge. You should also have guidelines on which pitfalls to avoid as you move forward.

Chapter 3 provides the next step in this process. What follows is a four-phase process—a framework for achieving business transformation by focusing on processes that touch the customer. Each phase requires voice-of-the-customer input to focus the effort, although some are more formal or rigorous than others. This framework resulted from extensive research, the Coopers & Lybrand IDEAS study described earlier, and an investigation of the best practices of organizations that have successfully achieved what customers value most:

- an organization that is easy to do business with;
- an organization that has devoted time and attention to improving processes that touch the customer (both internal and external customers); and

- an organization that is not afraid to learn from the best practices of others, not for the purpose of decreasing costs, but for the purposes of increasing revenue and profitability.

This framework is not complicated, but rather straightforward and logical. These phases can be described as follows:

Phase 1: Align Align senior management to the organization's commitment to excellence. Most organizations seem to jump into their performance improvement initiative without spending sufficient time ensuring that both senior management and support staff are aligned, that they talk the same language, seek the same goals, and have the same priorities and similar measures of success. In contrast, organizations that are successful have devoted significant time and effort to attaining organizational alignment.

Phase 2: Explore Listen to the voice of the customer. Too many failures are attributed to focusing efforts in the wrong direction and ignoring the drivers of customer satisfaction and dissatisfaction. By listening to the voice of the customer—which includes equally the internal customer as well as the external customer—issues of importance can be explored, priorities can be set, and the goals of revenue enhancement and improved profitability can be achieved. Successful organizations devote considerable attention and budget to this concept to help set direction and identify if they are going off course. Less-than-successful organizations prefer to guess and operate on instinct.

Phase 3: Focus Focus on processes that touch the customer and add value. Reengineering is an important component in this phase and is used quite effectively by organizations that provide what customers value most. A logical methodology is required. (I recommend *Best Practices in Reengineering* by David Carr and Henry Johansson.) Equally as important is a good understanding of when to use Big "R" rather than little "r" reengineering, which we will discuss in more detail later. This is a make-or-break stage so we will spend more time providing a framework for a methodology. Less-than-successful companies have focused on less appropriate areas and have reengineered processes that may have reduced costs, but unfortunately also alienated the customer. The organization may be operating more efficiently, but it is doing so with fewer customers.

Phase 4: Commit/Support Provide support for a culture of continuous improvement. This does not come at the end of this four-phase process, but rather starts right at the beginning. Not only must management be aligned, but so must the tools (rewards, awards, and incentives) that ultimately support the customer-focused behaviour. Organizations that customers value most do not regard this as a haphazard pat on the back for their employees, but rather as a tool to achieve internal customer satisfaction, which translates to external customer satisfaction.

In the following chapters, we provide tips on factors such as teams, leadership, and training, that affect an organization's ability to use this four-phase process, as well as the tools that must be used to progress through these phases. The final chapter summarizes key elements of this process and provides further valuable suggestions. But first, we will look at an organization that followed this best practices model.

Case Study: Gas Turbine Corporation—Putting the Process to Action

In this example, Gas Turbine Corporation (GTC) used a modified version of the four-phase approach to become more focused on customer needs and to better represent what customers value most. The success of its initiative is a direct result of the organization's passion to listen to the voice of the customer and align the total organization towards customer-focused process improvement.

The Company

Gas Turbine Corporation, a subsidiary of Chromalloy Gas Turbine Corporation (a Sequa Company), was founded in 1972 and is located in East Granby, Connecticut. It is the leading supplier in the jet aircraft industrial engine and land-based turbine repair market and also ranks as a principal supplier to the world's leading manufacturers of jet engines.

The Challenge—Call to Action

Operating in a highly competitive industry, GTC had been proactively looking for new ways to improve. GTC's president, Graham Bell, and his senior management team, had determined that in order for the company to survive and continue to succeed, there had to be a greater focus on the customer and its needs, with every employee assuming responsibility for changing GTC to more reflect these goals. Thus, the entire company became fully committed to customer-focused performance improvement as a strategic business initiative.

As Bell explains, "This allows us to take advantage of our employee resources...The current economic climate puts increased pressure on pricing and quality and our employees have a direct effect in making sure we meet the customers' demands. Employee empowerment increases our competitiveness in the marketplace."

Action Taken
Assessment (Align and Explore)

The first task involved identifying the magnitude of the task ahead of them. To do this, a multi-levelled, cross-functional team conducted a 10-week assessment. This assessment provided factual baseline measures of customer satisfaction with products and services, which were used to gauge current performance and to identify opportunities for improvement. Then, specific assessment methodologies were selected to determine customer satisfaction and cost of quality.

First, the assessment team conducted a customer satisfaction assessment. Thirty-five external customers were surveyed using various methods to measure their level of satisfaction with GTC's products and services.

Then a cost of quality assessment was conducted within one of GTC's most critical business areas—component repair. The team established a data collection plan for each cost of quality driver within the area. Data were collected, aggregated, and analyzed by the team over a two-week period.

Finally, the assessment team delivered the results to senior management. The team showed that GTC had not only established a factual baseline of internal and external performance, but had also successfully introduced employee involvement to the GTC workforce.

Planning and Implementation (Focus)

With the data to assist in quantifying current performance, GTC's senior management team—now called the Quality Council—could more effectively agree on organizational objectives for their improvement efforts. Coopers & Lybrand facilitated a two-day planning session, during which the Quality Council identified key elements of a corporate strategic plan. This session produced specific opportunities for improvement and actions plans and led GTC directly into the implementation phase of its performance improvement effort. Although many organizations begin their performance improvement effort in this phase, GTC realized that their investment in assessment and planning would provide a better basis for achieving breakthrough improvement.

Since March 1992, seven GTC Process Improvement Teams (PITs) have been chartered, trained, and supported on improvement methodologies. Since then, the Quality Council has chartered additional teams as a result of other team recommendations. Improvement efforts have focused on such processes as task planning, invoicing, external communications, material handling, and component repair. For example, the component repair team showed that its personnel were losing 12 per cent of available person-hours looking for tooling. As a result of this team's recommendations, an attended tool crib was built, thereby recovering more than $120,000 in billable hours per year. Four of the seven PITs have presented their results to the Quality Council. Implemented recommendations have resulted in measurable annual savings to GTC of more than $1 million.

Management's commitment to employee empowerment is most clearly evident in GTC's High-Performance Work Teams (HPWTs). A HPWT consists primarily of non-management employees associated with a common product, process, or customer, who are given the opportunity to manage, measure, and continuously improve their business. One of the main features of these teams is that they have no set duration. They exist as long as their customers are satisfied, their quality is continuously improving, their productivity is optimal, and, most importantly, they are valuable and profitable. Less than a year after introducing its performance improvement initiative, GTC is lending structure to the concepts of empowerment and self-management in key operating areas. Jim Von, a mechanic and a member of a HPWT states, "This approach has enabled us to make considerable gains in reducing our product costs to the customer without dampening quality. Each member plays an active role within the team and increases the overall effectiveness of the group."

Institutionalization (Commit/Support)

In the next phase, GTC enlisted Coopers & Lybrand to train a team of internal facilitators. The role of these facilitators, who came from different areas of GTC, was to support the ever-expanding team structure. The success of existing teams has resulted in PITs and HPWTs being planned and chartered to address processes throughout the company. This snowball effect is making success a way of life at GTC.

GTC has achieved continuous improvement through a business strategy focused on employee empowerment: employees measure their own process performance; conduct their own planning; order their own material; determine their own schedules; and set their own priorities. This business strategy has expedited progress and has resulted from GTC's initiatives. By recognizing that operating in an environment of autonomous employee work teams requires an organization that can successfully plan and implement change, GTC is benefitting from the methodology. Most organizations agree that the principles of customer- focused performance improvement make business sense, but many spend years trying to create an environment that successfully supports the concepts. At GTC, they have created such an environment and have seen results in less than 12 months. In fact, today over 60 per cent of GTC personnel have been directly involved in training and improvement initiatives.

Lessons Learned from GTC

GTC has taught us some very important implementation lessons. Its procedure was simple and straightforward:

Align and Explore

1. Quantify current performance to establish factual baseline measures, which can be used to gauge improvement and identify opportunities for improvement.
2. Align management and define specific opportunities for improvement as well as action plans.

Focus

3. Charter, train, and support internal process improvement teams (PITs).
4. Empower these teams to manage, measure, and continuously improve their processes.

Commit/Support

    5. Institutionalize the process. GTC employees measure their own process performance, conduct their own planning, order their own material, determine their own schedules, and set their own priorities.

TQM (Little "r" Reengineering) and BPR (Big "R" Reengineering): Different?

Before we discuss our examples further, it is important to pause and reflect on a frequently asked question: What is the difference between Big "R" and little "r" reengineering and when should each be used? Certainly the terms are more alike than different. Understanding this concept is critical to employing the appropriate methodology in the most effective way. In fact, the following case study on PHH will provide you with a concrete example of how both terms were used to achieve positive transformation.

The Differences

The differences between the two terms are best summarized in an article in Coopers & Lybrand's *TQM Quarterly* (Winter/Spring 1992), which describes little "r" reengineering, more commonly known as TQM, as *evolutionary*—continuous incremental change, and characterizes Business Process Reengineering (BPR), Big "R" reengineering, as *revolutionary*—occasional and drastic (quantum leap) change.

    Little "r" reengineering, or TQM, places the highest value on gradual but continuous improvements to processes. Most of these improvements are low cost or free, and many do not involve new technology. According to Paul O'Neil, President of ALCOA, "...[Incremental, little 'r' reengineering] improvement is exactly the right idea if you are a world leader in everything you do...It is probably a disastrous idea if you are far behind the world standard."

    Big "R" reengineering, or BPR, becomes important when an organization needs a quantum leap in improvement, but the current process is incapable of meeting this requirement. The need for extreme improvement may be prompted by a major change in customer expectations, a competitor's progress, or an opportunity promised by new technology.

"Quantum-leap" breakthroughs do not result from a gradual improvement mindset. While a TQM improvement team accepts many assumptions about a process, a BPR team challenges all assumptions and is prepared to completely redesign a process from the top down. While the redesigned process may satisfy the same needs as the old, (that is, to produce an accurate invoice as soon as goods are shipped), the process itself will be radically different (invoices will be sent electronically to the customer through the shipping department rather than the sales order clerk). Producing the output also usually requires only a fraction of previous labour and other costs. BPR is as much a break from the past as a thrust toward the future.

The Similarities

In the past, major redesign initiatives were driven by technological changes, with the sole aim of reducing costs or cycle time. However, the primary objective of both TQM and BPR should be to increase customer service and satisfaction. This requires up-front identification of external and internal customers and their expectations. The tools used for this process should include customer surveys and analysis (Chapter 5), benchmarking, and environmental scans (Chapter 8). Strategic and business planning based on this information sets process improvement priorities for both BPR and TQM. This planning is critical since often it determines how resources will be invested.

But simply knowing what should be done does not guarantee success. A process methodology to make positive change in performance improvement is required—our four-phase methodology described earlier.

The following case studies provide additional best practices examples and variations of the four-phase methodology described earlier and how it was used by the following organizations:

- PHH—to achieve continuous improvement;
- Hewlett Packard—in achieving business transformation; and
- Procter & Gamble—in becoming more customer focused and becoming what customers value most.

Case Study: PHH—Once May Not Always be Enough

The following is the first of a series of case studies that demonstrate the importance of a structured approach to business transformation. These examples have a number of common elements: a recognition of the importance of customer information and a process for achieving positive business transformation by focusing on processes that touch the customer. The obvious corollary to each of these examples is that these organizations did not follow a proven methodology or choose inappropriate processes for business transformation. Although there are many such examples, they are the fatalities described earlier. Since we have already discussed the common pitfalls in earlier chapters, it is now time to talk about positive transformation.

The Company

Founded in 1946, PHH is a North American leader in the fields of vehicle management services, relocation and real estate services, and mortgage banking services. On behalf of its clients, the organization manages supplier networks of automobile dealers, fuel and automotive parts and services suppliers, real estate brokers, attorneys, appraisers, moving companies, and financial institutions.

The Challenge—Call to Action

A wise person once said, "You never get a second chance to make a good first impression." The first impression for most of PHH's clients comes during the new business start-up process. That's why the organization set out to ensure that this process was as quick and as painless for its clients as possible.

In 1992, PHH began the business transformation of its sales through client set-up,—one of five core business processes. "Through the initial analysis, we found that if we could do a better job setting up a new client, we would eliminate a lot of service problems further down the road," explains Beverly Cain, Vice President, Account Management, and sponsor of the original business transformation project. Since then, several of the projects recommended by the initial team have been implemented. One of the most significant projects was the creation of the new business development team in fleet services.

In 1994, the reengineering of sales through client set-up entered a new phase—this time under the umbrella of North American integration and the service delivery business process reengineering (BPR) project.

Actually, new business set-up was just one element of its service delivery process, which begins during the sales process and ends only when its relationship with a client ends. When they first began reengineering service delivery, their goal was to design a system that would help to better manage its ongoing business. But as PHH became involved more deeply in reengineering, it realized that it really needed better information on its clients as well as a way to capture that information earlier in the relationship. That's when PHH went back and reviewed the work done by the original BPR team and changed its direction—from application design to process redesign.

Action Taken

By using the four-phase process and easily available internal voice-of-the-customer research, the team identified three major problems with its existing new business set-up process: poor communication, poor implementation of services, and too many hand-offs. Their research revealed the following findings:

- new business activity generated only a 25 per cent FRY (first-run yield). That meant 75 per cent of its clients experienced delays because of missing or incorrect information;
- cycle time ranged from five to 123 days, even though the process required only 48 hours of touch time;
- follow-up, rework, and other resource draining activities accounted for nearly one-third of the time it took to set up a new client.

Using information from the previous BPR project as well as data gathered through its own analysis, the service delivery team began the task of finding solutions.

The team held three days of visioning sessions and brought in more than 25 people from all areas of the company to help define what the new business set-up process should look like. In fact, the team took visioning sessions a step further. It combined traditional BPR methodology with a more detailed approach that is normally used in developing computer applications. Consequently the meetings were more rigorous and detailed than usual, but the company was better able to implement the recommendations that were developed.

From the visioning sessions emerged not only an improved new business set-up process, but also a broader one. The process now consists of five key activities and a method for monitoring results and providing continual feedback.

One of the first recommendations to be implemented was the formation of a new business consulting team. In partnership with account management, these "experts" now guide the set-up process from start to finish including developing and managing a timeline and strategy, facilitating communication between PHH and the client, and providing new client training.

However, PHH recognized that still more had to be done, including streamlining contract negotiation and finalization and ensuring that closure is brought to the contract stage. A contract management team was formed with a focus on simplifying contract approval. Its goal was to create a one-stop approval process that would eliminate many of the delays that resulted from its present multi-step approval process.

Both teams were in place January 1, 1995 and assumed responsibility for new service activation in March.

By centralizing the coordination of the new business set-up process, PHH expects to see significant improvement in both productivity and cycle time, which will favourably impact its bottom line. But even more important is the impact that it expects this streamlined process will have on client service, both in the short and long term. And, after all, isn't that what reengineering is all about?

As part of its business transformation process PHH embraced some key principles as described below:

Align
- Concentrate the organization to contribute to and achieve superior value generation.

Explore
- Listen to what the customer wants and understand what it needs. More than any other principle, this step ensured that although

processes were transformed, customer value and benefit were always the key focus.

Focus

- Focus on business processes that contribute to competitive advantage. Customer research provided a clear definition of competitive advantage and the changes necessary to achieve superior PHH performance.
- Utilize breakthrough strategies in the key competitive dimensions for industry leadership. The voice-of-the-customer research was a key enabler in this process.

Commit/Support

- Create reengineered organizations that satisfy customer and shareholder requirements for greater efficiency. PHH's new business set-up process embodies this principle.
- Achieve quantum leaps in improvement through empowered team work.
- Employ performance measurements geared to the desired process improvement measurements of its FRY and cycle time led to an urgency for change.

PHH now has a process that it can use whenever it needs to address customer-focused process improvement. But most importantly, it established a culture within its organization that encouraged the use of this process in order to achieve continuous improvement and "What Customers Value Most."

Case Study: Hewlett-Packard—Going from Process-Based to Customer-Focused

The following example shows an organization that recognized the value of positioning the customer not only at the start but also throughout the entire supply chain. Hewlett-Packard used customer research to identify the root cause of its customer concerns. Then it refocused its process with a view to constantly delight its customers. Its three-step process, which is a variation of our four-step process, was not surprisingly entitled "Design-Deliver-Delight."

The Company

Hewlett-Packard (H-P), a $25-billion organization, is known for a variety of products and services within the computer field. In 1991, the company reorganized into various independent organizations that could draw on the resources of the corporate giant, yet operate in a more entrepreneurial fashion. At the same time, each division now became responsible for its own sales and marketing. This restructuring forced each operating division to become more focused on, and responsive to, the customer.

The Challenge—Call to Action

When H-P restructured its business organization in 1991, the company discovered that its order fulfilment process was not meeting customers' needs.

The company's vision was to be the preferred supplier of information technology solutions to the top 1,000 customers worldwide. Unfortunately the organization was too hard to do business with.

Company data and surveys revealed that H-P's order fulfilment process was too complex. John C. Kenny, Manager of Logistics, explains, "We had far too many defects throughout the entire order fulfilment process." These "defects" occurred from taking the order all the way to providing complete "solutions" (including support) to customers. Furthermore the process took more than eight weeks from the time the order was taken until the product was delivered.

The impact on H-P was that the company was losing business. Customers were refusing to place orders because of the long order fulfilment process cycle time and because of the quality problems of the process.

Action Taken

The company created the following three-step process:
- setting customer order fulfilment goals;
- identifying the root causes of current problems; and

- "Design-Deliver-Delight"—H-P's organization of its customer value-chain.

Setting Customer Order Fulfilment Goals.

The company set out to reengineer the process with the following four goals in mind:

- to increase customer satisfaction;
- to achieve profitable growth of the business;
- to increase productivity of sales representatives by taking the burden off them when dealing with a dysfunctional customer order fulfilment process;
- to decrease the overall cost of its order fulfilment process as a percentage of both the total revenue, and the total expense of the business.

H-P characterized its vision in two simple ways:

1) The process had to provide customers with the information they wanted, where they wanted it, and when they wanted it through consolidated points of contact with the company.

2) The process was to take perfect orders. In many cases, these orders might consist of 12 to 15 individual boxes from 15 different suppliers being merged together. Furthermore, the process was to provide next-day delivery if needed, all in a matter of "seconds."

Identifying the Root Causes

During the initial analysis, the company quickly recognized that it was not customer-focused. In fact it did not have a single customer-based measure in its entire performance measurement review process.

In addition, the organization's laboratory and design activities were not focused on the order fulfilment process; assembly of the final order for shipping and set-up at the customer site was not of concern during product development.

"Design - Deliver - Delight"

To reengineer the order fulfilment activity, it was necessary to approach it as a process that spans the entire supply chain. Were the products and processes designed with order fulfilment in mind? By subsequently breaking down each component of the supply chain, the company considered how each element of the supply chain drove a customer metric or customer value.

According to Kenny, everyone is now participating in the supply chain to basically "delight" the customer—which is their goal. Certainly the R&D aspect of developing products will delight the customer technologically, but if the organization cannot deliver these products when customers want them, how they want them, and where they want them, then the organization is only providing partial service. They may be a superb technology company but not necessarily a great company in terms of meeting the customer's wants or needs.

The customer value chain is tied to the root cause—the organization must drive its business based on customer metrics rather than internal process or management metrics.

"What we're trying to do is provide the customer with an easy means of understanding what they need to meet their business problems, and allow the customer access to information they need in order for them to make good business decisions as well," Kenny says. "We need to have an organization in place across this supply chain that basically understands what those customer needs are and is tuned to those."

Lessons Learned from Hewlett-Packard

1. Research customer needs and potential drivers of dissatisfaction.
2. Set goals.
3. Identify root causes of failures.
4. Consider the entire supply chain for reengineering—break down silos.
5. Always keep the customer in the forefront.

Case Study: The Procter & Gamble Approach to Improved Customer Satisfaction

Our final example again deals with the customer order fulfilment process. Note the consistency in terms and strategy; specifically, customer satisfaction measurement, achieving value-added customer benefits, and seeking to identify and eliminate customer dissatisfiers. Here's how Procter and Gamble drove their process.

The Company

Most people would credit Procter & Gamble (P&G) as one of today's marketing leaders. Graduates of the P&G school, as it is sometimes known, are leaders of many of Fortune 500 organizations. But P & G was not aleader in customer satisfaction—neither internally or externally.

The Challenge—Call to Action

The root of P&G's problem lay with the front end and back end of its customer order fulfilment process. What were the symptoms of the problem? Each day the company made about 55 price and promotion changes with 30 per cent of the promotion changes occurring after the first order date. Each division (paper, soap, food and beverage, health and beauty aids) also operated with different and incompatible databases to enter price promotions and product specification. This combination of problems made the order entry process extremely complicated and time-consuming and increased the potential for invoicing errors. In brief, the company was not one that was easy to do business with. The processes that touched its customers were not customer friendly.

P & G took a simple approach to the business transformation that touched its customer: simplify, standardize, streamline, and then automate. Bill Pierre, Manager of Total Quality Management and leader of the process improvement effort, explains "Identify the business results you want to achieve and then use the knowledge of the process to drive improvements."

Align and Explore

P&G recognized that attention to this core business process would result in improved volume and profit for the company as well as for the trade. It would also result in better value for their mutual customer— the consumer. Thus, their strategy became one of focusing on the customer by eliminating customer dissatisfiers, optimizing total logistics systems costs, and developing value-added customer benefits.

The company did that by changing the rules—their own rules. P&G began measuring service as the customer saw it. As problems were identified, root-cause analysis was conducted. This helped P & G to prioritize efforts. But more than this was needed. Roles and responsibilities were expanded to ensure that individuals on the front line acted quickly to customer needs.

Focus

High commitment interdepartmental work teams were formed and given a mandate to improve the processes they now owned. As a result, new systems for order capture, shipment, and billing were created as well as a new system for continuous replenishment.

Commit/Support

The company adopted a unique attitude: customer satisfaction can be achieved by better meeting customer needs and delivering greater value by driving out non-value-added costs — not only in internal systems but also in systems that are shared with their customers.

The results of their efforts were spectacular. Perfect orders (traditionally called fill rate) increased from 50 per cent to 75 per cent; billing accuracy increased six points to 93 per cent; price and promotion changes were now averaging less than one per day (down from 55); and the number of invoice discrepencies were dramatically reduced. Due to its staged implementation, which included eliminating several databases, system development costs were significantly reduced.

As you can see, it's all a matter of focus...customer focus.

Lessons Learned from Procter & Gamble

1. Measure service as the customer sees it.
2. Empower front-line staff to act quickly on customer needs.
3. Drive out non-value-added costs—particularly in those systems that the company shares jointly with its customers.

——— CHECKLIST ———

Five "Make or Break" Factors When Improving the Processes that Touch the Customer

Hewlett-Packard's experience with customer-focused process improvement revealed that it's a difficult process but an absolutely necessary one. According to H-P, if you're going to take on a customer-focused business transformation project and can't answer "yes" to the following five questions, then you're not going to achieve customer satisfaction, and you'll probably fall into the 70 per cent failure category.

The following are the five critical success factors. Note the correlation to our four-phase best practices process.

Align
1. Is there shared vision and goals? The management team must agree on the attributes of the business transformation initiative.
2. Is there sponsorship, leadership, and ownership for driving change? Often, one particular part of the organization will attempt to take ownership of the project, but other parts are too busy or don't feel the same sense of urgency.

Focus
3. Is there agreement to the business transformation process at the global process level? It needs to be a "starting over" methodology as opposed to "tweaking the process a little bit here and there."
4. Are resources (i.e., the best people, full-time) allocated to the business transformation project? Part-time people tend to move on to other jobs during the course of the project, may have other, more pressing priorities, or tend to think of it as a part-time project.

Commit/Support
5. Is there commitment to implement the transformed process? This step can cause failure or disaster if, at the end of the day, the organization is not willing to go along with the program.

How did you fare?

4

The Align Phase: Aligning the Organization to Deliver

This chapter differs in focus and style from the previous chapters. As the title suggests, it deals with the first phase of our four-phase process—alignment—but approaches it from various perspectives. We will discuss senior management, organizational, and even customer alignment. We have included relevant examples and case studies rather than explanations through instructional "how to's." In this case, it is easier to show than to tell.

We will first examine mission/vision; why it is important to create a mission as well as examples developed by organizations. The mission/vision, or what we will call the statement of purpose, is a clear statement of what the organization stands for and in what direction it is going. This document may appear in the organization's annual report or be framed and hung on the walls of the organization. I have even seen some printed on the back of business cards. Review the examples, take the parts you like, adapt or modify them, and fine-tune them to the culture of your organization.

Next we will discuss the concept of the Customer Bill of Rights (CBR). The CBR is a clear statement of what your customers—internal, external, and stakeholders—can expect from your organization. It is a statement of what you are prepared to be measured against and how you expect to differentiate yourself from your competition. Organizations that are truly committed to their CBR will often print this on the backs of their invoices or in their newsletters. Their philosophy is simple: the CBR is a statement of what we will strive to exceed. Some might say that that is a subset of the mission/vision, but I believe that it stands alone as a testament to the commitment of the organization. Examples of these are provided but good ones are scarce. They are, however, a major communication device, a key alignment tool, and perhaps the heart and soul of the ISO quality assurance standards that will be briefly discussed in Chapter 9.

Lastly, we will focus on service guarantees, the true test of alignment, and, most importantly, *what customers value most*. When an organization can deliver on its promises in a consistent manner, its processes and people are in alignment. Only then can it be so bold as to guarantee that it will deliver...or else. Only then can it advertise and promote itself as the organization that will give *what customers value most*—an organization that is easy to do business with. But before we deal with the statement of purpose, let's first examine the importance of internal organizational alignment.

The First Steps

The Importance of Alignment

For Jack Welch, CEO of General Electric, the only way to achieve more productivity was to get people involved and excited about their jobs. He believed that it was a matter of understanding the customer's needs instead of merely producing something and putting it into a box. Welch explains,

> It's a matter of seeing the importance of your role in the total process. When people see that their ideas count, their dignity is raised. Instead of feeling numb, like robots, they feel important. They are important. I stand by my belief that a satisfied workforce is a productive workforce. Back when jobs were plentiful and there wasn't any foreign competition, people were content just to hang

around. Now people come to work with a different agenda: they want to beat the competition, because they know that the competition is the enemy and that customers are their only source of job security. They don't like weak managers, because they know that the weak managers of the 1970s and 1980s cost millions of people their jobs.

From Welch's perspective, trust is enormously powerful in a corporation. People won't do their best unless they believe they will be treated fairly. The only way to create that kind of trust is by laying out your values and then walking the talk. You've got to do what you say you'll do, consistently, over time.

> "People do not care to know how much you know until they know how much you care."

The Statement of Purpose

The statement of purpose, or mission/vision, can be structured in various ways. In fact, several hundred books address this subject alone. The following is a quick summary of the statement of purpose: what it is, why you need one, and how to develop it.

The statement of purpose should include some basic components:

- a vision statement for the future of the business;
- a statement explaining how the organization expects to do business;
- a core values statement explaining what is essential to the accomplishment of the mission and the fulfilment of the vision; and
- a description of standards against which it dares to be measured.

More than any other document, the statement of purpose is a reference point for those within the organization (the internal customers) as well as those outside it (external customers). It is something around which the organization can rally. Without a strong commitment to it, which must start at the top, the organization will wander aimlessly and without purpose. Departmental silos will appear, corporate investment may be misdirected, and employees will become unfocused. The result will be labour unrest, staff turnover, less-than-adequate customer service, and less-than-potential revenue and earnings growth.

You must ask yourself these key questions when creating this statement of purpose.

COMPONENTS OF A MISSION STATEMENT

Component	Key Questions that must be Addressed
Vision	What is our over-riding goal and desired future state? What is our commitment to survival, growth, profitability? Why are we in business and what business are we in? Should we be in a single-business or diversified enterprise? If we opt for diversification, should our lines of business be related or unrelated?
Target Customers and Markets	What markets do we want to target? Who should our customers be and which of their needs should we try to satisfy?
Geographic Coverage	What geographic domain should we serve? Should we compete regionally, nationally, multinationally, or globally?
Principal Products and Services	What range of products and services will we offer?
Core Technologies	What kinds of technologies do we want to be involved in?
Basis of Competitive Advantage	What distinctive competencies will we maintain relative to competitors? What values will customers obtain from buying our products and services?
Values	What key corporate values and shared beliefs do we hold dear?

Courtesy: Coopers & Lybrand

Although the answers to these questions provide the substance of the statement of purpose, we will now look at how to create the document. First, you must recognize that it cannot be created by consensus. This document must be created and fine-tuned by senior management and must be revisited at least annually. It must be compatible with your current and/or future customer base and, for that reason, some level of customer needs research or environmental scanning must be conducted before preparing this statement. As it drives the alignment of resources of the organization (human, financial, and physical), the heads of these divisions must be involved in the process.

Some organizations find it helpful to start with a template, or a copy of another organization's statement, to start the process and then modify it to their needs. For that reason, we have provided models later in this chapter. Other organizations prefer to start fresh and not be influenced by these examples. Both methods work well, as long as the goal is to produce a simple statement that is realistic, written in plain language, and will be taken seriously. If it is not believable, it will not be followed.

Once you have this statement—and it will probably need various iterations before you are completely satisfied—then it must be communicated. Although many organizations invest significant effort in communicating this statement—using posters, plaques, and newsletters—many do not invest sufficient time explaining why the statement is important, how it will be used, and how it will affect the organization as a whole. My experience has shown that small focus groups or town-hall-type meetings are an effective forum for this purpose. Similarly, it is equally important to introduce the document to your customers, either through special meetings/forums or one-on-one sessions. Finally, senior management—the creators of the statement—must visibly show their support. They must actively demonstrate to employees that this statement truly guides the organization in its current and future direction.

The following will provide you with some examples of effective statements of purpose as well as my comments on why I believe they warrant your attention. Your final product may be a variation of these examples. Choose the parts that best suit your needs.

This first example is excerpted from NCR (now AT&T Global Information Systems).

NCR—A Focus On Customer Satisfaction

Because quality and customer satisfaction are viewed as one and the same, our near-term quality goal is to achieve world-class customer satisfaction.

Our long-term quality goal also relates to customer satisfaction and is based on the fact that Total Quality Management drives continuous improvement. As our organization achieves excellence in the execution of all of its processes and relationships, there will come a time when all operations should be defect-free, and when every employee can "guarantee" his or her customer's satisfaction. Thus, our supreme goal is "guaranteed customer satisfaction"—doing the right things right, the first time, and every time!

We Are Relentless in...

* Focusing on the customer
* Ensuring that quality systems are under control
* Performing benchmarks against the world's best
* Performing ongoing self-assessments
* Adopting Malcolm Baldrige quality award criteria as its own measure of excellence
* Improving everything we do

This statement, which appeared in the company's annual reports and also in the company's training materials, left little to misinterpretation. It clearly identified both the organization's short- and long-term objectives as well as its ultimate goal of "guaranteeing customer satisfaction." Within the statement is a subliminal message that the organization may not have quite reached its ultimate goal.

What makes this statement unique are the closing statements, introduced by the heading, "We Are Relentless In..." The organization clearly presents a checklist, against which it is prepared to be measured, and a set of priorities for the organization as a whole.

The following is Texas Instruments' mission statement for the 1990s, which appears in their training catalogue and various marketing materials. It also sets the standards for their benchmarking initiatives.

Texas Instruments—A Mission for the '90s

The fundamental objective of Texas Instruments (TI)— *Customer Satisfaction Through Total Quality*—emphasizes the organization's commitment to excellence. TI strives to achieve this goal through people involvement, continuous improvement, and customer focus. In keeping with these objectives, TI has reaffirmed its determination to offer state-of-the-art training and development to all its employees, customers, and suppliers. TI seeks to prepare people for the jobs of the future, jobs which will require new skills and concepts to ensure quality management, products, and processes.

Benchmarking to Achieve Total Customer Satisfaction

At Texas Instruments, benchmarking has gone beyond merely improving internal processes to satisfy customers' needs. It has evolved into an ongoing learning tool.

Although the statement is simple and straightforward, Texas Instruments' commitment to the internal customer, the employee, is particularly noteworthy. The organization obviously believes that the key to achieving success is through well-trained and satisfied employees. It has also outlined the organization's commitment to continuously learn from the best practices of others.

Southam Inc.'s mission statement on the following page, is also distinguished by the fact that it includes a message for its three key stakeholders: its employees, customers, and suppliers.

It has been selected to demonstrate simplicity and a clear focus. More than the others, the statement has been written for the organization's investors and employees. It highlights the company's focus, key business units, and expectations. Note that it is not written from a customer perspective. Southam's businesses are so diverse and service so many customer segments, that no single customer perspective can be presented.

Southam Inc.

Our aim is to be a leader in the communications and information industry.

Within this industry we will concentrate on newspapers, commercial printing, magazine publishing, book publishing and retailing, and business, trade and professional information and services in print and electronic form.

We will pursue growth opportunities in these fields, either internally or through acquisition, to ensure consistent, appropriate, long-term growth in earnings for our shareholders.

Note the strong "customer" focus in the following statement from Amdahl and the use of this statement as a rallying point of reference. It sets out what the organization is to stand for, its key principles and practices, and an internal Customer Bill of Rights—what you can and should expect to help you assist the organization in achieving customer satisfaction.

Amdahl's Quality Commitments

Amdahl employees recognize that each of us has a customer, internal or external, for everything we do, and for every business process. We are each committed to provide products and services:
• That consistently meet our customers' agreed-to requirements; and
• That add substantial value in comparison to our competition.
  We are committed to do the right thing, the right way, every time. No level of defect is acceptable.

Amdahl's Quality Fundamentals

To help every employee meet our quality commitments, each Amdahl organization applies these quality fundamentals:
• We understand and appreciate our customers, know their requirements, and strive to satisfy their needs and expectations.
• We work in partnership with our suppliers and our customers to add maximum value to our products and services.

- We understand and manage our work processes, using proactive prevention-based measurements to make certain each process is in control.
- We keep planning for improvement with stretch goals based on benchmarks of the world's best.
- We dedicate ourselves to continuous improvement, reducing costs, and eliminating waste and non-value-adding activities. No level of process or output defect is acceptable.
- We involve everyone in quality. Everyone makes a difference.

How Best to Communicate the Statement of Purpose

If your internal and external customers know what you stand for and where you are going, your chances of alignment are increased significantly. The statement of purpose should not be just something that looks impressive hanging on the wall. It should be a confirmation that you are committed to what customers/stakeholders value most. Although advance communication is critical, in the form of customer needs assessment, communication once the statement has been created is equally important. Aside from stating your beliefs, you are sending another message: you are listening to what customers need you to be. Remember, it's impossible to overcommunicate.

Designing a communications campaign requires tailoring messages, media, and timing for each stakeholder group. In some cases, it's necessary to communicate what won't change. Hallmark Cards' senior managers found that before they could change the company's product development and other key processes, they had to reassure employees that the company's core values and beliefs would not falter. Over several months, the company's chairman communicated nine beliefs and values to all 22,000 employees. Company managers said that reinforcing those long-held beliefs put people at ease, helping to gain their support for reengineering.

Yet employees represent only one important stakeholder group that requires communication. Much more work needs to be done with other key stakeholder groups: management, suppliers, customers, shareholders, and Boards of Directors. While there is only one mission statement, the identification of stakeholder issues shapes the message to be communicated and the medium to be used for each.

Sometimes focus group sessions with stakeholder groups are necessary to fully understand their concerns. These interviews can also provide valuable feedback on the communication efforts to date. When a large company conducted these types of sessions, it found that half of the employees did not understand why the statement of purpose was even necessary.

The most effective communications campaigns are consistent in message, simple to understand by all levels of the organization, and honest yet enthusiastic. To underscore senior management's resolve for change, the campaigns should be unrelenting. They must also honestly present matters ranging from the company's current competitive standing to the need to eliminate jobs and redefine roles.

> Keeping secrets or providing misinformation is far worse than disclosing painful realities.

Need a Change?—Create a Crisis

Although communication is an important part of presenting the message, sometimes an organization needs a crisis to give new meaning and urgency to their statement of purpose.

Most organizations, like most people, won't change fundamentally until they absolutely have to. Smart managers don't wait for the crisis to overtake them. They see it from afar and tell other employees about it so persuasively that everybody gets scared.

In practice, the worst types of crises can be grouped into two categories:

- a financial crisis or a crisis in the industry; and
- a crisis with customers.

Financial Crisis: Craig Weatherup, President of Pepsico Division, created a crisis. During a three-day meeting with his top 11 managers, Weatherup bluntly explained that although most executives would be satisfied with 10 per cent annual growth in earnings, he was not. From now on, it was 15 per cent or bust. "There's a freight train out there," he explained to the startled group, "and it's called 15 per cent earnings. We're standing on the track, and we'd better figure out something or it will run us right over."

To emphasize his point, he gave each manager a model train that had an engine with 15 per cent painted on its side. On the accompanying train tracks, facing the oncoming train, were 11 tiny, frightened figures.

It didn't take long for Weatherup's managers to get the message. Over the next two years, he and his team restructured the organization, redesigned how it did its work, and redefined jobs. The change included breaking the division into 107 customer-focused units and dramatically revising processes like beverage delivery and special sales promotions—moves that ended up saving Pepsi-Cola tens of millions of dollars. The division, says Weatherup, will make its 15 per cent earnings growth target by the end of this year, three years after he declared the crisis. Profits for the first quarter of 1993 rose 22 per cent, and employees are changing the organization with gusto.

A Crisis with Customers: Peter Lewis is the CEO of Progressive, a highly successful Cleveland auto insurer that sells policies mostly to high-risk drivers. To make employees believe that they had to change, Lewis communicated a message guaranteed to get their attention: "I told them that our customers actually hate us."

Allstate, a new competitor, was starting to steal market share by offering lower prices. To stay competitive, Lewis believed that Progressive had to revamp its claims process and cut prices. But he could only cut prices by firing some 1,300 employees—19 per cent of the workforce. All this at a time when the company was enjoying healthy growth.

The company found that by settling claims faster—in 11 days on average compared with 18 before—there would be less paperwork, fewer hours spent by claims adjusters on each case, and fewer lawyers involved. All these changes added up to big savings for Progressive. And customers were happy to get their money faster. The company's stock even appreciated 70 per cent over the next 12 months.

Gaining Commitment to the Mission

One organization used a novel approach to ensure that their performance improvement effort received senior and middle management support. They made them sign for it!

As shown earlier, Amdahl takes its performance improvement efforts seriously. It recognized that without the full support and co-operation of all levels of management, it could not expect to be successful. It also recognized the need for a commitment of resources to its performance improvement teams—not just people who had time, but creative people who could make a positive contribution. This would not be feasible unless the managers of those assigned to the performance improvement teams were also committed to the process.

The following statement was signed by both Amdahl staff assigned to performance improvement teams and their immediate supervisors, who are also drafted into service.

Amdahl Canada Limited

Manager's Quality Pledge

I accept ownership of the processes I manage. I fully recognize that everyone downstream is my customer and deserves to receive defect-free work. Therefore, I will make certain that I and the people I manage fully understand the requirements of our jobs and the systems that support us. I will conform to those requirements at all times or see to it that the requirements are officially changed to what I and my customers really need.

I accept zero defects as my performance standard and agree to continuously monitor my processes to identify causes for error and to take corrective action to permanently remove those causes.

Quality Objective

To have our customers and prospects agree that we meet or exceed their expectations and are superior to the competition in everything we do.

Service Quality Council—Commitment to Serve

As an appointed member to the Service Quality Council, I understand that my responsibilities are as follows:

---

1) To attend meetings as scheduled giving my full participation. of service quality.
2) To hold confidential any information gained through my membership on the Council, which otherwise would not be known to me.
3) To diligently perform all duties for which I volunteer or am assigned by the Council.
4) To continually reflect in all my actions and words, the principles of service quality.

I hereby agree to the above and understand that my term of service will be for a period of at least one year beginning in August of 1992 and ending in August of 1993.

_____

Witness:_____

As the manager of_____I hereby agree to support the activities of the Service Quality Council and to consider the duties required by_____as a member of this Council, as a normal duty of their position until August 1993. _____

Witness:_____

Setting the Course—The Role of the Leader

Senior management must set the direction for the entire organization—whether it is a crisis or not. The following example illustrates that an "outrageous goal" can send a key message and achieve organizational alignment.

Case Study: Lincoln Life

The Company

Lincoln Life is one of the largest diversified financial services companies in the United States, recognized for its strong earnings performance, high-quality investment portfolio, excellent liquidity, and overall financial strength.

Lincoln Life is a subsidiary of Lincoln National Corporation, whose headquarters are based in Fort Wayne, Indiana. It is one of the nation's largest holding companies whose subsidiaries are engaged primarily in insurance and investment services. The corporation has assets of more than $48 billion and annual revenues of approximately $7 billion.

The Challenge—Call to Action

"Lincoln Life must redefine and restructure itself within the next calendar year, if the company is to remain among the leaders in the financial services marketplace." This was the call to action by John Boscia, President of Lincoln Life. "Major banks, mutual funds and investment brokers have joined insurers among our competitors, and they're ahead of us in being customer-focused and service-oriented."

In an effort to reach out and communicate his vision to every employee, Boscia used the organization's company newsletter to outline his goals, vision, and plan of action (including responsibilities) for Lincoln Life. The following is his message to employees.

Our "Outrageous" Goals

To create our future, the Lincoln Life Leadership Team has set these goals for completion by December 31, 1996. These goals establish the sense of urgency with which we must act. They are called "outrageous" because they are stretch goals with a short timeline for completion.

Vision Sets Direction for Change

Achieving Lincoln Life's vision to be the best customer-focused, service-led company in America will set the direction for all of the Company's change efforts. It will demonstrate our commitment to become a true customer-focused marketing organization that will measure future success in a variety of ways:

- Customers who are delighted.
- Agents who are genuine partners in our business.
- Associates who are involved, valued and have a passion for serving customers.
- Shareholders whose investment in us grows in value.
- Products and services that provide value and profit.
- Financial results that provide ever improving returns.
- Culture/Values that embody empowerment and a focus toward the customer.

How We Achieve Our Vision

Essentially, we'll achieve the Lincoln Life vision by directing our efforts toward the following important principles:

• **We will focus on our customers and ways we can best serve them.** That means decisions will be made in the best interest of customers. We need to put ourselves in the customers' shoes and ask ourselves what the customer would want. We will be asking for more feedback from customers and support them in ways that will make them advocates for Lincoln Life.

• **We will be process-based.** We will create value for our customers by continually examining each of our processes front to end. We'll rework them, measure our results and modify them again where necessary—whatever it takes to meet the changing needs of our customers, create operating efficiencies or reduce costs.

Today, Lincoln Life is organized around the various products we offer our customers—life insurance, annuities, pensions, disability income, and longterm care insurance. This arrangement focuses on development and delivery of products and services in product line "silos," which do not serve comprehensive customer needs.

In a process-based organization, the focus is on continuous identification, anticipation and fulfilment of customer needs.

The resulting process orientation coordinates and integrates similar processes that flow through all product areas. This achieves efficiencies that translate into faster and better service to customers.

Our goal is to develop new products, services and distribution combinations and approaches that make us the most customer-focused, service-led company in the Americas.

Achieving our vision will require a total transformation of Lincoln Life—our structure, the work itself, job responsibilities, culture and our people.

Teams Guide Lincoln Life Revitalization

The Leadership Team is responsible for establishing vision, setting direction and providing overall guidance for Lincoln Life's renewal efforts.

The Transformation Team is responsible for developing and implementing strategies that transform Lincoln Life into a totally integrated, process-based organization.

Process Design Teams are responsible for redesigning Lincoln Life's work processes.

Action Taken

In the first two months of Lincoln Life's transformation process, it made the following amazing accomplishments:

- A new vision was developed.
- "Outrageous" goals were established (they were stretch goals with a short timeline for completion).
- A high-level road map for achieving the "outrageous" goals was defined.
- Close to 20 town hall meetings (mass gatherings of employees) were conducted.
- A customer survey was conducted, and the results were analyzed

and assembled for decision-making.
- Current process data were gathered, analyzed, and assembled for decision-making.
- Workshops were conducted to determine points of contact with customers and how associates and agents evaluated Lincoln's performance. A random telephone survey of individual and employer-sponsored customers tested this information.
- Data on the more than 350 current initiatives were collected and analyzed; decisions were made to stop or delay; and additional decisions regarding current initiatives were considered.
- A new high-level life underwriting and issue process was developed.
- "Leadership through Action," a two-day transformation training intervention was developed.

Outrageous goals can set direction and urgency, but they will only be words if there is no leader of the charge.

It's Not Only What You Say, But Where You Deliver It That Counts

Leaders must often provide visible support for an organization's performance improvement initiative. One leader, Philippe Tafelmacher, President of Tetra Pak Canada chose an interesting venue to present his message. Tetra Pak, which develops, manufactures, and markets equipment, process lines, packaging machines, and complete plants for the handling of liquid food products, is best known by consumers for its juice boxes and milk cartons.

Tafelmacher rented the SkyDome, Toronto's world-renowned entertainment complex, to hold a meeting to address company employees. As he stood in the middle of the playing field, he made the following powerful presentation:

I don't know how many of you are baseball fans, but even if you aren't, you probably did, at some point, see the home run scored by Joe Carter in the 1993 World Series, which allowed the Toronto Blue Jays to become world champions for the second consecutive year.

That happened right here on the field behind me.

Ladies and gentlemen, I welcome you to the first-ever Canadian Mixco event, and I invite you all to think about Joe Carter. Bottom of the ninth inning...the Blue Jays losing the game that would give them the World Series...Joe Carter at the plate...then...BANG...a home run that gave it all to the Jays.

Tetra Pak Canada is a team just like the Blue Jays, and we have our own Joe Carters, John Oleruds, and Roberto Alomars. When the going gets tough and when we need to win, I know that each and every one of you has the ability to score that home run!

One of my missions as president of our company will be to make Tetra Pak a 100% quality and customer-focused organization, and I take this opportunity to personally ask each of you to join me in this, for it is a job that will require all of our efforts.

Tetra Pak Canada has made a commitment to Total Quality Service:

Total: Make everyone in the organization responsible for quality, and everything in the organization fair game for improvement.

Quality: Provide products or services which consistently meet or exceed customer expectations the first time; reduce the cost of poor quality.

Service: Manage for focus on customer service in all aspects of operation, vision, values, goals, policies, process improvement, financial support, measurements, communication, participative supervision, training and education, rewards and recognition and above all management involvement.

We have a long way to go. When examining the TQS scale it begins at the awareness level, moves to understanding, then to competence, and finally to excellence. We have been graded at the first level of awareness. Being at level one is nothing to be ashamed of, I think we should all be proud of the fact that Tetra Pak wants to be better, that we have acknowledged we need help to do this, and that we found the help to move us up the scale.

I would like to leave you with one message which I really have been saying all along in my talk to you. I will borrow some words and graphics from our former President Uno Kjellberg who made a very thought-provoking presentation at the first Mixco event held in Sweden (Author's note: you should be able to visualize the following without the pictures).

The hand is a very powerful element of the human body. It is strong, and graceful, and very necessary. Look at the hand in this picture and notice the fingers. They are not attached to the palm. You could equate this to the different Tetra Pak divisions, regions, and people. They all belong to one unit, yet often operate separately. Now look at this picture. The fingers are attached to the palm indicating that there is some coming together, yet they are spread apart and all pointing outwards in different directions. Now look at this picture: it is the same hand but it has changed into a fist—very powerful now. The fingers are all folded together as ONE.

All that I have said to you over the last several minutes feeds into this thought. Tetra Pak, with all of its different people, locations around the world, customers, and packaging systems, will only operate successfully if it operates as this fist, as ONE company. Please take this thought with you: we are the ONE company.

The Role of the Customer Bill of Rights

Do your customers know what they should expect from you? Do they know what your core service offering is? Do your internal customers know what customer standards you expect them to deliver and what standards you, as management, will meet in delivering quality service to them? Do you have a service strategy and Customer Bill of Rights? Do you post it prominently on the wall so that customers can see it?

Regardless of the industry sector, a Customer Bill of Rights has two purposes. First, it tells your internal customers what is expected of them as routine standards of performance. Secondly, it is a bold commitment to your customers concerning how they will be treated.

Unlike the statement of purpose, which is traditionally a top-down document (prepared by senior management with limited, if any, input from the front line), the Customer Bill of Rights (CBR) is generally a bottom-up document, with significant input from the customer and front-line staff. It clearly states what the company is prepared to deliver to the customer and the standards against which it is prepared to be measured. It is a public document that is circulated to customers and sometimes even printed on the back of all invoices or business cards.

Your Customer Bill of Rights should state clearly and concisely the services that your organization is prepared to deliver to the customer. For example, a hotel might have the following CBR.

Our customers have a right to...

- get through to reservations without waiting and to receive prompt, courteous service and accurate information in the official language of choice.
- receive the best room available at time of reservation in the price range requested.
- receive cheerful, efficient, and hassle-free service and be treated with care and compassion during their stay.
- stay in a clean, comfortable room with basic amenities that include soap, hand lotion, and a shower cap, and in-room devices such as telephones, mini-bars, televisions, and convertors that are in working order and are user-friendly.
- be informed of the availability and cost of all services before use and receive accurate, timely, and consistent billing for services used.
- have confidentiality respected.
- receive value-for-money in all their food-related experiences.
- be informed when there are delays or when things go wrong and be treated with extra care in these circumstances.
- comment on his/her guest experience and receive prompt response to comments, concerns, and suggestions.

I came across the following CBR in a health care facility recently. It seems that many health care facilities have been reluctant to create a similar statement, although U.S.-based organizations seem to be more progressive than Canadian-based organizations in this area. This could be explained by the fact that service is a key differentiator in the highly competitive U.S. market.

Mount Sinai Hospital, Toronto, Canada
Our Philosophy of Patient Care

It is our objective and commitment that:

1. All patients should receive considerate and respectful care.

2. All patients know the name(s) of the physician(s) in charge of their care.

3. Medical staff keep patients informed about their care, their diagnosis, anticipated treatment and prognosis. This information should be made understandable to the patient. When it is not, in the opinion of the physician, advisable to give such information to the patient, the information should be made available to the appropriate person on his or her behalf, when so requested.

4. The right of the patient to refuse treatment be recognized after the patient has been informed of the possible medical consequences of such refusal.

5. The hospital and its staff ensure that there is not undue invasion of patient privacy in delivery of medical care.

6. Confidentiality of patient information be preserved. The patient should be apprised of the fact that Mount Sinai Hospital is a University affiliated hospital, undergraduate and postgraduate medical students may be involved in his or her care under supervision of his or her own physician.

7. Within the capacity of the hospital, patients' requests for services be respected.

8. Coordination of patient care be ensured.

9. Policies and procedures affecting patient conduct within the hospital be made known to the patient on admission.

Follow this simple step-by-step process to create your own Customer Bill of Rights.

I. Form a Team

Using the principles to be discussed in Chapter 6, form a cross-functional and cross-hierarchial team that will be responsible for creating and validating the Customer Bill of Rights. The team should be given a short time frame of less than 90 days to accomplish their mandate.

2. Conduct and Interpret Customer Research

Conduct research to identify customer needs and expectations from your organization. Conduct internal research to identify what the organization appears to be willing to deliver. Then prepare a gap analysis. Are you willing to, and can you afford to, meet all of these expectations?

3. Prepare a First Draft of a CBR

Using the research, your gap analysis, and the examples provided in this chapter, draft a Customer Bill of Rights. Be prepared to go through several iterations before it is finalized.

4. Obtain Organizational and Customer Input and Buy-in

Through a series of workshops or town hall meetings, review this document with the organization as a whole. Explain why you have chosen the terms of this CBR, how conformance will be measured and the implications for your organization. Make the appropriate modifications and additions. Undertake the same process with a group of customers. Then prepare an action plan to ensure that the organization can deliver the terms of the CBR.

5. Communicate, Communicate, Communicate

Once you can consistently deliver all the elements in the Customer Bill of Rights, you are ready to aggressively communicate your message. Post it on your walls, put it on the back of your invoices and send a special communication, through possibly a newsletter, to your customers. Do not hesitate to overcommunicate.

6. Measure and Take Corrective Action

Your CBR is the standard against which you must constantly measure your performance. Listen to customer complaints and take the appropriate corrective action. Perform regular research to identify how effectively you are delivering against these standards and where you must improve. This document must be respected by the organization and your customer base.

Many organizations have discovered that they cannot live up to their customers' expectations. Yet many of these organizations do not have a Customer Bill of Rights that states what they are prepared to deliver. Consequently, it's not surprising that confusion and disappointment exist.

Case Study: Canadian Pacific Hotels & Resorts

This case study provides a good example of an organization that identified a vision and established core values. What is more noteworthy, however, is that the organization did not create this vision in the belief that it would achieve a quick-fix in a difficult market.

For Canadian Pacific Hotels & Resorts (CPH&R), the company's vision set the guideposts along the road. The company had to make significant investments in training, technology, and culture change to ensure that its employees had the tools to achieve this vision. From the onset of their path towards Total Quality Service (TQS), the company viewed TQS as an extended journey, not simply as a weekend trip. The rewards, as shown below, have been well worth the investment.

The Company

Canadian Pacific Hotels & Resorts is one of Canada's leading hotel companies, operating 25 distinctive properties across the country. With world-renowned hotels such as The Banff Springs, Le Château Frontenac, The Château Lake Louise, and The Empress, Canadian Pacific Hotels & Resorts has one of the largest collections of landmark hotels in the world and has become an internationally recognized symbol of Canada.

The Challenge—Call to Action

According to Chairman & CEO, R.S. DeMone, "Achieving success is an ongoing process. Our employees, and the organization as a whole, must constantly strive to achieve success through improved productivity, more effective service delivery, and quality products. It is important to provide a consistent guest experience at every one of our hotels and resorts."

Action Taken

In 1991, Canadian Pacific Hotels & Resorts received a call to action and responded quickly with an initiative called Total Quality Service (TQS). From the outset of the TQS journey, employees have been active participants.

As a result of over 40 employee workshops held across Canada last year, CPH&R is currently implementing recommendations for over 100 potential improvements in guest service and productivity. These improvements are above and beyond the company's current service levels, which have continually received high marks. They reflect its desire for continuous improvement.

One of the recommendations from these workshops was the need for a set of core standards to support the company's mission. In response, CPH&R quickly developed system-wide core standards, which provided employees with clear guidelines when serving their guests' needs, yet also allowed for individual flexibility and discretion.

The core standards were designed to fully meet guests' expectations. Over the years, the organization had learned that when standards were not properly developed, communicated, and consistently managed, guests suffered and costs increased because employees spent their time reacting to crises and correcting errors. The core standards provided clear guidelines to establish a more proactive approach to guests' needs. They addressed every aspect of a guest's stay such as check-in, room service, amenities, guest confidentiality, and check-out (including standard response times, standard responses, and specific procedures to respond to various situations).

The following examples highlight some of CPH&R's core standards:
- Reservation calls will be answered within three rings;
- From the time of the guest's arrival in the lobby, the check-in process will take no more than five minutes;
- Servers will acknowledge the guest within three minutes of the guest being seated; and

- Guest room deficiencies reported by a guest will be corrected within 30 minutes.

In conjunction with the core standards, measurement and corrective action committees were also formed. These committees monitor guest satisfaction through a guest satisfaction index, a mystery guest program and the special service plus helpline (for customers who had comments or concerns). Another subcommittee, known as the quality assurance committee, performs service audits to ensure that core standards are maintained. In addition to these initiatives, every department performs a self-audit program at least once a year. These audits cover every aspect of the department's function, with particular emphasis on the performance of the core standards.

"The creation of core standards is a direct result of our front-line employees assessing our guests' needs and developing their recommendations for service improvement," comments Carolyn Clark, Vice President, Human Resources. "With these core standards, we are confident that we have a quality tool to assist in fulfilling our guests' needs together with employees who have the skills to make it happen!"

And was this initiative successful? Not only have occupancy, revenues and profits improved through its TQS initiative, but so has recognition from its peers.

While the focus of its service initiative was to consistently exceed its guests' expectations, CPH&R also recognized that it could only achieve this goal through motivated, trained, and service-oriented employees. In response to this need, CPH&R established a comprehensive training program to help employees achieve their full potential. Recently, the Educational Institute of the American Hotel and Motel Association (AH&MA) awarded CPH&R with the Lamp of Knowledge award for an outstanding corporate training program.

At CPH&R, this support has resulted in an enthusiastic employee base, where people are committed to standards and values, as is evident in the following anecdotes:

Take me out to the Ball Game
A family of four was enjoying a baseball game from one of the Skyboxes at the SkyDome Hotel when the two young boys noticed that fans in a nearby box were enjoying candy floss and giant pretzels. The children asked

Susan Roylance, Skybox Coordinator, if they could have some, too. Although Susan explained that these snacks were only available in the SkyDome and not to hotel guests, their disappointment inspired her to be creative. Flashing her employee badge and sweet-talking security officers, Susan managed to get their treats. The young fans were so excited about their delicacies, they didn't even watch the rest of the game!

Elvis takes the Cake
Mr. & Mrs. Whiteway used to frequent the Outport Restaurant at Hotel Newfoundland every evening for dinner. But the week before Valentine's Day, the elderly couple was surprisingly absent. Elvis Dumaresque, a host in the restaurant, called Mrs. Whiteway to check on the couple and discovered that her husband had been ill. To wish Mr. Whiteway a speedy recovery, Elvis asked the kitchen to bake a special Valentine cake, which he delivered along with a get-well card signed by the restaurant's staff.

Laundry to go
After a few weeks of travel, some guests of Le Château Frontenac needed clean clothes. Unfortunately, it was late and the laundry at the hotel was closed. But Pierre Lapointe, Bellman, offered to take their dirty laundry and wash it in his washer and dryer at home. The next morning, the guests awoke to a basket of clean clothes.

Alignment/Empowerment and Guarantees... How to Set it Up

Earlier in this chapter we talked about the importance of a Customer Bill of Rights as a tool to align the organization. But a CBR can also be used as a competitive strategy. Consider the impact of guaranteeing to your customers that you will deliver the terms in the Customer Bill of Rights. If you do not deliver, your customer either does not have to pay or perhaps receives a significant discount. Why would they want to go elsewhere? This was the strategy of U.S.-based Northrim Bank, described below.

Northrim Bank opened for business in 1990, with a goal of creating a different kind of bank—a bank that is totally committed to customer service.

In 1994, in a report in *Executive Report on Customer Satisfaction*,

Northrim reported that its key to success was its "Customer First Service Guarantee," in which customers were guaranteed excellent service or they would receive an "Oops card" that could be redeemed for $5.

In addition to the customer service guarantee, the bank developed an employee pledge. Every employee signed this pledge—from the courier to the chairman—and made a commitment to follow the stated standards and practise Customer First Service. The pledge is framed and displayed in every department of the bank, and each employee has a copy in his or her personnel file.

The following is the bank's "Customer First Employee Pledge."

Northrim Bank's Customer First Employee Pledge

Customers deserve the very best service I can give them. I will do everything I can to meet or exceed Northrim Bank's customer service standards, not just today, but every day.

"Customer First" means I treat each customer as an individual who has special circumstances and needs and his/her own personal and financial goals. Before I make a decision or take an action, I will always consider how it will impact the customer.

I recognize that each customer has made a conscious choice to bank with Northrim. A satisfied customer is a loyal customer. By giving caring, personal attention and showing concern for my customers at every opportunity, I can do my part to keep our customers satisfied.

Quality service is my personal priority and my pledge.

According to Lori Philo Cook, Vice President/Marketing Director, Northrim employees attend customer service training at least once a year to review the company's service standards, the customer pledge, customer service guarantee, and other commitments to service. In addition, the organization provides training in sales, setting goals, and product lines.

Educating Customers About Service

Northrim has also differentiated itself in the marketplace through its customer communication program. The bank uses the following methods to educate customers about its commitment to service.

- The bank's positioning and commitment to service is regularly communicated to shareholders and potential investors. Quarterly and annual reports outline enhancements and performance.
- Customers receive explanations of the "service guarantee" with their statements. The guarantee is also promoted with counter cards, which are placed in the lobby, as well as employees wearing "Customer First Guaranteed" buttons.
- Every customer receives a letter from the president, reinforcing the commitment to service and encouraging customers to call him if they experience a problem.
- Reminders of the service guarantee are printed on statements.

And, for a more personal approach, three or four times a year, eight to 10 customers are invited to lunch with the president and a few other bank officers to let them know how the company is doing. In addition, every month the president lunches with a group of internal customers to reinforce the commitment to service.

More on Guaranteeing Your Customer's Bill of Rights

A Customer Bill of Rights should not only stand for something, but the organization must also stand behind it.

In fact, in some organizations, the fact that service guarantees are being offered has more impact than the Customer Bill of Rights itself. Nobody wants to admit that they have failed, and the fear itself does more to encourage excellence and align the organization than anything else.

Here's how Georgia Power Co. in Atlanta, backed its customer service with its own guarantee in the form of a payment policy:

> **We will provide timely, courteous customer service.** We are committed to giving extraordinary, world-class customer service. If we are ever discourteous or if your inquiry isn't handled in a timely manner, please let us know. Your comments will help us service you better.

We will connect your service by the date promised. We will do everything in our power to connect your service on the date promised. If we fail, our customer service representatives are authorized to credit your account $100 per day for every day late (maximum of $500) or pay reasonable expenses up to $500.

We will install your outdoor light or street light by the date promised. We will repair a broken light within three calendar days. We will do everything possible to install or repair your outdoor light as promised. If we fail, our customer service representatives are authorized to credit your account an amount equal to one month's service on the light. If we fail to provide service on a street light as promised, a credit of $5 per lamp will be provided.

We will provide you with an accurate bill. We always strive to give our customers 100% accurate bills. If you are over-billed, we will correct it, plus credit your account an amount equal to 10% of the corrected bill. If you are ever under-billed, we will correct it plus credit your account an amount equal to 10% of the corrected bill, up to six months. Any credit will be a minimum of $5 and a maximum of $500, not to exceed the amount of error.

We will respect your property. We know how important it is to have respect for the property of others. If our employees damage your property, they are expected to initiate prompt resolution of the problem. They are authorized to repair or replace damaged property up to $1,000.

A Personal Experience and a Bold Guarantee

On a recent visit to Harrisburg, Pennsylvania, I stayed in the local Marriott Hotel. Similar to many other hotel rooms, various materials and tent cards were placed on the bedside table. However, one certificate in particular caught my eye as I turned on the light switch. The statement on the following page was printed on this certificate.

Guarantees are important to the customer because they provide a standard of excellence against which an organization can be measured.

If the organization fails to perform for some reason, a system is already in place to respond. More importantly, the customer will not be further inconvenienced.

Even more important, however, in order for the organization to offer this guarantee, it must believe that their processes that touch the customer are so well tuned that the chance of failure is remote. That is the ultimate objective.

Incidentally, I had the opportunity to test this Customer Bill of Rights at least three times during my overnight stay at this hotel. However, I did not get an opportunity to see how they would handle service recovery—they consistently delivered on their guarantee.

When Companies Don't Take Their Guarantees Seriously

When companies make hollow service promises, with no real intention of backing them, unfortunately they not only affect their own ability to achieve improved customer retention and loyalty, but they also negatively affect the industry as a whole and the power of the guarantee as a true market differentiator.

According to Christopher Hart, President of Spire Group, and former Harvard Business School professor, in general, there are three categories of companies: The first two types use guarantees to align the organization, while the third uses guarantees to mask misalignment.

First, there are companies that offer great service and guarantee it explicitly—or the "rare" companies from which you don't even have to ask about a guarantee.

Next, there are companies that are good, and offer a guarantee—and they use it as a symbol of the value that they place on customer service and the value they place on customers.

Finally, there are companies that are falling behind in market share and offer a service guarantee because they think it's what they need to do. Unfortunately, in these companies, the systems, policies and employee buy-ins aren't in place. Hart explains, "So, to the employees, it's a joke. And if employees think it's a joke, customers will certainly think it's a joke—because this is a company that can't deliver on its guarantee promise. Companies in this category tend to put a lot of conditions on their guarantees, because if they have too many problems, they would lose too much money. And every time that happens, that debases the guarantee."

When there is nothing to substantiate the guarantee, that is, the organization cannot consistently deliver against this promise, problems

HARRISBURG Marriott

THE FINEST FULL SERVICE HOTEL IN HARRISBURG... WE GUARANTEE IT!

When we provide you with AIRPORT TRANSPORTATION:
If our van takes over twenty minutes to pick you up at the airport, we will pay for a taxi to transport you to the Hotel.

Your requested WAKE-UP CALL:
Will come at the correct time or your room will be complimentary.

When we cater your MEETING OR FUNCTION:
All meeting rooms will be properly set, according to your banquet event order, on schedule including Audio/Visual requirements or there will be no charge for the Room Rental. All coffee breaks will be set properly and on time or the break will be complimentary.

When you dine in Ashley's:
From the time your order is taken the Five-in-Five breakfast will be delivered on time or it will be our compliments. No lunch entree will take over 20 minutes or we will be responsible for the bill.

When you join us in Cahoot's:
Any food ordered in the lounge will be delivered in twenty minutes or we take the check.

When we serve you with ROOM SERVICE:
A delivery time will be quoted with every order, and your order will be delivered on time or it will be free.

occur. Customers become skeptical of any promise. And those that can truly offer differentiated service cannot get their message across…it's no longer believable.

Let's understand what happens and why this occurs.

First, if an organization offers a guarantee without a corresponding customer-focused process change, it is unlikely that employees will have the process capabilities to consistently deliver to customers' expectations. If process failure is the rule rather than the exception, customers become wary of any companies that make similar promises. And every time that happens, it reduces the power of the guarantee concept.

Customers want to do business with companies that they know from personal experience, that they have heard about by word-of-mouth, or ones that provide superior value. In other words, they want to do business with an organization they trust. When organizations make similar promises in an effort to duplicate their competition's guarantee without the corresponding ability to deliver, customer confusion and skepticism arise. Numerous surveys have shown that there are very few companies that people completely trust to do whatever it takes to satisfy them, regardless of the situation. Without this level of trust, an organization cannot use guarantees to differentiate itself in the marketplace, as it should, and correspondingly the incentive to strive for this level of differentiation is extremely low.

Lastly, too many companies use the guarantee as a marketing tool rather than using it to increase pressure on the organization to consistently deliver to customers' expectations. If a company offers a guarantee and doesn't meet its self-imposed standard, it's like waving a red flag in front of a bull: customers will get even more angry if they get lousy service. But if the guarantee is used as a means not only of measuring performance but also of identifying process failure, then the opportunity for customer-focused process improvement is a reality.

Case Study: AMP Incorporated—An Example of Total Alignment

Offering guarantees is a critical part of organizational alignment. It is the ultimate reflection of an organization that has its act together. But you cannot just offer it, you must ensure that your organization is aligned to deliver error-free service.

The Company

AMP is the world's leading supplier of connectors and interconnection systems. As the leader, it sets the industry standards in a wide range of areas, including customer service. AMP Incorporated is committed to offering a level of customer service that makes them the supplier of choice.

In March 1994, AMP brought this commitment to an even higher level by attaining ISO 9002 certification. This goal was reached through the hard work and dedication of all customer-service employees. This achievement, coupled with their unsurpassed technological systems and comprehensive customized programs, reinforces AMP's position as the leader in the electronics industry.

The Challenge—Call to Action

Escalating customer expectations and increased global competition presented a challenge to AMP Incorporated's customer-service organization. AMP's strategic response was simple—develop a well-trained team of customer-service professionals who are committed to AMP's customer-service efforts. Providing total customer satisfaction had to be the focal point at AMP Incorporated from which all products and services would be derived.

Action Taken

AMP took a number of steps to achieve its goals. Here are a few of these activities and some of the results achieved.

Teams and Teamwork

In Harrisburg, the customer-service department is divided into industry teams. The department floor plan groups teams into "corrals" with a supervisor in the centre of each work team. This structure gives a continuous opportunity for two-way communication throughout their day-to-day activities. Previously, customers had to communicate with different representatives for each transaction, now they contact one person for all dealings. In fact, 80 per cent of customers are assigned to a specific representative or team.

Measurement

AMP has two customer-service locations in the United States—one in Harrisburg on the East Coast, and the other in Diamond Bar, California. The two sites are networked to give customers a continuous 12 hours of service. Customer calls that come in before 7 a.m. are answered in Harrisburg; after 5 p.m., calls are answered on the West Coast. In October 1994, the Harrisburg site was honoured by the International Customer Service Association with its 1994 Award of Excellence for quality customer-service efforts in the manufacturing category.

From 1988 to 1991 the company made great headway in completed calls by enhancing its call management system. Earlier, by monitoring abandonment rates, the company had discovered that a disturbing 70 per cent of the time, customers were hanging up before representatives answered the phone. To remedy this, the department installed a new system with some enhancements. Small strobe lights were installed above each customer-service team. When a particular team is saturated with incoming calls, the light blinks to let customer service representatives in that team know that customers are trying to get through. When the lights were first installed, the ceiling looked like an airport landing strip—the lights were flashing continuously.

Today, the customer-service department has a call abandoned rate of .5 per cent—and calls are answered in five to six seconds—three rings would take 14 seconds.

Early Warning Systems

AMP measures the number of orders processed without having to call the production control unit for a delivery date—or "available to promise." They found that approximately 73 per cent of AMP's order schedules are processed automatically from the computer system. However, if the items are not available to promise, customer service must call or E-mail production control. Over the years, AMP has found that the most frequent customer complaint has been not being notified when a delivery might be late. The unit then has a commitment to respond to reps within four hours. In fact, all of the various operating divisions have made that commitment—and AMP tracks their progress.

To respond, AMP developed an early-warning system: when the computer system attempts to release a shipment and no inventory is available, "whistles go off." Both the customer-service representative and the production control department are then notified. Production control checks the situation to determine if the inventory is in process and might still make the ship date. If not, that unit receives a revised ship date. The production control department has the commitment to contact the representative within four hours, who can then notify the customer if AMP will miss the ship date.

Quality/Error-free Service

Another goal for AMP's customer-service department is error-free service. By first tracking the number of errors by customer-service representatives that caused materials to be returned, AMP could then analyze that the predominant cause was typographical mistakes and incorrect account numbers. To motivate representatives to reduce errors, AMP developed a recognition program that includes "spot bonuses." At the end of 1993, representatives who had gone 18 months with no errors received a spot bonus of $300. Those who went 12 months error-free received $100.

Today, the error-tracking system has been expanded beyond returned materials to include refused shipments, billing adjustments, de-releases (when customer service has to recall a product from the factory or distribution centre), and corrective action requests that reflect an error by customer service. The results are impressive: in 1994 customer service has processed almost two million transactions and has logged only 800 errors—for an accuracy rate of 99.96 per cent.

Customer Complaint Management

AMP began a "Delivery Manager" program in the early 1980s to respond to customer complaints about late shipments. The company developed a scorecard that tracks the company's shipping date back to the original promised delivery date. However, the company's perception of how well it's doing and the customers' viewpoint don't always agree.

So AMP developed a "Customer Perception" program in which customers are encouraged to send in similar scorecards to show how they perceived the company's performance.

By comparing the company's ratings with the customers' score, they found that, in many cases, there was a significant difference in results. In this case, the customer-service representative works with the customer to try to close the gaps.

AMP customer service representatives continually focus on early involvement in and immediate response to customer requirements. AMP standards are achieved by improving quality, delivery, value, and service. In the words of AMP's Larry Brandt, Associate Director of Customer Service and Corporate Logistics, "Value to our customers can only be achieved through the monitoring and continuous improvement of each business area, meeting customers' requirements, and maintaining committed suppliers, empowered employees, and enthusiastic leadership."

And, of course, AMP carefully tracks how that department performs in responding to early warnings. AMP brings new meaning to the expression, "If it moves, measure it."

How Important is Alignment?

In summary, senior management, organizational, and even customer alignment are necessary if an organization is to be recognized as an organization that *customers value most*.

It all starts with the organization's mission/vision, which must be created and sponsored from the top. From that point, the organization must live and breathe this philosophy and direction. From that document and the values it espouses comes the Customer Bill of Rights (CBR). Developed in concert with your customer base, the CBR is a clear statement of what your customers (internal, external, and stakeholders) can expect from you. It is a statement of what you are prepared to be measured against and how you expect to differentiate yourself from your competition. As expressed earlier, it stands alone as a testament to the commitment of the organization. Those organizations that are truly those that *customers value most* go one step further and offer service guarantees—the true test of alignment.

But alignment is only the first step in our four-phase process. Once the organization is in alignment for the business transformation process, care must be taken to address those processes that touch the customer in order of customer priority and impact on revenue enhancement and improved profitability. That is the purpose of the Explore phase as described in our next chapter. But first, take the challenge posed in the checklist that follows.

—— CHECKLIST ——

Do You Have the Personal Ability to Encourage Alignment?

Achieving organizational alignment requires special leadership. The leader plays a key role in defining the mission/vision and values of the organization. The leader must also be capable of generating enthusiasm and support for the Customer Bill of Rights. In brief, for alignment to be successful, the leader must be capable of communicating a believable message and the charisma to garner support throughout the business transformation process.

What Type of Leader Are You?

Personal Leadership

1. I treat both my peers and my subordinates fairly and with respect.

Rarely			Sometimes				Always		
1	2	3	4	5	6	7	8	9	10

2. I actively listen to my peers and direct reports and don't interupt to give my point of view.

Rarely			Sometimes				Always		
1	2	3	4	5	6	7	8	9	10

3. I take responsibility for my actions.

Rarely			Sometimes				Always		
1	2	3	4	5	6	7	8	9	10

4. I prefer to coach my subordinates rather than direct them.

Rarely			Sometimes				Always		
1	2	3	4	5	6	7	8	9	10

—— CHECKLIST ——

5. I maintain a healthy, positive outlook.

Rarely			Sometimes				Always		
I	2	3	4	5	6	7	8	9	10

6. I understand the organization's mission/vision and values and apply them in my dealings with all staff in the organization.

Rarely			Sometimes				Always		
I	2	3	4	5	6	7	8	9	10

7. I try not to lose sight of the fact that the organization has both long-and short-term goals.

Rarely			Sometimes				Always		
I	2	3	4	5	6	7	8	9	10

8. My personal practices and behaviour are in harmony with the organization's corporate values.

Rarely			Sometimes				Always		
I	2	3	4	5	6	7	8	9	10

9. I enjoy working with my peers and subordinates towards a common goal.

Rarely			Sometimes				Always		
I	2	3	4	5	6	7	8	9	10

10. I practise good customer service with both my internal and external customers.

Rarely			Sometimes				Always		
I	2	3	4	5	6	7	8	9	10

—— CHECKLIST ——

Planning

11. I take time to plan my daily activities around key personal and corporate objectives.

Rarely			Sometimes				Always		
1	2	3	4	5	6	7	8	9	10

12. I try to align my long- and short-term goals with those of our corporate goals.

Rarely			Sometimes				Always		
1	2	3	4	5	6	7	8	9	10

13. During my planning time, I prioritize those activities that I need to accomplish.

Rarely			Sometimes				Always		
1	2	3	4	5	6	7	8	9	10

14. Each day I plan to accomplish only those activities for which I have allocated enough time.

Rarely			Sometimes				Always		
1	2	3	4	5	6	7	8	9	10

15. I strive for continuous learning and have plans to further my competencies in areas that assist me in reaching my corporate and personal goals.

Rarely			Sometimes				Always		
1	2	3	4	5	6	7	8	9	10

16. I strive to work to the standards as set out explicitly (through our CBR) and implicitly through our mission/vision.

Rarely			Sometimes				Always		
1	2	3	4	5	6	7	8	9	10

CHECKLIST

17. I try to exceed the expectations of all the customers with whom I come into contact in my activities.

Rarely			Sometimes				Always		
1	2	3	4	5	6	7	8	9	10

18. When I plan my activities, I have knowledge of my environment and take any changing elements into consideration.

Rarely			Sometimes				Always		
1	2	3	4	5	6	7	8	9	10

19. I have a good sense of how my personal values, strengths, and weaknesses align with those required to support our corporate direction.

Rarely			Sometimes				Always		
1	2	3	4	5	6	7	8	9	10

20. I have realistic goals with achievable targets for my major activities.

Rarely			Sometimes				Always		
1	2	3	4	5	6	7	8	9	10

Improvement

21. I have a clear idea of which processes affect my ability to deliver *what customers value most.*

Rarely			Sometimes				Always		
1	2	3	4	5	6	7	8	9	10

22. I constantly strive to improve those processes identified above.

Rarely			Sometimes				Always		
1	2	3	4	5	6	7	8	9	10

CHECKLIST

23. I constantly strive to measure whether I am meeting my own and my department's performance objectives.

Rarely			Sometimes				Always		
1	2	3	4	5	6	7	8	9	10

24. I constantly strive to eliminate non-value-adding activities.

Rarely			Sometimes				Always		
1	2	3	4	5	6	7	8	9	10

25. I admit my mistakes, acknowledge the reasons, and then move on with the goal to not make the same mistakes again.

Rarely			Sometimes				Always		
1	2	3	4	5	6	7	8	9	10

26. I encourage communicating and celebrating successes as well as failures.

Rarely			Sometimes				Always		
1	2	3	4	5	6	7	8	9	10

27. I consistently strive to measure performance against customer expectations.

Rarely			Sometimes				Always		
1	2	3	4	5	6	7	8	9	10

28. I constantly strive to improve in areas that are important to the organization as a whole.

Rarely			Sometimes				Always		
1	2	3	4	5	6	7	8	9	10

——— CHECKLIST ———

29. I am a role model for continuous improvement in everything I do.

Rarely			Sometimes				Always		
1	2	3	4	5	6	7	8	9	10

30. I am open to changes in my life that will enable me to learn new things.

Rarely			Sometimes				Always		
1	2	3	4	5	6	7	8	9	10

Scoring

Add up the numbers you have circled and write the total in the space provided.

Your Score:_____

Maximum points: 300

How to Interpret Your Score

60-89 points:
Grade F. You might choose to adopt some of these strategies to get your leadership focus back on track.

90-128 points:
Grade D. You should analyze your personal practices and goals in life. You do not currently demonstrate a leadership philosophy.

129-158 points:
Grade C. You demonstrate some patterns of leadership but need to be more consistent on a daily basis if you are to play a significant role in organizational alignment.

159-229 points:
Grade B. You have a good foundation in leadership principles and practices, and could serve as a role model for others.

230-300 points:
Grade A. You are a strong role model, with a solid set of principles in leadership, planning, and continuous improvement. You should have great success in encouraging organizational alignment.

5

The Explore Phase: How to Use the Voice of the Customer

This chapter is dedicated to the voice of the customer. As expressed in earlier chapters, too many failures are attributed to focusing efforts in the wrong direction and ignoring the drivers of customer satisfaction and dissatisfaction. Although there is no single best listening device that can or should be used in all situations, this chapter will explain why this is the case and will provide a checklist to help you in the selection process.

As we will discuss, research on the voice of the customer must be used to identify customer satisfiers and dissatisfiers as well as customer-focused processes that require immediate attention. This research must also be used to monitor the effectiveness of the process changes that are being implemented so that corrective action, if appropriate, can be made.

Why the Voice of the Customer Sets the Direction and Focus

As we discussed earlier, your organization has internal customers—your employees—and external customers—your clients, associates, suppliers, or stakeholders. Regardless of the term you use (I will call them customers), their collective voices and degree of satisfaction with the processes that touch them, as well as isolated activities within these processes, must be heard.

The results of the IDEAS study indicated that successful organizations survey their customers regularly and extensively not only to determine their needs, but also the extent to which the company is meeting or exceeding these needs. As shown in the following figure, successful companies are more likely to survey customers on a variety of issues, including the effectiveness of handling complaints; customer satisfaction; conformance to standards; customer needs; and new product ideas.

Organizations that are Successful in Achieving Improved Customer Satisfaction Listen to the Voice of the Customer in a Number of Key Areas

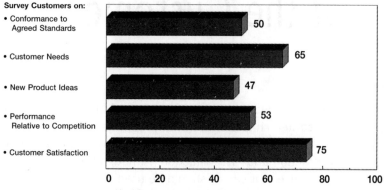

Source: 1994 C&L I.D.E.A.S. Study

But successful companies don't stop there. Not only do they measure their actual performance against standards they have established for themselves, but they also research and compare themselves to their competition. In short, the companies that satisfy their customers are the companies that do their homework. They know that a commitment to customer satisfaction must be supported by a complete understanding of three key elements: the customer, the competition, and the marketplace. Furthermore, they also need the ability to identify and respond to areas where change is needed.

"If you know the enemy and know yourself, you need not fear the result of a hundred battles. If you know yourself but not the enemy, for every victory gained, you will also suffer a defeat. If you know neither the enemy nor yourself, you will succumb in every battle."

Sun Tzu
The Art of War

Who Are My Customers and What Are Their Needs?

This is not a strange question; rather, it is one that must be asked regularly. Customers' needs change and are influenced by competitive offerings, market changes, technology, or the environment.

Here's a new perspective for organizations that are concerned about customer satisfaction, and it's one that applies to all organizations—large and small, domestic and international. It deals with a concept that many of us learned in school—Maslow's Hierarchy of Needs. If applied properly, this exciting and effective approach will lead to a more focused marketing strategy and, in turn, to improved customer satisfaction and increased profitability.

In brief, Abraham Maslow proposed that a hierarchy of needs exists for all humans, starting with basic biological needs and ascending to more complex psychological motivations that become important only after basic needs have been satisfied.

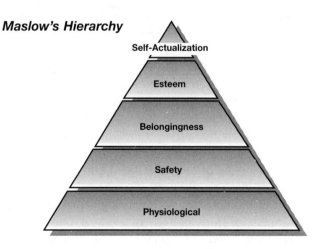

Maslow's Hierarchy

Self-Actualization

Esteem

Belongingness

Safety

Physiological

Maslow proposed that the needs at one level must be at least partially satisfied before those at the next level become important determiners of action. For example, when physiological/basic and safety needs are difficult to fulfil, a person's time and effort become consumed with trying to satisfy these needs, and higher motives become less significant. According to Maslow, only when basic needs are easily satisfied will the individual have time and energy to devote to the more aesthetic and intellectual interests. The highest motive—self-actualization—can be achieved only after all other needs have been completely fulfilled.

Customer satisfaction is analogous to Maslow's Hierarchy of Needs. Customers similarly operate on a hierarchy of needs when they are considering purchasing goods or services from a supplier. We will refer to this hierarchy as "Stages of Customer Need."[1] More specifically, customers, or customer groups (e.g., local, regional, or international), have a priority of needs and a particular degree of satisfaction with their current supplier, based on how well the supplier meets those needs, as shown in the following figure.

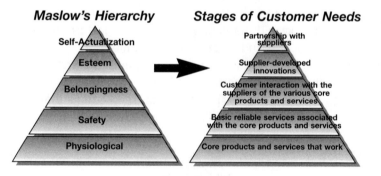

The level at which the customers' needs fall within the hierarchy, together with their level of satisfaction with the supplier, will affect the marketing and customer satisfaction strategies required to attract and maintain these customers. This highlights the importance of a well-designed and institutionalized market/customer satisfaction research program.

Let's look at each stage of customer need and the corresponding customer/market research required for it.

The lowest-level human need is physiological—food, sleep, etc. The analogous need for someone considering a purchase is core products or services that work. By reviewing your customer list, you should be able to identify which customers fall into this category. Most likely they will be commodity purchasers. Ongoing monitoring should be simple—perhaps a mail survey or periodic telephone surveys.

Maslow's next level of basic needs is safety—security, protection, reliability, freedom from anxiety, and so forth. The corresponding customer need is a set of basic services associated with the core offering. For instance, delivering products that are on time and are undamaged. In a service business, the safety equivalent is accessibility, timely hours of operation, or localized service access. A combination of focus groups and well-designed telephone research will help you segment your customers into this "need" level or one of the next three levels on the hierarchy. Because customers in this segment will most likely be in a growth stage of their business, monitoring through a combination of telephone and in-person interviews is suggested. Customers within this group may quickly move into one of the next two levels as they gain market share and require market differentiation to maintain their market presence.

Maslow's third basic need, belongingness, can be equated to a customer's need for an accessible, two-way relationship. A supplier's employees must listen to, and communicate with, a customer's employees to understand unique expectations and solve problems. Research must be focused on several levels within the customer's organization.

The fourth need in Maslow's hierarchy is esteem—the need for acknowledgement, or for having a favourable reputation, prestige, or expertise. In business, suppliers grant the customer prestige and stature by committing resources to understanding and anticipating the forces of change affecting them and then developing new products and/or services to accommodate these forces. There is a primary need on the hierarchy for suppliers that are proactive and knowledgeable of market conditions and that operate as an extension of the customer's field salesforce. Research must therefore now be focused on the external market with an eye on the suppliers' ability to meet product quality and delivery needs.

Maslow's highest need level is self-actualization. The self-actualized individual has mastery in what he or she does. The self-actualized customer relationship is often described as a true partnership, where the customer has made the supplier a complete and open participant in the detailed, long-term conduct of his or her business.

Customers at this level require the most extensive forms of research that must be designed to assess performance at all the lower levels on the needs hierarchy. One-on-one customer interviews on a regularly scheduled basis are paramount. Customer intelligence must be contained within a versatile contact management system and not only updated, but also analyzed regularly.

Now that you understand this concept, watch out! Customers may migrate to a new level in a short period, as their business matures and the competition changes. Only through a well-focused and flexible customer/market research program will these shifts and changes be noticed.

Consequently, you must answer the following question: On what levels are my customers? Most likely they will cluster in different stages. They may differ by region, product offering, and price point. Internationally, customers in different countries might either have a different order of priorities, or different degrees of satisfaction. Your challenge is to find the answers and to stay ahead of the competition by satisfying the higher-level needs.

> Whether it be your existing customers, or those that you seek to win over, the key components of the research design will revolve around achieving answers to the following questions:
>
> What is the customer's current "need" level?
>
> How does the customer rate your organization's performance relative to satisfying this and all lower need levels?
>
> How well are competitors currently satisfying the customers' needs at this level, or alternatively, would they be capable of satisfying them to a greater extent than you?

Priorities for Improvement: Mapping the Service Cycle

Before you can actually create a research questionnaire, you must first understand the strengths and weaknesses of the processes that touch the customer. This will help you to identify the process improvement opportunities that eventually lead to revenue enhancement and improved profitability. One of the most effective and cost-efficient ways of gathering this information is through Service Cycle Mapping. There are actually two parts to this mapping process: an internal and an external part.

Before we start, we must first clarify the meaning of a key term in this mapping process. This term, "moment of truth," (MOT) was made popular by Jan Carlzen, President of SAS Airlines. Carlzen defined a "moment of truth" as any activity in which the customer gets an impression (positive or negative) of the service you deliver. Although Carlzen popularized the definition, the term originates from bullfighting. The moment of truth occurs when the bullfighter sees the approaching bull and must make a split-second decision— to move the red cape and get out of the way or be gored by the bull.

> Moment of truth (MOT)-The moment when the customer comes in contact with any aspect of your business and, on the basis of that contact, forms an opinion (positive or negative) about the quality of your service.

Regardless of the term's origin, every employee experiences hundreds, if not thousands, of moments of truth in the course of a day, week, or month. A MOT that is managed successfully helps to create a positive perception of quality and service. But each moment of truth can also be a potential failure point that can make the customer decide to shift his or her business to a competitor.

How do you harness this potential for success and/or failure? How do you use it to identify strengths and weaknesses in current customer-focused processes?

The first phase of the Service Cycle Mapping process must be focused internally. For each market segment served, assemble a group of eight to 10 individuals who have direct and indirect contact with the customer. The individuals that are brought together should represent three groups:

  i) people who provide input into the process under consideration;
  ii) people who are on the receiving end of the process—the output (in some cases, it may be the actual external customer); and
  iii) people who are responsible for activities within the process.

Since your goal is to encourage open and honest communication, senior management is typically not invited to this session.

A number of issues should be explored in this session. First, identify where the moments of truth exist. You can either chart these on the Cycle of Service itself (as shown below) in its proper sequence or create a list on a flipchart or white board.

Cycle of Service

Moments of Truth - Distributor

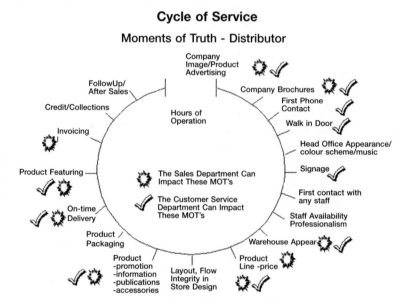

Second, identify what you believe to be the top 10 priorities in the eyes of your customers. That is, determine which MOTs have the greatest impact on your customers' perception of your organization. Write them down in any order on a chart similar to the one that follows.

Moment of Truth	Rating Scale of 5 to 1 5 is Excellent	Priority Scale of 10 to 1 10 is Highest Priority

Now that you have identified these MOTs, ask group members to rate your organization's performance on each of those moments of truth using a scale of 1 to 5, where 5 is excellent and 1 is poor. Then ask them to rank the MOT in terms of priority to the customer: 10 is the activity of highest priority, 1 is the lowest.

Now comes the real challenge. For each of these top 10 issues, ask your group to answer the following questions:

i)   What do we do well within this MOT?
ii) What do we do poorly?
iii) What improvement opportunities exist?
iv) What are the impediments to success?

This exercise should highlight a number of issues surrounding your process and identify drivers of satisfaction and dissatisfaction that should be investigated within your customer research questionnaire.

The following figure shows one organization's results, to the chart described above.

Moment of Truth	Rating Scale of 5 to 1 5 is Excellent	Priority Scale of 10 to 1 10 is Highest Priority
On-time delivery	4.2	1
Invoicing accuracy	3.2	4
Brochure/product literature	4.8	3
Technical support	4.5	9
Order accuracy	3.8	8
Reception	3.9	6
Phonemail	2.5	5
Back order fulfilment	4.9	2
Inventory availability	2.9	10
Salesperson contact	3.4	7

As this figure shows, the areas that require the most significant attention—high-priority items—are also areas where the organization has less-than-satisfactory performance. Too often organizations spend an inordinate amount of time fine-tuning areas that have little effect on their customers and their changing needs. Focusing time, energy, and resources on an area in which you already excel (even if it does add value) will not improve your performance or customer satisfaction, as much as improving something high in value that you do not do very well.

Remember, however, that we are considering the internal organization's perspective of its ability to deliver to customers' needs. This internal perception must be matched against your customers' actual perceptions. Therefore, before we start the process of developing a questionnaire, a final validation step is required.

To achieve this, bring together a group of eight to 10 customers in a focus group. You may require several groups that represent different customer segments. Start the discussion by outlining your service cycle mapping exercise and presenting your top 10 priorities. Give each customer a blank chart, similar to the one you used with your internal group, and ask him or her to rate each moment of truth. Then ask each participant to prioritize the MOTs on a scale of one to 10. Finally, ask if there are other MOTs not mentioned that have higher priority. Spend the rest of your time with this group to discuss why these scores have been assigned.

Compare these scores to the scores prepared by your internal team and you then have the start of what is called a gap analysis. This initial step in identifying which customer-focused processes will have to be addressed first.

Service cycle workshops are an effective tool for listening to customers:

The "Voice of the External Customer" is heard through participation of not only front-line employees who have the best understanding of the needs and expectations of external customers, but also through the external customer directly;

The "Voice of the Internal Customer" is heard through participation from the various functional areas involved in the organization as they articulate issues, expectations, and barriers to effective cross-functional cooperation.

Creating the High-Level "Quick" Map

Now that we have a qualitative appreciation of customer needs (through our mapping of the service cycle), it is now time to obtain a pictorial representation of the processes that touch the customer. We must do this before we develop a questionnaire. The organization must be able to describe, in general terms, its operating practices and the processes that directly and indirectly touch the customer. This requires an understanding of the processes as they exist today, as well as an efficient way of representing this information.

Most companies are organized around the various products that they offer to their customers. This type of structure focuses on the development and delivery of products and services in product line "silos." One department enters the order, another sends the invoice, and the third is responsible for collections, but no one is responsible for the entire customer experience—not a very customer-friendly approach.

In contrast, customer-oriented organizations focus on continuous identification, anticipation, and fulfilment of customer needs. The resulting process coordinates and integrates similar processes that flow through all product areas. This helps to achieve efficiencies that translate into faster and better service to customers. For example, at Oxychem, a major manufacturer and distributor of chemical products, the customer-service department does not just process orders. This department anticipates customer needs (occasionally contacting customers if an out-of-stock situation is imminent), takes responsibility for ensuring that the order is accurate, and ensures that all invoicing is accurate and that credits and mispricing do not occur.

How your organization defines and describes these processes is critical, so let's first start with a definition of process.

What is a Process?

The heart of managing a business is managing its processes. After all, a company is defined not only by its products and services, but also by its processes. How a company creates and delivers value to customers is the core of a business enterprise.

Since this chapter deals primarily with processes and process improvement, we will start by defining the term "process."

A process is a series of interrelated transactions that convert inputs into outputs (results) that offer value to the customer. Processes consume resources and require standards and documentation for repeatable performance.

Process Map
A Process is...

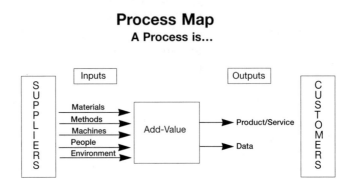

One of the most fundamental and critical processes that affect customer satisfaction is the Customer Order Fulfilment (COF) Process. The process map below illustrates the traditional approach to customer order fulfilment, in which different individuals or departments deal with the customer at each stage of the process.

Traditional Approach to
Customer Order Fulfilment

This is traditionally viewed as a process that converts an order to a received good or service with an accompanying invoice. But as you can see, the process is actually made up of a number of subprocesses:

- order acquisition (obtaining the order from the customer)
- order processing (processing the physical order through the organization, including pricing)
- order delivery (from receipt of the order at the warehouse, assembling the order, and arranging shipping to the customer)
- billing (preparing the invoice and sending it to the customer)

This traditional view, however, has been reengineered by enlightened organizations. These organizations have adopted a more expanded approach that has greater impact on revenue enhancement and improved profitability. This new approach adds a number of subprocesses at the front and back end of the traditional COF process.

**Potential Expanded Approach to
Address Revenue Enhancement**

Business/ Marketing Planning	→	Order Acquisition	→	Traditional COF Approach	→	After Sales Service

Let's first examine the Sales Acquisition subprocess. This process traditionally includes the following key activities:

- marketing planning/budgeting (preparing an overall plan for marketing the products and/or services of the organization);
- promotional program development (a subset of the marketing plan that ensures that maximum benefit is received for the promotional dollar);
- account/contact management (to ensure that appropriate coverage is given to all customers and that it can be monitored);
- salesforce training (to ensure that a training cycle is built into the process and that both the internal and external salesforce are sufficiently versed in product knowledge and corporate operating practices); and
- advertising planning and evaluation (as with promotion, to ensure that advertising dollars are allocated appropriately and that the impact of these expenditures is evaluated appropriately).

At the other end of the COF process is the Customer "After Sales" Service subprocess that includes the following activities:

- complaint management (discussed further in Chapter 8);
- billing enquiry (to ensure that rapid response can be provided to the customer on any and all enquiries);
- order status reporting (to provide the customer with timely, accurate response to the delivery status of orders and back orders); and

- new product information dissemination (a market research mechanism that can feed back to the start of the process and possibly initiate new product development or refinement).

Finally, don't forget the internal customers and how subprocesses will ultimately affect their willingness to implement them. Poor implementation of improvements by internal customers will affect external customer satisfaction. These subprocesses include the following:

- recruitment;
- training and employee development;
- performance management;
- suggestion systems;
- rewards and awards systems; and
- communication systems.

The message is simple: a business enterprise is composed of a series of processes, some of which are interrelated and some of which are independent. Although massive change may be necessary, an organization obviously cannot make changes in all areas at the same time.

A Process for Mapping the Process

You can use many tools—either manual or computer-generated—to assist you in drawing these processes. However, I recommend the following, highly effective horizontal mapping procedure.

You need these items to proceed:

- a long roll of brown paper
- a marker pen
- a pad of sticky papers (size 2" x 2"), which we will call process blocks (PBs).

Roll out the paper on the top of a long meeting-room table and ask the team to gather around the table. List the departments or divisions that touch this process in rows on the paper. Now you are ready to draw/describe your process flow.

For each activity within the process, write the name of the activity on a piece of "sticky paper." Do this for each activity until you have described the process, from end to end. You may find that you will need to move these PBs, either because you found out that the PB is done earlier or later in the process or because it may be handled by a different department. At some points in your process flow, you may reach a point where there are a number of activities or routes that could be followed. We call this a branch in the process flow. At these times, turn the PB sideways to form a diamond shape. These should be the only PB shapes that will be required.

Once you are comfortable with the process flow, draw in the lines with your marker pen. Next, using a flowchart software package, recreate the map and distribute it to your team members. Your final diagram should look something like this.

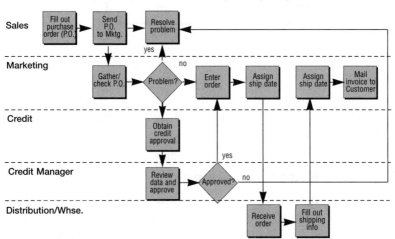

The Customer Order Fulfilment (COF) Process

You are not quite finished yet. Circulate this map to your colleagues in the departments involved in this process. Then meet with them to ensure that you have not missed a step. Finally, reconvene the team and, using coloured markers, do the following:

i) Use a red marker to mark with an asterisk all hot spots where roadblocks or customer dissatisfaction/complaints occur (i.e., credit approval takes too long). These become priority areas for investigation within your research program.

ii) Use a green marker to mark with a checkmark all PBs where obvious redundancies or non-value-added activities occur (i.e., marketing gathers or checks the P.O.). These are obvious areas where quick hits can occur.

Now this activity is complete—that's all there is to it. This process should be repeated for each core business process that touches the customer such as product development, customer relationship management, customer service, new customer set-up, customer acquisition and sales process.

Process Maps

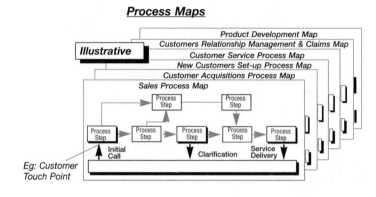

By completing this exercise, you will have identified major customer-focused processes and where they touch the customer. Linkages to other processes will have also been defined.

You are now ready to input this information into the "Voice of the Customer" research design that will be explained in the following section.

Designing a Research Questionnaire

Now that we have defined the processes, we need to develop the research instrument (either to be administered by telephone or in person), to identify the drivers of external customer satisfaction and dissatisfaction. The questions used in your qualitative and quantitative portions of research should always keep a focus on the customer in mind (more on this in the next section of this chapter).

You may wish to consider the following guidelines when designing or reviewing these questionnaires. The questionnaire should address the following primary issues:

Satisfaction and Loyalty Attributes

The questionnaire should include the attributes that the process mapping and MOT Cycle of Service exercises, described above, may have indicated are important to verify. This may include delays in credit approval, the knowledge and competencies of the customer-service representative (CSR), and timing and notice with respect to back orders. Wherever possible, try to assess your customer's rating of the service you provide on each attribute as well as the priority they assign to your improvement of this attribute. For example, you should not focus on an attribute that customers have defined as low value.

Complaint Resolution Experience

Some issues will require detailed probing within your questionnaire. It should address some of the following issues:

- reasons why customers contact your company with questions or problems
- reasons why customers who have problems do not complain
- the average number of questions/problems experienced per customer
- the most serious problems/questions from the customer's perspective
- satisfaction with the action taken
- ratings of the contact experience in terms of access, professionalism, knowledge, courtesy, resolution, etc.

Points of Contact for Complaints

Capturing complaints is critical for your organization. However, because these complaints typically have a number of entry points, they can be difficult to capture and track consistently. Therefore, you must acknowledge these entry points and use them as a source for further probing. The questionnaire can help to determine the following:

- the points of contact that customers actually use to complain, access the company, or request assistance.
- the typical number of contacts that will have to be made in order to resolve the problem; and
- the average response time for final resolution.

Impact on Customer Retention and Positive Word-of-Mouth

Consider again the Customer Satisfaction/Revenue Enhancement Model described in Chapter 1. Customers' experiences play an important role in terms of loyalty and positive word-of-mouth. Through customer satisfaction research, you must be able to identify the impact of complaint behaviour, problem resolution, and customer satisfaction on overall satisfaction and loyalty to your organization. You can accomplish this by assessing your customers' willingness to recommend your company to others (See Chapter 8-IBM Rochester example) as well as through their willingness to repurchase.

Suggested Improvements

Your customers are a tremendous source of new ideas and suggestions for service improvement. Tap into this resource by including questions that probe your customers on this issue.

The following can be used as a guide as you construct your questionnaire. Note the sequence of questions for both General Impressions and Business Interaction. Also note how the final line of questions is to deal with Suggested Improvements.

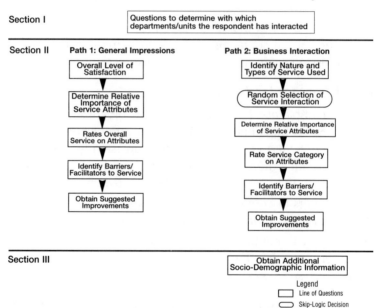

Questionnaire Flow Model External Survey

Section I — Questions to determine with which departments/units the respondent has interacted

Section II

Path 1: General Impressions
- Overall Level of Satisfaction
- Determine Relative Importance of Service Attributes
- Rates Overall Service on Attributes
- Identify Barriers/Facilitators to Service
- Obtain Suggested Improvements

Path 2: Business Interaction
- Identify Nature and Types of Service Used
- Random Selection of Service Interaction
- Determine Relative Importance of Service Attributes
- Rate Service Category on Attributes
- Identify Barriers/Facilitators to Service
- Obtain Suggested Improvements

Section III — Obtain Additional Socio-Demographic Information

Legend
- ☐ Line of Questions
- ⬭ Skip-Logic Decision

Relevant Versus Irrelevant Questions

Despite your best intentions, you may be inclined to include some off-topic questions (such as questions related to advertising or product versus process questions). Try to ensure that these types of questions do not distract the respondent, and limit them to fewer than 10 per cent of the questions asked).

Before you use the questionnaire, we recommend a trial run with a small sample of six to eight customers. During this trial run, check for ambiguities, redundancy, and jargon (technical terms and expressions). Correct any problems, even if it means delaying your questionnaire launch.

When you have completed all these steps, it is now time to launch the questionnaire. Although you may choose to use your own resources to conduct the survey, ensure an objective assessment by out-sourcing the conduct of the research to an independent third party. Tabulation can be done externally, but the analysis should be done by those who must use this information to make changes within the orga-nization. In most cases, this analysis can be done by working with skilled consultants who can help you to interpret the key findings of the research. The analysis must focus on identifying the processes that affect customer satisfaction and dissatisfaction. Your first-level graphical inter-pretation representation of the data might look like this.

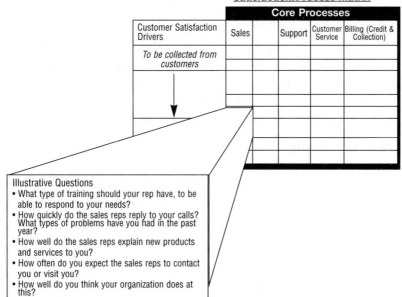

Satisfaction/Process Matrix

Customer Satisfaction Drivers	Core Processes				
	Sales		Support	Customer Service	Billing (Credit & Collection)
To be collected from customers					

Illustrative Questions
• What type of training should your rep have, to be able to respond to your needs?
• How quickly do the sales reps reply to your calls? What types of problems have you had in the past year?
• How well do the sales reps explain new products and services to you?
• How often do you expect the sales reps to contact you or visit you?
• How well do you think your organization does at this?

Capture Candid Customer Feedback with Focus Groups

Before you introduce new marketing campaigns, value-added services, or products, or before you design customer satisfaction surveys, step back and assess your company—from your customers' point of view. One of the most effective ways of doing this is by means of a focus group. This face-to-face research tool is typically used to ask your cus-tomers what you do well, what you do wrong, what they expect from you, and for suggestions on how to improve your weak areas. Following are some guidelines for using this research tool effectively.

Number of Groups

For every market segment that you wish to research, you should conduct two sets of focus groups. A market segment could be defined in terms of sex, age group, buying preferences, current or past customers, or some other criterion. Why do you need two focus groups? Because one group may not be a true reflection of customer behaviour and perceptions. Two focus groups offer a more balanced viewpoint.

Preparation

Research customer issues in advance. Even if you have used customer focus groups to get "preview" data for a product or service, you should do some preliminary research before conducting the discussion. For instance, some companies prefer to send participants a prequalifying questionnaire (which might contain questions related to their attitudes and perceptions on topics that will be probed in more detail during the focus group) before the meeting so that they have a preview of issues that may arise. This background research can help you to develop a topic guide or agenda, which will provide a framework for the moderator conducting the session.

Discussion Guide

Your primary objective is to stimulate discussion among the participants. Consequently, you have to be selective and restrict your discussion to relevant information rather than less relevant issues. Furthermore, phrase your questions carefully. Many organizations make the common mistake of using jargon instead of plain language that customers will understand.

Audio- and Videotaping

Audio-and videotaping are common practices nowadays. Even so, ask participants' permission to videotape—or at least audiotape—focus sessions. Videotapes in particular serve as a useful record of the proceedings and a portion of the videotape can be part of a presentation or report of the results for senior management. Managers can also review the tapes as they design the customer surveys to ensure that they are staying on target.

What to Ask

You may choose to pose some of the following sample questions to your focus group:

- How do you feel our management team has done in providing you with products and services on a timely basis to help you stay competitive?
- Tell us which of our value-added services are most beneficial to you.
- Are there some services we should discontinue? Are there some we should add?
- Would you prefer to have the cost of these services rolled into the product pricing or pay for them separately?
- How do you feel our customer service, sales, and technical staff do in meeting your needs on a timely basis? Are there any people who you feel deserve special recognition for their efforts?
- How do we do in filling your orders correctly the first time? Do you get them on time?
- Is our method of packaging and shipping products acceptable? Any suggestions?
- Are we getting all of your business? If not, why? What do we need to do to get it all?
- Do you feel that implementing technologies like bar coding and EDI (Electronic Data Interface) would be helpful to you? Would you be willing to pay slightly higher prices in the beginning if we implemented these technologies?
- What are our biggest strengths as a business partner?
- In what areas do we need to improve? Which of these areas should we work on first?
- What are the biggest challenges you face in your business? How can we work together to help you make more money in the upcoming year?

Data Analysis: Matching Drivers of Satisfaction to Process Improvement

Once you have the results from both the focus groups and questionnaires, what do they really tell us?

Although there are many approaches to the analysis of this data, the approach you use should be one that is easy to follow. In essence, the research must give you answers to the questions you developed earlier and, in particular, to the question, "What are the drivers of satisfaction and dissatisfaction?" Basically, you need to know where customers see value and where improvements are necessary, which processes and activities within these processes add value, and which ones have no appreciable value. The following figure is a graphical representation of the analysis that I have found to be most useful.

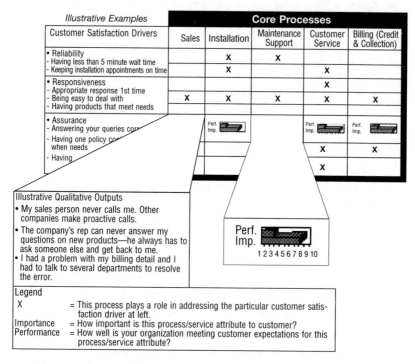

The matrix provides a representation of the customer satisfaction drivers as rows and the core processes as columns. As shown on the matrix, the "x's" identify which processes play a role in addressing the particular customer satisfaction driver (in simple terms, where an "x" appears, the process touches the customer). The research should tell us how important this process service attribute is to the customer. More importantly, the research should tell you how well the organization is meeting customer expectations.

But this is only the first step. Next, we must prioritize what must be done. High-priority items—drivers that are important to the customer but

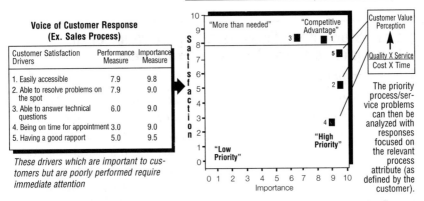

**Voice of Customer Response
(Ex. Sales Process)**

Customer Satisfaction Drivers	Performance Measure	Importance Measure
1. Easily accessible	7.9	9.8
2. Able to resolve problems on the spot	7.9	9.0
3. Able to answer technical questions	6.0	9.0
4. Being on time for appointment	3.0	9.0
5. Having a good rapport	5.0	9.5

These drivers which are important to customers but are poorly performed require immediate attention

Customer Driver Prioritization (Ex. Sales Process)

Customer Value Perception

Quality X Service / Cost X Time

The priority process/service problems can then be analyzed with responses focused on the relevant process attribute (as defined by the customer).

are poorly performed—should obviously receive primary consideration (the following chapter will give you some direction on what you must do). The following is a graphical representation of that analysis.

Note the information on performance rating and customer priority. The graphical representation now allows you to identify how well the organization is doing in areas that the *customer values most*. As a result of this analysis, the organization can clearly identify what process points can provide it with a competitive advantage and then focus on these priority issues.

High-priority items that drive customer satisfaction and provide a competitive advantage must obviously be addressed first. However, a number of quick-fixes may also require attention.

Graphs alone will not ensure management buy-in. These graphical representations, which summarize your research findings and point to process improvement priorities, are just the tools to help you to identify the trouble or opportunity spots and help prioritize them in moving forward. They must, however, be presented in a clear, concise manner, properly identifying all linkages.

Graphs and pictorial charts work well for this purpose, since to quote a popular saying, "A picture is worth a thousand words." A word of caution, however. This representation must be easy to explain to all levels within your organization. Employee buy-in is essential and that will not be achieved if you do not consider their needs and level of understanding. Think of both senior management and front-line staff as your customers, and develop your summary analysis accordingly.

Case Study: Kelly Services: Using the Voice of the Customer to Drive Process Improvement

The Company

Kelly Services operates a worldwide network of more than 1000 offices in 12 countries, serving the needs of virtually every Fortune 500 company.

A full-service, human resource company, Kelly Services is committed to partnerships with customers that help them achieve their corporate goals in a globally competitive business environment. By the nature of its mandate, Kelly Services is a people-oriented company. It is dedicated to developing a diverse and highly skilled workforce that is capable of responding quickly to the needs of its customers.

Its Canadian subsidiary, Kelly Services (Canada) Ltd., is one of the company's more progressive divisions. This division has been serving Canada's business community for over 25 years, bringing its customers all the benefits of its global network. From its head office in Toronto, Kelly Services Canada oversees the activities of a country-wide network of 46 branches, in all major cities and in various smaller communities.

The Challenge—Call to Action

Kelly Canada's entry into customer satisfaction research was based on an effort to understand a phenomenon that existed throughout the staffing industry: organizations were finding it easier to acquire new customers than to retain existing ones. However, the cost of signing new customers was significantly higher than the cost of maintaining existing ones. Taking a long-term view, Kelly Canada decided to redesign its existing processes through an effective quality management system, which was integrated with its overall business plan and based on continuous improvement.

Action Taken

Kelly believed that an effective quality system embodied three key elements:

- customer focus;
- employee involvement; and
- a strong element of continuous improvement.

In response, Kelly Canada developed a three-year plan to implement a Total Quality Management system. Making customer satisfaction research the first step, Kelly enlisted the help of experts to determine its customers' true needs and expectations, and how the organization was performing in those key areas.

Kelly could choose from a number of customer satisfaction research tools. Ultimately, the company opted to use a questionnaire. The questionnaire could provide the kind of detailed information the company needed, and was more cost-effective than some other methods.

To develop the questionnaire, Kelly held a series of customer focus groups across Canada to identify key satisfaction issues. A cross-functional employee team, representing corporate and field staff, then used the results of the focus group session to design the final questionnaires. The Kelly team was particularly interested in the correlation between Kelly's five key business processes (hiring, order taking, assigning, customer satisfaction in general, and temporary employee satisfaction) and what their customers identified as important.

Questionnaires were mailed to more than 6,500 customers and temporary employees across Canada—approximately 3,500 to customers and 3,000 to temporary employees.

The data outlined what Kelly's customers perceived as important and the company's actual performance in those areas.

At that point, Kelly set about closing the gap between customer expectations and the services it provided. Another employee team was formed to examine Kelly's key business processes, based on the customer and temporary employee feedback. Over time, the team reengineered all of Kelly's key processes based on the "voice of the customer."

Information was shared throughout the company from field staff to senior management and their feedback was solicited as part of the reengineering process.

The Results

The survey data have aided Kelly Services in its reengineering initiatives, enabling the company to streamline procedures and reduce costs. For example, the temporary employee hiring process has been reduced from 10 to five steps. A more effective and timely process has resulted—a process focused on what is important to Kelly's customers as well as to its temporary employees.

Concurrent with Kelly Canada's three-year quality plan, Kelly's international operations have been committed to the establishment of a global Total Quality Management system, using the ISO 9000 quality standard as part of the framework.

The objective of the ISO activity in Canada was to have Kelly headquarters, and each of its 46 branches, registered to ISO 9002 by mid-1995. Now that this has been achieved Kelly has become the single largest Canadian service operation receiving ISO certification. (ISO will be discussed further in Chapter 9). By reengineering its processes prior to registration, Kelly Canada has ensured that it is certifying a quality system that meets its customers' needs. As customer needs continue to change, Kelly processes will be adapted to respond to those needs.

——CHECKLIST——

Tools to Use—When and Why

Confused about what to use and when? Here's a guide.

Service Cycle Mapping (A process to map your moments of truth)

• To improve customer satisfaction through an improved understanding and analysis of all moments of truth that make up a Service Cycle.

• To help define the intended deliverable of key business processes (i.e., on-time delivery, error-free order processing, accurate invoicing).

• To promote cross-functional cooperation and interdepartmental communication.

• To kick-start, feed, or accelerate a Continuous Improvement Process.

• To provide input into questionnaire design.

Quantitative Research (Large sample surveys of more than 100 people, but more likely more than 500 people)

• Used to collect "hard numbers" or representative data on the entire customer base (ratings on all aspects of quality service; direct comments and opinions on the service experience).

• Can be used on an ongoing basis for tracking or monitoring purposes, and as input to a CSI (Customer Satisfaction Index).

Mystery Shopper Surveys (A tool used to test service levels. A trained individual will observe the service practices of an organization and then report in a standard report format)

• To assist in defining all the contact points, service features, and problems associated with each.

── CHECKLIST ──

- Provides verification of problem points, and can be used as part of an incentive or appraisal program for service personnel.

- Used for large customer base, low relationship, many or few transactions.

Customer Service Audit

- Used to collect information on a specific service experience.

- Can supplement market research surveys by providing information from selected individuals on a few key areas.

- Provides opportunity for direct feedback to service provider, and for ensuring that quality standards are continuously maintained.

- Suitable for large population, few transactions, high relationship type.

Individual Personal Interviews

- To monitor the quality of service provided through personal observation and to show customers and employees that the company cares.

- Can be useful in uncovering problems or needs that are difficult to identify.

- Used for small population, high transaction value, and high relationship situations.

Team Visits (Personal visits using cross-functional members of an organization—sales, purchasing, distribution—to observe customers first hand)

- To provide insight into how the customer uses the product/service and the problems or unmet needs that may exist.

- Allows employees to develop value-added solutions designed specifically for each customer.

- Used for small customer-base, high relationship, many transactions.

────CHECKLIST────

Customer Panels (A group of customers invited on a regularly defined schedule to comment on new product, service, or strategy enhancements)

- An opportunity to communicate on an ongoing basis with key customers, experts, etc.

- A relatively inexpensive means of obtaining feedback on changing needs and reactions to newly initiated improvements (especially high technology).

- Suitable for large customer base, low relationship, many or few transactions.

Toll-free telephone line (1-800 number for customers to use to contact their supplier to report on customer service issues)

- A means of obtaining many types of information from customers as a supplement to market research, as well as providing information to customers.

- Represents a point of entry into what may be perceived as a "faceless" organization used for large customer base, low relationship, many or few transactions.

- Used for large customer base, low relationship, many or few transactions.

Warranty/Registration/Comment Cards (mailed surveys—having a brief set of questions)

- Assists in providing information defining the customer base to management, and may solicit customer opinions.

- Useful as a further supplement to market research, and as a means of tracking customer problems and complaints, as well as perceived product strengths.

- Suitable for large customer base, low transaction volume, low or high relationship.

—— CHECKLIST ——

Customer Service Department/Customer Call Centre

- Key opportunity to "get close to customers" and to win their loyalty.

- Important source of information on problems and unmet needs. Future opportunities to improve performance and increase customer satisfaction can be identified.

- Suitable for large customer base, high or low relationship, few or many transactions.

Conventions and Trade Shows (Held by your organization or industry—maybe even competition)

- Useful means of communicating with "hard to reach" customers (e.g., doctors, scientists).

- Direct information on current satisfaction levels, unmet needs, etc. (may be combined with quantitative survey).

- Suitable for large customer base, high or low relationship, low transaction.

The following chart may help you determine what tool you may wish to use and when it is most appropriate.

	Strategic Planning	Competitive Intelligence	Process Improvement Opportunity	Customer Satisfaction Measurement	Root Cause Analysis	Performance Evaluation
Tools Found Effective						
Service Cycle Mapping	X		X	X	X	X
Quantitative Research						
Mystery Shopper Surveys		X				

── CHECKLIST ──

	Strategic Planning	Competitive Intelligence	Process Improvement Opportunity	Customer Satisfaction Measurement	Root Cause Analysis	Performance Evaluation
One-on-One Management Contract	X	X	X	X	X	X
Team Visits			X	X	X	X
Toll-free Telephone Line			X	X	X	X
Customer Service Department	X	X	X	X	X	X
Warranty/ Registration/ Comment Cards	X		X	X	X	X
Panels	X	X	X	X	X	X
Conventions Trade Shows	X	X				X

6

The Focus Phase: The Importance of Teams and Training

Focusing on processes that touch the customer and add value is an important component in this phase. A multitude of logical and effective reengineering methodologies can be used to accomplish this. Unfortunately, there are far fewer publications that provide guidance on how to use teams to assist you in this, big "R" or little "r" reengineering initiative. Thus the purpose of this chapter and the third phase of our methodology.

Forming Teams: The One-Third Rule

Teams are necessary to design, implement, and achieve performance improvement. In working with a wide variety of organizations, I have seen many companies struggle with team structure and composition. There is traditionally a debate regarding who should be included and whose feelings will be hurt if an individual or department is not involved.

Your primary purpose when forming a team is to gather together individuals who can help you achieve success. To that end, you must recognize some fundamental truisms within all organizations. Knowing them can save you a lot of time and increase your chances for success.

One these truisms is that employees in most organizations can be divided into three groups.

In the first group, which I will call the achievers or the leader/pioneer group, are employees who readily recognize the benefits of the initiative and are ready, willing, and able to assist in the process. It is not important to them whether their role is to be part of the team or just to provide support. They are your advocates.

The second groups is composed of the sceptics. These individuals are fence-sitters. They have heard the benefits and pitfalls of embarking on an initiative of this magnitude. They have probably read articles that address the potential risks as well as possible failure and success rates. They may even have business associates whose organizations have also been through similar activities with mixed success. Yet they are not prepared to take sides at this time. They want proof that this initiative can work. If they see some semblance of success, they will probably be willing to shift their position.

The final group comprises the cynics. They view the new initiative as the "flavour of the month" or the latest fad, and want no part of it because they view it as a waste of time.

Most organizations that have not yet embarked on a performance improvement initiative believe that all three groups will be represented on a team. After all, they are trying to achieve change throughout the whole organization, not just in parts of it. They believe that the cynics are probably the most important members and if they can be converted, then success is guaranteed. However, organizations that have undertaken these initiatives will tell you a different story.

As stated earlier, your objective when forming teams is to achieve success and therefore you must cheat the system. Your teams should be composed of only leaders and sceptics. When cynics are part of the team, the process is slowed down. Time is wasted trying to convince the cynics and bring them on board. The balance of the team becomes frustrated and loses interest, and the cynics end up the winners. Either a less-than-satisfactory compromise is created or the process crawls to a stop. The cynics' self-fulfilling prophesy—that this initiative will fail—comes true.

The solution is simple: ignore the cynics and form teams composed of only sceptics and achievers. Since the cynics don't want to be a part of the solution, why include them in the redesign? Although this may appear harsh, your objective is to achieve success. The cynic is a roadblock to that success.

> When forming teams...ignore the cynics.

What Else You Need to Know About Teams

You must consider a number of other factors when forming teams. Some of these criteria change depending on the ultimate purpose or goal of the team. In general, however, the following criteria should be considered.

Team member selection criteria:

Team members should...

- Be stakeholders in the process being reviewed with a vested interest in the outcome
- Have good practical knowledge of at least one component of the process
- Should represent the cross-functional groups involved
- Have high credibility, seen by their work group as representing them
- Possess strong analytical skills. Have strong persuasive and interpersonal skills (for interviews, focus groups, etc.)
- Be creative, capable of thinking "outside the box"
- Have enthusiasm for the assignment, based on a belief that significant improvements are possible. Be somewhat frustrated with the current situation and see this as an opportunity
- Be recognized as team players who thrive on empowerment, are willing to take risks, and are ready for change
- Be seen as winners with potential for growth and upward movement in the organization
- Have good work habits, be self-starters not needing a lot of direction

- Possess a willingness and ability to commit the time necessary for the team to achieve its mandate. Is most likely too busy to be on the team but will make the time available

Team structure and composition are critical if success is to be achieved. You must put your best people on these teams. They must be the ones who are the stars of the fast track—your highly skilled people, the best leaders. These people have the greatest credibility and will generate the required enthusiasm.

The Pyramid Approach to Team Co-ordination

Now that you have given considerable thought to team membership, you should also consider what these teams should be doing and how their activities should be co-ordinated.

One of the most effective ways of creating a co-ordinated action plan is through the use of the following pyramid structure.

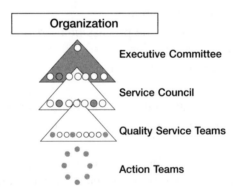

Executive Committee

At the top of the pyramid is the senior management team, which I will call the Executive Committee. This group should include the President/COO and the people who report directly to him or her. The primary role of this group is to set the direction of the performance improvement initiative. It also has three other responsibilities:

1. to provide input and guidance to the Performance Improvement Council;
2. to help establish priorities; and
3. to ensure that middle management blockage does not occur.

Performance Improvement Council

In the next level, the Performance Improvement Council exists. This Council is composed primarily of six to eight employees who represent a cross-section of the organization. However one, or possibly two, members of the Executive Committee are also members of the Performance Improvement Council. Although they cannot be team leaders, they represent the views of the Executive Committee and facilitate communication between the two groups.

The employees comprising the Performance Improvement Council must be carefully selected from the top two-thirds of the organization: the achievers and the sceptics. They must also be regarded as "up-and-comers," that is, well-respected and creative individuals who will understand their role but will also know when to ask for help. Third, although not every department within the organization can participate, the composition of the Council should fairly represent a cross-section of departments within your organization. Two departments in particular must be represented on this Council: human resources and information technology/systems, since decisions and information related to both of these areas will be required on an ongoing basis. Finally, Council membership must represent all levels of the employee hierarchy, from front-line staff to senior management.

The Council has two basic roles. One of its roles, as a team, is to coordinate all activities of the teams at the next level. The second role, as individuals, is basically one of representation. Each member of the Performance Improvement Council will also be a member of one of the teams at the next level (Quality Service Teams), which are responsible for redesigning processes and implementing change. The Council is also responsible for formal communication of team progress to the Executive Committee. My experience has shown that this group should meet approximately once a month for typically one half-day, while the Executive Committee might meet only quarterly. Performance Improvement Council members carry out the following roles and responsibilities:

- Develop and communicate the performance improvement, strategic goals, and improvement strategy and plan for the organization to be the "best."
- Provide and use a process for prioritizing projects for improvement.

- Establish methods that enable employees to identify problems and make suggestions for improvement.
- Periodically review all major processes, process improvement teams, key quality data, analysis and measurements to provide encouragement and support.
- Develop and implement a plan for appropriate education and training of all employees.
- Ensure that appropriate plans for awareness and communication to all employees are in place.

Quality Service and Action Teams

Throughout the initiative, various teams and task forces will be required (referred to in the pyramid diagram as Quality Service Teams and Action Teams). Quality Service Teams have a long-term mandate, typically lasting up to one year, and generally deal with major customer-focused process issues. Action teams, however, have a shorter-term mandate, less than three months, and deal with implementation-type projects (i.e., a suggestion for improvement). As part of their membership, both Quality Service and Action teams must have at least one member of the Performance Improvement Council to represent their views and to facilitate communications between them and the Council and Executive Committee.

Amdahl provides a good example of a company that effectively uses teams for both long- and short-term changes. Amdahl manufactures and sells large-scale mainframe computers, data storage devices, communications products, and unique software products to business and governments throughout most of the industrialized world. Amdahl calls its teams PIGs and CATs. PIGs is an acronym for Process Improvement Groups, and corresponds to the Quality Service Teams in the pyramid diagram. These teams are formed annually and are led by a divisional vice president. The role of the Process Improvement Group is to review, identify, and implement change in processes that are under the control of the divisional vice president. These improvements must be implemented within the team's one-year mandate. The following are their defined roles:

The role of the process owner is to improve the effectiveness, efficiency, control, and adaptability of the process for which he or she is responsible.

- Effectiveness means achieving the intended business results—getting the job done as viewed by the customer and management.
- Efficiency means that the process operates with minimum resources. Running at optimal efficiency means that no additional investment in process improvement is justified.
- Control means the process is documented, data are verified, separation and understanding of duties is adequate, assets are accounted for and protected, and measurements are in place.
- Adaptability means identifying future constraints and deficiencies and putting process changes in place before the business is impacted.

The process owner is responsible for these activities:

- Defining and documenting the process boundaries and interfaces.
- Documenting operational flow and work tasks.
- Establishing control points and continuous measurements.
- Defining cycle times and schedules.
- Developing criteria for measuring satisfaction of customer requirements.
- Continuously reviewing and analyzing the process and its measurements.
- Initiating and managing corrective action or process improvement.
- Reporting to management on process capability and efficiency.

CATs is an acronym for Corrective Action Teams, which correspond to the Action Teams in the pyramid diagram. These teams are formed to quickly implement projects resulting from their in-house suggestion system. The size of the group is smaller than a PIG—probably only three to four members—and its duration is more short term—most likely two to three months.

Amdahl has formed teams or subcommittees within the context of both PIGs and CATs. Some of these teams are described as follows:

- **Education and Training**—promoting the quality-related education and training of the organization. This may include tracking quality training for employees, offering quality seminars and workshops, developing and teaching advanced quality training classes, and providing specialized "how-to" training programs (CATs).

- **Awareness and Recognition**—assuring that all employees remain aware of quality-related projects and are informed of quality successes. This may include establishing and managing an organizational process to formally recognize individuals or groups for quality contributions (PIGs).
- **Measurement**—providing analysis and process measurement support to the Council and to individual Process Improvement Groups or Corrective Action Teams. This includes assisting teams and the Council in identifying meaningful process measurements that will initiate corrective action. Benchmarking to identify reasonable goals and quantifying cost of quality are also appropriate (CATs).
- **Corrective Action**—providing a methodology to allow defects to be identified, corrected, and prevented. This includes tracking and reporting on the status of the organization's corrective action projects (PIGs).

In the organization's orientation manual, Amdahl also provides the following description of the the role of the individual.

Continuous quality improvement is the job of every Amdahl employee.

These are the individual's responsibilities:

- Take responsibility for individual work processes. Know who the customers for the process are and understand their requirements.
- Take the initiative to apply the Continuous Improvement Process to work processes.
- Identify appropriate improvement tools and get training in their use.
- Ask for coaching and guidance as needed.
- Participate in improvement teams.
- Demonstrate personal leadership by identifying problems and opportunities for improvement.
- Make suggestions for improvement.
- Be willing and open to make change.

Everyone makes a difference in Quality, and active participation in carrying out these responsibilities is the key to Amdahl's success.

Lessons Learned from Amdahl

- There must be specific leadership responsibilities that cannot be delegated down the organization.
- Work processes flow horizontally and are often cross-functional or interdepartmental in nature. While process ownership may be difficult, given this business reality, it is still important. When in doubt, the process owner is the individual who is responsible for the final deliverable of the process.
- The use of teams and committees can provide better communication, leverage of resources, expertise, and seamless integration.
- The never-ending nature of continuous improvement requires organizational permanence for continual focus and reinforcement. Specifically, the organization structure defined by the reengineered process must be maintained, otherwise improvement opportunities will not be maintained in the long term.
- All employees should nurture performance improvement concepts and activities.
- Problem resolution and improvement activities should be done by those closest to where the work is actually done.

Teams Need Senior Management Involvement and Leadership

Organizations that are converting to a team structure must rely on their leaders to make that transition a success. "As with most paradigm shifts, we rarely recognize the change when we're living through it; as a result, we fail to successfully manage the transition," says Glenn Parker, author of *Cross-Functional Teams.*

He suggests that senior management can take the following steps to create an organization that has quality and customer satisfaction as their goals and cross-functional teamwork as their strategy.

- **Talk the talk.** The company leaders must send out a clear and consistent message that cross-functional teamwork is its strategy for achieving world-class quality. This message must be communicated in all written presentations and publications.
- **Walk the talk.** Words are not enough. The leadership team must not only live by the words, but they must also act and work like a team—serving as a model of cross-functional teamwork.

- **Focus on performance.** The company's performance appraisal, compensation, and promotion policies must support the goal of teamwork as a business strategy.
- **Be a storyteller.** Any organizational culture is composed of a series of stories, norms, and myths that enhance and shape the behaviour of employees. Stories give people a sense of the company; they tell people what type of behaviour is valued. Leaders should take every opportunity to tell and retell stories that praise cross-functional teamwork.
- **Provide resources.** In order to survive, teams need resources. Resources come in many forms:
  Space—provide team meeting rooms with basic equipment like flip charts, overhead projectors, etc.
  Technology—provide electronic methods that can improve team communication such as E-mail, local area networks, tele-conferencing, faxing, voice mail, etc.
  Training—equip team members with the skills and knowledge to help them be successful. Topics could include the following: basic leadership skills; planning and facilitating meetings; decision-making; problem-solving; conflict resolution; communication, etc.
  Time—allocate time for the staff to work on the team. Only senior management has the authority to ensure that this allocated time is respected by the team members' superiors.

Put the Customer on Your Team

Wouldn't it be great if you could put a customer on every team in your organization? Although this may not be practical, some companies that have restructured into cross-functional teams have given their customers a loud voice on their teams.

For example, Chrysler recorded its restructuring process in the documentary film *Reinventing Chrysler.* Previously, work was divided into functions and design plans were passed along from department to department. If any problems emerged, the plans were returned to the original department—and the whole process began again. This process caused constant conflicts among the departments about issues such as time, cost, supplier relationships, etc. The company began to lose sight of what the real customer wanted.

In a similar situation but a different industry, Schering-Plough Health Care Products also had a functionally focused structure. In its customer-support department, each function (order entry, accounts receivable, promotional payments, deduction resolutions, credit and collections, etc.) worked at its own tasks led by a manager.

"It seemed like there was a constant turf war going on," says Trine Aanensen Lyman, Associate Director of Customer Support. "There was a lack of team effort, and very little communication." In fact, each function worked so independently that it didn't even know what the others did.

Restructuring into Customer-Focused Teams

Both companies believed that their environments were compromising customers' needs. By restructuring into cross-functional teams, both companies have successfully brought their customers' wants and expectations to the forefront.

Chrysler achieved this by merging its departments into four teams that were focused on a particular type of customer: large car, small car, mini-van, and jeep. Those teams were then further broken down into smaller teams. All of the functions were represented— finance, design, engineering, manufacturing, etc.

Schering-Plough's customer support also restructured into four customer teams that were divided by geographical location. Representatives from all of the functions—order entry, accounts receivable, promotional payments, etc.—were included on each team. Their objectives were to satisfy customers' particular requirements and to capitalize on customer partnership opportunities.

Let the Teams Take Control

An important component of the success of both companies was team empowerment. "Team members have to understand that they make the difference. They have to be responsible and accountable," explains Lyman. "When they feel 100 per cent responsible for what they do, this is when the power of creativity or applications of techniques comes into play."

This belief was certainly evident at Chrysler. The company believed that decisions made at a lower level will be better decisions, because the people at this level are closest to all the facts. Senior management set the tone by tossing out the former top-down management style. In other words, supervisors stopped being the "boss," and instead became teachers and coaches. As a result, employees work with a new spirit: they try to anticipate problems and solve them before they become a problem.

Bringing the Customer on Board

A significant advantage of cross-functional teams is the ability to make the customer's voice heard—within the team and company. Schering-Plough specifically trained team members to reorganize customer expectations and solicit feedback.

"On a daily basis, team members ask specific questions of buyers, executives—whomever they deal with," stresses Lyman. "They ask questions to clarify what the customer expects, and from that information we understand their expectations and standards." Part of that concept includes gathering as much information as possible about each customer. "You have to know your customer in order to meet their expectations," she adds.

For instance, Lyman's team creates customer profiles. Team members research whether their companies are publicly or privately held, the value of their stock, any past business with Schering-Plough, the customer's outstanding balance, their deduction level, and the executives who are leading the company. All of this information is then entered on a shared database, which is available to everyone within the organization. Profiles are continually updated and expanded as new information becomes available.

At Chrysler, teams get to know their customers by focusing on a particular customer type such as jeep customers or truck owners. This way, workers can not only meet customers' expectations, but they can also tailor special products and options to that customer. What is the result of restructuring? The first Chrysler automobile built entirely by a team—known as the LH—received rave reviews in the industry. It was also developed with fewer people for less money and in less time than it used to take to design and build a new car.

Schering-Plough's customer support department is more "customer friendly," says Lyman. "Teamwork is truly the way of the future in management and performance."

How to Make Teams More Effective

Despite the best intentions, teams run into problems because of either a reluctance to address potential problems or a tendency to let troubling issues fester. I like to present the analogy of a "moose check" in these situations.

The moose, as most people know, is a large, awkward animal. Even in the early stages of growth, it is a fairly large animal. Imagine a problem or an unresolved issue as a young moose making a home under your table. Everybody knows the moose is there, but no one is willing to talk about it.

If you leave it alone, one of two things may happen. First, the moose may continue to grow. If you leave it long enough, eventually it may stand up, topple the table, and cause mayhem. Alternatively, if not fed, it may die and decompose underneath the table—not a pleasant thought or odour.

What do you do? As a team leader, here's a suggestion. At the start of each meeting do a moose check. Ask if any issues need to be discussed. There may be an issue about team membership, mandates created by senior management, unrealistic goals, or someone even may ask, "Will anything we are doing make a difference?"

Did anyone do a Moose check?

Regardless of the issue or question, it is best to get your team to discuss it and reach some resolution. The alternatives are not pleasant nor desirable.

How to Allocate Team Responsibilities...Don't Choose a Team Chairperson

Here's a twist on a popular theme. Your group or team will be more cohesive if you give more of the members roles and responsibilities. But no one should be assigned the position of chairperson.

Actually, individuals within the team should volunteer for roles and responsibilities, rather than being assigned them. Once these roles are accepted, the individuals hold onto these responsibilities until they determine that they can no longer handle it (that is, if they no longer fit the role, they can resign or be asked to step aside) or until the "moose is loose."

The following lists some of the potential roles for team members, provided by Peter Lawton, an associate at Coopers & Lybrand, and an authority on teams and culture change.

- **The Minute Taker** records the meeting. The style and content of the minutes are determined by the needs of the team. The minute taker is also usually the group communicator.

- **The Administrator** organizes the meeting. The administrator is also responsible for identifying the meeting location, booking the room, and ensuring that the proper facilities are available.

- **The Performer** ensures that the task is clearly defined. The performer's job is to ensure that the task gets done, to keep the team focused on the task, and to maintain the pace.

- **The Integrator** ensures that everyone is included in the task and that no one is left out or ignored. Good integrators work to identify the unique strengths that each person brings and makes sure that the team draws on those strengths.

- **The Scribe** creates a focus for the team during the meeting by noting the key points on a flipchart or overhead projector. A good scribe can summarize discussions into one or two words or phrases. He or she will summarize the main points, draw inferences and conclusions, and ensure closure of an item before moving on to the next.

- **The Friendly Sceptic** is the team's reality checker and stops the team from "running away with itself." A good friendly sceptic is not afraid to take an unpopular position and "take on" the rest of the team because of what he or she believes to be in the best interests of the team.

- **The Team Leader** makes sure that the mandate is achieved and periodically evaluates the team's progress. The team leader oversees the role assignment process to ensure that the required roles of the team are established, understood, and assigned appropriately.

A Non-Traditional Approach to Training

Although it may seem strange, I believe that training is the wrong approach. Follow this analogy with me.

Fold your arms across your chest.

Typically, you will take your right hand and cross it over your left biceps and then tuck your left hand over your right biceps. Check it out, am I right? Now, cross your arms in the opposite direction and hold it there.

How does it feel? Awkward? Uncomfortable? That is analogous to how your teams will feel after you have trained them for the new skills that they will require for carrying out their team mandate.

Now, put your hands by your side, and then quickly raise them and fold them across your chest again. Most people will cross them the same way they did originally—right over left, then left over right. You have naturally reverted to your old practices. That's the potential downfall of training. There is a strong likelihood that the training will soon be forgotten, unless there is some follow-up or reinforcement.

What would have happened if instead, I had instructed you, "Now be careful, remember how I asked you to change your method of folding your arms? Let's do it." The likelihood of you doing it differently would have increased tremendously.

Training is too short term. What is required is education and coaching.

The issue of training and education has always posed a significant challenge for most organizations—more so today than ever before. Constant pressures exist to control or reduce costs, while also providing more competent, customer-focused front-line staff. Are these two goals in conflict? Perhaps not. Should we relent to corporate pressure and reduce spending on education and training? Hopefully not.

Based on my work with a wide variety of organizations and my research on this topic, I have identified a number of best practices to help those who must address these issues and rise to this new challenge.

Which Path Should You Follow?

Most organizations have a choice of following one of two paths, each leading in a different direction. The first path is the more traditional one: train and educate employees along functional boundaries (i.e., customer service, finance, marketing). This has been an accepted practice with many organizations. While the path may be known, the result may be less than effective. For organizations that follow this path, one of two objectives should be met:

1. All employees must receive a certain number of hours within that functional area (i.e., 40 hours per year per employee); or

2. That there is 100 per cent compliance to a core curriculum of programs, which all employees within the organization must receive.

Both of these goals are self-gratifying rather than benefits-oriented. Consequently, this approach is too limiting and is incorrectly focused. Not all employees need to be exposed to the same curriculum or exactly the same number of training hours—some require more or less. Depending on the employee's position in the organization's hierarchy, a different form of training may be required, which leads us down another path.

The second path requires more discipline to follow and as a result, is not as widely used. However, this path is generally followed by best-in-class organizations. It is based on the belief that training requirements should be built on the following foundation:

1. training objectives should be based on individual needs;
2. these needs should be mapped against required competencies to identify gaps; and
3. consideration should be given to non-functional needs through both training and coaching.

Why a One-Size-Fits-All Approach Will Not Work

Each employee in your organization is a unique individual. Best-in-class organizations, particularly those that achieve improved customer satisfaction, recognize this fact and base their training programs on this truism. Of course, some training programs must be given to employees within a particular functional group—which typically relates to new technology, or changing rules, regulations, or procedures. But beyond this, consistency is not necessarily required.

Your approach to training (customized to individual needs) is an example of listening to the voice of the internal customer (their needs and ambitions). Developing a training curriculum customized to their needs is one way of keeping them satisfied and happy (which will rub off positively on your external customers, as discussed earlier in our Customer Satisfaction/Revenue Enhancement Model. Consider, for example, the training curriculum for one of the winners of the 1994 ICSA Award of Excellence—First Chicago Cash Management Services. Its course catalogue consists of almost 20 courses in the following four categories:

1. basic skills such as keyboarding and analytical skills;
2. core competency skills such as working in teams and achieving service culture;
3. professional development skills such as writing skills, supervision, or time-management; and

4. functional skills such as typing, cost management, and risk management.

Not all employees, however, require training in the complete curriculum.

How to Identify and Fill the Training Gap

In order to identify gaps, a training grid must be created.

In organizations that achieve outstanding customer satisfaction ratings, an assessment is first made of the skills and competencies required to ensure individual growth and functional proficiency. This assessment forms the rows of the grid and identifies both fundamental training requirements as well as new competencies required. Employees are listed in columns, from senior management down to front-line staff, and whether training has been or should be conducted. This grid is then reviewed with employees as part of the annual performance review. The employee and manager then agree on and develop a personalized short-term (one year) and long-term (two to three year) training plan.

What More Can Be Done?

Although every employee may play a role in achieving customer satisfaction and performance improvement, the skills that each will require may be quite different depending on his or her position in the management hierarchy.

The IDEAS study highlighted a number of the new and upgraded skills that may be required. The following is a summary of the study's main findings.

Employees may need technical skills such as the following:

i) **process mapping**—a procedure for mapping the entire service delivery chain to identify waste, redundancy, and improvement opportunities;

ii) **benchmarking**—a process for looking outside of your organization—even outside of your industry segment—and continuously comparing and measuring your organization against business leaders anywhere in the world. This enables an organization to gain information that will help it to take action to improve its performance.

iii) **performance measurement**—which must include statistical process control (SPC), as well as analysis techniques such as histograms, parieto analysis, bar charts, fishbone diagrams, etc.

The IDEAS study also highlighted some enabler skills—soft skills that affect internal culture and change.

Middle and senior management require enhanced people skills in areas involving:

i) problem solving;

ii) communication; and

iii) change management or coping with change.

Beyond all this, however, is the fact that employees need courses that provide education, not training.

Perhaps the best way to differentiate between training and education is through a simple analogy. In school, children are given in-class sex education, not training. Education heightens awareness; training provides hands-on experience. Not surprisingly, most organizations fall into the trap of providing training, not education. And, even more damaging, coaching is not provided at all.

A Word On Coaching

Because of its importance, the concept of coaching requires further discussion. After all, coaching reflects the fact that the leader is listening to the voice of the internal customer and providing training in a form preferred by the internal customer. But training, regardless of how strong the course content and instructor, can be ineffective if it is not reinforced by a good coach.

Let me expand on this by using a childhood example. Remember when you were a child learning to ride a bike? You were not sent out by yourself to learn this new skill. Instead, you were coached through the process. Someone initially stood behind you, told you what you had to do, then held onto the seat until you were comfortable in the new environment. When you were let go, he or she still ran behind you just in case you needed some additional help. When, or if, you fell off, he or she gave you words of encouragement and got you right back on the bike. That was the role of the coach and mentor—not unlike what your staff may need today.

The Path to Success and Improved Customer Satisfaction

In summary, you face a fork in the road ahead and must make a strategic decision on which training path to follow. One path—one-size-fits-all training—is fairly easy to follow, simple to track, has short-term impact, but may be ineffective in the long term. The second path—customized training and education—is more difficult, requires a substantial investment of time and dollars, and needs more intensive post-training and coaching support.

Success depends upon dedication and perseverance. This is no doubt difficult given all the pressures on you today. But take it from those who have reaped the benefits—it's worth the challenge.

> Training and education must be tailored to the needs and competencies of the team members. A one-size-fits-all approach will not work. A training grid must be created and a program designed to fill critical gaps.

A Different Perspective on Coaching

Barry Wittacker, President of AMP Canada, a worldwide leader in the manufacture and distribution of electrical connectors, has a unique way of making a point. Here's his view on coaching, as he expressed it in *CMA Magazine* in April 1993:

> For many organizations, the middle manager has become as obsolete as the Berlin Wall. The traditional multi-layered management hierarchy slows response time, increases costs, and opens gaps in quality performance. In a bid to become more responsive to customer needs, leading organizations are reengineering their processes, building their employees' skills, and removing top-down decision-making and control structures. And they're finding that a far more effective way to transfer needed skills to employees is by doing more coaching instead of managing.
>
> On a much smaller scale, I see the distinction between managing and coaching as I watch the potty-training of my two 18-month-old grandsons, Jake and Dalton. For their parents, "managing" involves looking after the diapers—planning, buying, inspection, application, checking and re-checking. "Coaching" involves shifting practices from parent to child for strategic advantage. The results of self-reliance, once the boys are out of diapers and putting themselves on the toilet: things are accomplished easier, better, faster, and cheaper.
>
> In organizations, traditional "management" has included similar tasks—planning, organizing, controlling, problem solving, and decision-making. Under this model, the thinking occurs in one place, the action in another. The result: time is wasted in communication breakdowns between the "planners" and the "doers."

Under this model, most organizations' training expenses are wasted. Whether in the form of periodic lecture or procedures manuals, traditional training treats learning as if it were merely a transfer of information, not the building of new skills. It's like trying to potty-train the grandchildren by holding lectures at the kitchen table. To use another analogy, talking about riding a bike does not demonstrate how to ride a bike. It merely demonstrates competence in talking about riding a bike. Without an illustration of competent practice, the learner misses the expected standard. Coaching works through shared experience, not shared information. The coach's authority is grounded in demonstrated competence, not hierarchical authority or mere information transfer.

The manager must allow employees a time and place for practising their skills. Practise allows employees to build on their capabilities and understanding in a systematic way. Errors are welcomed with understanding and compassion, and employees are redirected toward improved performance. The fact that the grandchild (and the first set of training pants) will suffer indignities are essential to the learning experience. While we are less willing to risk our pride later in life, we must be willing to do so today while building new capabilities.

Managers must constantly coach and assess their employees until they demonstrate the ability to carry out the task themselves to an acceptable standard of performance. Detecting the point at which this occurs is not an easy task. People learn at different rates, and thus must be considered individually in assessing their readiness for a task. When employees have retained a reliable set of practices, show sincere commitment to the new practice, and demonstrate the necessary level of competence, then the coach can trust and empower them.

Few organizations can promise job security to their employees these days. However, leading-edge companies show a genuine interest in expanding their employees' abilities and value. A commitment to coaching for independence, and commitment to the continual transfer of relevant skills, ensures both sides a return on their investment. Self-reliance leads to accelerated personal growth for the learner — and it helps enhance performance and maintains a competitive organization.

A Coach's Viewpoint on Coaching for Success

When challenged to describe the essential elements in his formula for winning, Lou Holtz, former Notre Dame coach came up with the following 10 principles that can produce a winning team both on and off the football field.

1. **Do Right.**

   You know what's right, you know what's wrong. Too many people in this country talk about their personal rights. I'm still one of those old-fashioned people who believes in obligations and responsibilities.

2. **Do Your Best.**

   It is not enough to be born with the skill of an All-American. In order to succeed day in and day out, each individual must strive to do the best that he possibly can.

3. **Treat Others as You Want to be Treated.**

   I have never seen a business, a family, an organization, or a football team that cannot be turned around if you can generate love, mutual appreciation, and fellow feelings.

4. **Set Goals.**

   You have to have something that you wish to obtain. Everybody has to understand what we are trying to accomplish. Why are we here? There are a lot of reasons why these young players are here at Notre Dame: they are here to get an education and to win football games.

5. **Accept Your Role.**

   Not everybody can be the number-one quarterback at Notre Dame. But in order for the team to succeed, everybody from the water boy to the coach has to accept the hand that he or she has been dealt and make the best of it.

6. **Practise Fundamentals.**

   Our whole program is based on doing little things the right way. Let little things slide, and the whole foundation of your organization will collapse.

7. **Believe in Yourself.**

   I want a group of players that believe in themselves. You can't be a great coach, a great football player, or a great entrepreneur if you don't have faith in yourself.

8. Care About People.

Teamwork is the foundation of success. The three universal questions that an individual asks of his coach, player, employee, employer are: Can I trust you? Are you committed to excellence? And, do you care about me? If we don't care about one another, we don't stand a chance.

9. Overcome Adversity.

There is one thing in life that is universal. You're going to have problems, so be prepared for them.

10. Don't Flinch.

Believe that you're going to succeed. You cannot flinch, you cannot let people think that you are seriously in jeopardy of failure.

Lessons Learned from the Chinese

The Chinese have a symbol for learning that all of us should consider.

The first character means "to study." It is composed of two parts: the top symbol means "to accumulate knowledge," and it is standing over the symbol for a child in a doorway. The second character means "to practise constantly." It also comprises two parts: the top symbol is a feather, which represents flying, over the symbol of youth. These symbols translate literally as "as young birds fly, they practise constantly." Together, the characters stand for learning—to study and practise constantly.

This example presents an interesting point. Unlike in the English language, in Chinese it is impossible to use the past tense and say, "I have learned,"—one can only use the present tense and say, "I am learning." The message, "I am learning" is the equivalent of saying, "I do not know everything: I have more to learn."

How might the nature of our business meetings change if we walked into meetings thinking, "I am *still learning* how to interact with colleagues, how to problem solve, how to manage a project," rather than thinking, "I *have learned* how to interact with clients, etc."

What We Can Learn from Japanese Culture

Ask anyone which country excels in quality and service and nine out of 10 people will say Japan. What is their secret to success and why did North America fall so far behind? Is it the people, their culture, the books they read? Maybe it's their work ethic. After researching this issue, I have identified some central issues that differentiate Japanese from North American management.

Harmony and Conformity

There are many terms that describe Japanese operating principles and a brief primer on these fundamental terms is useful at this point in our reading.

Japanese Term	Definition
Andon Boards	Worker-illuminated electric boards that indicate what part of the production line has a problem.
Genba, Genbutsu, Genjitsu	Literally: actual place, actual thing, actual situation. Honda's tough-guy version of "management by walking around." Also known as the Three G's of the Three A's
Kaizen-Continuous Improvement	The idea that every job or process can be improved.
Kanban	Literally: card. Refers to the just-in-time system originated by Toyota in the early 1950s, in which boxes of parts come with inventory cards. New parts are not ordered until a worker uses a box and returns the cards.
Nemawashi	To cut a wide circle around the roots of a plant before transplanting it. The idea of building consensus before making an official decision.
Ringi	Shared decision-making.

Taiso	Calisthenic excercises done at the beginning of the work day.
Teian	A suggestion system in which workers recommend ways to increase the productivity or safety of their work.
The Five S's	Extreme cleanliness and reduction of clutter are the key to achieving quick-set up times and quality, according to Japanese managers. In Japan, they call it the Five S's: Seiri—arrange things properly; Seiton—keep things in their proper place; Seiso—clean the workplace; Seiketsu—maintain the above three principles; and Shitsuke—practise self-discipline and respect for fellow workers.

In Japan, the success of these principles is based on deeply ingrained cultural values that stress harmony and conformity at the expense of individual expression. But these principles are foreign to most North American workers, who thrive on a corporate-star system geared to personal recognition. Not surprisingly, therefore, attempts to implement these Japanese-style management principles in North America are not always successful. Consequently, Japanese manufacturers are developing hybrid systems of Japanese and North American management. When you consider these adaptations, familiar concepts emerge: listen to the voice of the internal customer and you will achieve positive results; improved productivity, retention, and customer satisfaction; and enhanced revenue and improved profitability—our Customer Satisfaction/Revenue Enhancement Model once again.

Some of these adaptations have been introduced at a HONDA car plant in Alliston, Ontario. For example, Japanese piano music was replaced by the "Miami Vice" theme song to summon workers to taiso exercises. Teian "suggestion" systems, long recognized as a key element in Japan's transformation, have also been adapted to reflect the North American passion for rewards. For example, Suzuki has implemented a much more lucrative and extensive program than their parent company in Japan. Employees accumulate points for each of their suggestions and redeem them for merchandise. Not surprisingly, money talks. Workers at their plant in Ingersoll, Ontario generate 4.1 suggestions per person per month on average, compared to 3.0 in a comparable plant in Japan.

Increasing numbers of employees at the plants are enthusiastically suggesting money-saving improvements through, as they say, "*Kaizen*ing" their job. As more improvements are implemented—particularly engineering changes—the employees are gradually Canadianizing Honda's manufacturing process and the ensuing results are quite impressive.

Japanese companies have long recognized the benefits of extreme cleanliness and tidiness. In Japan they call it the Five S's. When these words were originally posted in the plant of Honda Canada, workers were unresponsive, claiming that the concept was "too foreign." Management then challenged the workers to come up with five equivalent English words that would spell PRIDE. They did: Pick up, Remove, Inspect, Dust and sweep, and Eliminate clutter. But the prize for the best translation goes to the worker who posted his own version in his work zone: "Your mother does not work here. You will have to pick up after yourself."

Teamwork and Team Building

Teams take on a different meaning in many Japanese organizations. Most teams are run by a *kacho,* or middle manager, who answers to the *bucho*, who operates as the ultimate authority. The bucho commands the utmost respect of those below him or her in the hierarchy, has earned his or her responsibility, and is very influential in the organization.

One might think that this would have a negative impact on the organization, but it is the collective actions of the team that result in an opposite effect. Within a department, people have relatively defined roles. But as a member of a team, you are the supporting cast for all of the team's needs. You are responsible for other people's assignments or work loads, and they are responsible for yours. The challenge is to satisfy the group and yourself at the same time. The result, though, may be products or solutions that are partially "watered-down" by endless refinements. Nevertheless, the final submissions are generally well rounded in terms of serving a large audience of customers.

Consensus is revered above all else. The Japanese language itself distinguishes between the terms "to decide" and "to have been decided." The latter term implies that the group has reached consesus, although there has not been unanimous agreement. That is, if group members are unable to reach consensus, a decision is made nonetheless to preserve the sanctity of the group role. While this process may not differ from what might normally occur in the Western world, the motivations and implications of the Japanese are quite different. As described earlier, the larger issues of harmony and fairness are considered integral to the decision-making process.

Communication and Co-operation

There is a high degree of communication and co-operation between individuals and groups within the most successful organizations. As one Sony Corporation executive expressed,

> "I believe one factor that has led to Sony's success in introducing a stream of innovative products is the high degree of communication and co-opertion between individuals and groups in the company. On the most successful projects, there seems to be very little territoriality between groups. The spirit between design, product planning, engineering, and manufacturing is one of community. Information is shared informally on a daily basis from the start of a project. Groups work simultaneously and interactively as much as possible rather than working independently and passing along a treasured result to the next group along the line. There is healthy disagreement and debate on various issues as the product is developed, but it is accompanied by constant discussion and negotiation until agreement is reached."

Doubtless, much can be learned from the management style of the Japanese. The key, however, is to learn from the Japanese, rather than copy them. As we stated before, strict application of Japanese practices by themselves is not a panacea for success; innovative approaches to interpreting or applying these principles has definite advantages.

Case Study: An Approach to "Enabling" High Performance at Quaker Oats

The Company

With 1993 sales exceeding $5.7 billion, the Quaker Oats Company is a major force in the food and beverage segment of the consumer products industry. Supported by a deep and rich history, and by such well-known brands as Gatorade ®, Rice-A-Roni ®, Cap'n Crunch ®, Aunt Jemima ®, Ken-L Ration ®, and of course, Quaker Oats ®, the Chicago-based giant continues to expand its presence both in the United States and internationally.

The Challenge—Call to Action

In a fiercely competitive industry, recent moves by competitors and rising price-consciousness by consumers have intensified the battle for market share and the need for increased operational efficiency. Quaker Oats has reacted by focusing on creating value for its customers and consumers through an intense effort to create a high-performance organization. From the start, Quaker Oats recognized that it must do more than just say it needed change—it must provide those within the organization with the tools to make it happen. Quaker University was one of these tools.

Action Taken

To assist in implementing the required organizational change, Quaker Oats established Quaker University (QU). In September 1993, QU enlisted professional outside assistance (Coopers & Lybrand) to develop 11 courses for its high-performance school. The courses were to focus on process improvement, change management, project management, benchmarking, and team facilitation.

Development of these courses consisted of seven steps. The first step was to create an individual course design document outlining the course objectives, existing performance gap, module content, learning methods, and tools and skills covered. Once the design document was confirmed, a draft version of the course was developed. The draft was then reviewed by the QU program managers. As a key part of their review, these managers sent copies to key stakeholders throughout the company for their comments. The QU team consolidated stakeholder input and forwarded it to Coopers & Lybrand, where changes were made or negotiated. The pilot course was then finalized. At the time of writing this book, two pilot courses are being conducted for each of the 11 courses. The results from the pilot offerings will be incorporated into the final editions of the courses.

The 11-course series represents a significant investment for Quaker Oats. The courses within the series are consistent in methodology, terminology, and style. Each course consists of a participant guide, facilitator guide, and supporting course materials. Intense, up-front coordination regarding style (such as page layout, supporting graphics, type of electronic media desired, narrative tone) was absolutely necessary to avoid rework and other potentially costly changes. An important component of the development was extensive consultation with internal customers to clearly understand their training needs and preferred method of learning. Additionally, since QU received the complete series on electronic media, future modifications will be within the company's control.

The courses are application-oriented and designed to be facilitated rather than instructed. They are intended to be delivered primarily to teams that use their real work experience as a basis for immediate application of the skills and tools covered. Flexibility in delivery is critical. Although the consultants delivered the initial series of courses, Quaker Oats facilitators will ultimately facilitate the courses.

Quaker Oats now has a consistent, modular series of courses to help move them towards being a high-performance organization.

Summaries of Quaker University Courses

Process Mapping: A one-day course for teams or individuals designed to develop skills in four mapping techniques: Top-Down Process Flows, Detailed Flowcharting, Deployment Charts, and Product Process Mapping.

Priority Setting: A one-day course designed to assist individuals or teams in prioritizing work activities.

Problem Analysis: A two-day course for individuals or teams designed to impart a problem-solving methodology and the tools needed to carry it out.

Applied Problem Solving: A four- to five-day course for a team that has been chartered to solve a specific business problem. This course is divided into two separate sessions with team activities between sessions.

Applied Process Improvement: A six-day course for a team that has been chartered to improve a business process. The course is divided into three separate sessions with teamwork between sessions.

Responsibility-Charting: A half-day course for individuals or teams designed to impart basic and more advanced methods of responsibility-charting.

Project Management: A three-day course designed primarily for project teams that are about to embark (or have recently embarked) on a business project. The course presents a goal-oriented project management methodology and the tools needed to carry it out.

Managing Change: A three-day course that covers the theories of change management and the steps for successful planning and implementation of business/organizational change.

Benchmarking: A two-day course for individuals covering benchmarking methodologies and tools, with an optional third day for benchmarking project teams,

Team Feedback Skills: A one-and-a-half-day course designed for teams, team members, and team leaders to enhance feedback skills for improved team performance.

Advanced Facilitation Skills: An intense five-day course for individuals designated to become facilitators within the organization. The course takes a process consultation approach toward facilitation, and covers theories, tools, and skills for effective facilitation in a variety of situations.

Although not every organization has the financial resources to fund such an aggressive and well-thought-out training agenda, some lessons can be learned from the content of the Quaker program.

1. Define the end result you want to achieve before you define your curriculum.
2. Ensure that stakeholders—the internal customers—are involved in selecting or developing course curriculum.
3. If possible, pilot-test the courses with the internal customer and be prepared to make further refinements to ensure that your deliverables will be achieved.
4. Design your courses to be facilitated rather than instructed.
5. Draw from the industry's best practices and from the areas of process improvement, change management, project management, benchmarking, and team facilitation.

Lessons Learned from the External Customer—The 3M Approach

Although innovation has long been a part of research, product development, and manufacturing processes at 3M, it has not been as conspicuous in sales. Management believed that while training was high quality, it was not as well focused on customer needs as it might have been.

That changed in November 1993 when innovation struck sales training. The company started to ask customers in which areas salespeople needed to improve skills or get additional training. 3M's corporate training department developed a survey that would reveal how customers assessed 3M's sales force and training needs in terms of specific skills. What developed was a new way to integrate the "voice of the customer" into the training and development process of each salesperson.

3M called its customer-focused training process A.C.T.—an acronym for the three steps of its process: assessment and analysis; curriculum content; and training content.

The process started by providing each customer with a questionnaire. The questionnaire assessed sales skills in six areas: knowledge of products and services; strategic skills critical to leveraging time with the customer; interpersonal selling skills; sales negotiation; internal influence and teamwork; and customer-focused quality. The completed questionnaires were then summarized into a feedback report for each salesperson, showing the gap between customers' perception and application. This information was then used to suggest specific areas in which the salesperson could use additional training. With his or her sales manager, the salesperson could then determine a training curriculum focusing on the three most significant gaps according to the customer survey. The salesperson is also expected to return to customers who completed the survey to review the composite results. The salesperson is effectively stating, "Here's what a small group of my customers have said. Can you give me some direction on what I need to be doing to close these gaps?"

3M has developed five criteria for looking at "off-the-shelf" training programs. The primary focus is on customer needs. As you will note, the ultimate goal is to ensure that these programs will not be rigid but rather, flexible to customization. Their five criteria are as follows:

1. The curriculum must tie into customer needs and objectives.
2. The training must be facilitator-friendly. 3M must be able to certify its own people as facilitators rather than depend solely on vendors.
3. Training must be participant-friendly. It must be intelligible, interactive, and designed for adult learners.
4. There must be a mechanism to review and reinforce the application of newly learned skills in the field.
5. It has to be adaptable. There has to be an opportunity to customize the program to meet the needs of individual 3M business units.

How Much Should You Spend on Training?

North American companies must be urged to treat their workers as assets to be developed, rather than as costs to be cut.

Some of the best training in North America takes place at Motorola. Its factory workers study the fundamentals of computer-aided design, robotics, and customized manufacturing not only by reading manuals or attending lectures, but also by inventing and building their own plastic knick-knacks. The company runs its worldwide training programs from Motorola University—a collection of computer-equipped classrooms and laboratories at its corporate headquarters in Schaumburg, Illinois. Last year, Motorola University, which includes regional campuses in Phoenix and Austin delivered 102,000 days of training to employees, suppliers, and customers.

In a similar example of commitment to training and education, Corning executives expect all employees to spend five per cent of their time at work on formal in-class and on-the-job training. That mandate, which is tracked by the managers of each business unit, averages out to an extraordinary 92 hours per employee per year.

In a more technology-based environment at Federal Express, at least once a year every one of the company's 40,000 couriers and customer-service agents plugs into an interactive, PC-based program that tests their job knowledge. For example, a courier who handles dangerous goods must tap into the computer every six months to find out if she is aware of all current government regulations and company policies.

In terms of cost to employers, let's look again at Motorola. In 1994, Motorola's sales were a record $13.3 billion in 1994, and the company spent $120 million on education. That's equivalent to 3.6 per cent of payroll—more than double the goal of 1.5 per cent that President Clinton advocated during his election campaign. Motorola conducted extensive pre- and post-training research and found that for every $1 spent on training, it realized $30 in productivity gains within three years.

Teams at Motorola are putting this training into action. For example, before starting a project, one of Motorola's teams enrolled in a two-day class at Motorola University called High-Commitment, High-Performance Team Training. They covered topics such as setting priorities, conducting focused meetings, and disagreeing with colleagues without insulting them. Some of that training took place on the job, and some in classrooms. What better way to prepare workers for their new roles as teachers, coaches, and leaders.

—CHECKLIST—

A Team Inventory Evaluation Form

In this chapter, we have addressed a number of issues, from forming teams to guiding and coaching teams. We have also addressed the concepts of training and education and where and how teams have been used to facilitate this requirement. Given the importance of teams and structure, the following questionnaire should prove useful in providing you with a means of assessing the future effectiveness of your teams.

Here's what Xerox suggests for those wishing to evaluate their current team and plot a path to improved performance.

The following questionnaire has two parts. The first part allows you to score your team on a set of criteria. The second part allows you to plot your team's progress/growth on a number of scales.

TEAM INVENTORY EVALUATION FORM
Is Your Team an Excellent Team?

TEAM INTEGRITY

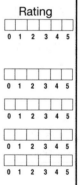

- Are the team goals well understood and actively supported by team members, colleagues, and management?
- Do these goals clearly contribute to Xerox efforts to increase market share, improve return on assets, and promote customer satisfaction?
- Is there at least 75% attendance at all team meetings?
- Do members understand and follow through on their responsibilities?
- Are meetings orderly and productive?

AVERAGE "SCORE" FOR TEAM INTEGRITY: _____

PROCESS DISCIPLINE

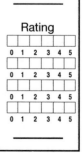

- Does the team use analytical tools effectively?
- Does the team stick to the problem-solving process?
- Has the team fully implemented the solution?
- Was the solution evaluated after implementation?

AVERAGE "SCORE" FOR PROCESS DISCIPLINE: _____

— CHECKLIST —

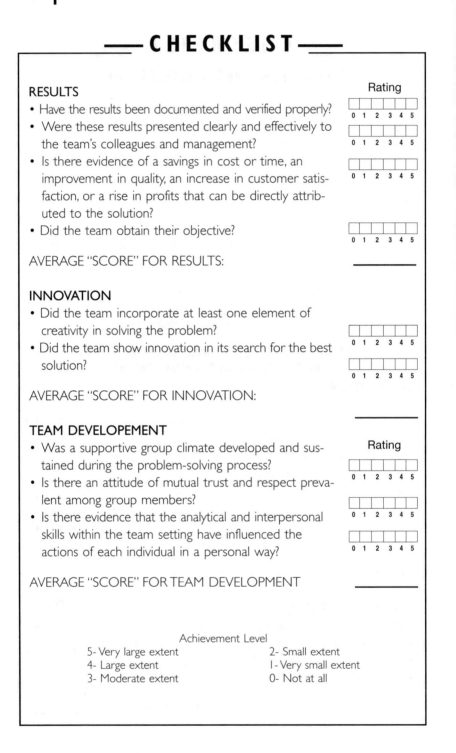

RESULTS

Rating

- Have the results been documented and verified properly?
  0 1 2 3 4 5
- Were these results presented clearly and effectively to the team's colleagues and management?
  0 1 2 3 4 5
- Is there evidence of a savings in cost or time, an improvement in quality, an increase in customer satisfaction, or a rise in profits that can be directly attributed to the solution?
  0 1 2 3 4 5
- Did the team obtain their objective?
  0 1 2 3 4 5

AVERAGE "SCORE" FOR RESULTS: _____

INNOVATION

- Did the team incorporate at least one element of creativity in solving the problem?
  0 1 2 3 4 5
- Did the team show innovation in its search for the best solution?
  0 1 2 3 4 5

AVERAGE "SCORE" FOR INNOVATION: _____

TEAM DEVELOPEMENT

Rating

- Was a supportive group climate developed and sustained during the problem-solving process?
  0 1 2 3 4 5
- Is there an attitude of mutual trust and respect prevalent among group members?
  0 1 2 3 4 5
- Is there evidence that the analytical and interpersonal skills within the team setting have influenced the actions of each individual in a personal way?
  0 1 2 3 4 5

AVERAGE "SCORE" FOR TEAM DEVELOPMENT _____

Achievement Level

5- Very large extent	2- Small extent
4- Large extent	1- Very small extent
3- Moderate extent	0- Not at all

— CHECKLIST —

Plot Your Growth

Once you have reviewed your team performance, you can keep track of your progress through a series of meetings. Every meeting, plot your average "Score" for each category on the appropriate chart below. You'll be able to see your strong points and spot problem areas, too.

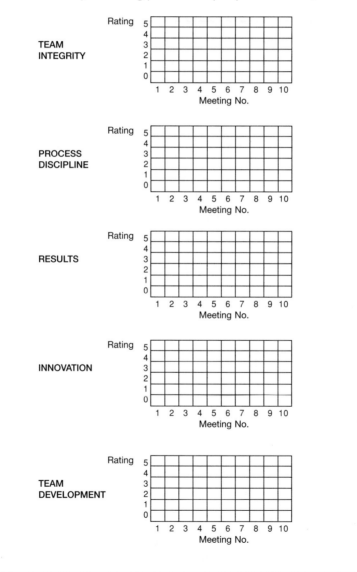

── CHECKLIST ──

Review your team performance on a meeting-by-meeting basis. Every meetings plot your average score for each category on the appropriate chart.

After you have plotted your results, review it with your team and establish objectives against these criteria, for your next series of meetings.

7

The Commit/Support Phase: Making It a Habit, Not an Act

Having the best, most efficient customer-focused processes cannot guarantee that the organization will achieve enhanced revenue and improved profitability. It's quite possible that some short-term goals may be accomplished, but not long-term success. Customer satisfaction must become a habit, not an act. That means that your organization must have a supportive culture, which will not happen without attention to the human/emotional needs of your internal customers. You can use various tools to help get you there, among them award and reward programs to create a service culture within the organization. However, some practices, if misused, will create havoc and an inappropriate focus within the organization.

This chapter differs somewhat in format from the previous chapters. It contains detailed examples of what others have done to create an internal service culture, excitement, and commitment within their respective organizations. There are fewer "how-to's" within this chapter—the onus is on you, the reader, to be innovative and to learn from the best practices of others.

The Tools Needed to Support a Culture of Continuous Improvement

Successful companies speak passionately about the importance of understanding that improving customer satisfaction is an ongoing process. They recognize that paying attention to the "human" aspects is essential. For them, this focus has to become part of the day-to-day operations of the organization, which means creating an internal service culture throughout the company. The IDEAS results indicate that companies with improved customer satisfaction use five main strategies to create an Internal Service Culture.

1. Communicate with employees to determine their needs and level of job satisfaction. Successful companies practise the Golden Rule of Service: "Do unto your internal customers (your employees) as you would have them do unto your external customers." Why? Because satisfied employees create satisfied customers. And satisfied customers (internal and external) create momentum. Customers help a company to innovate by giving it ideas on how to improve. As these ideas are implemented, improved customer satisfaction results that, in turn, will stimulate new ideas and keep the process alive.

2. Empower senior management with the responsibility for developing and maintaining the service culture. The commitment to improve customer satisfaction must begin at the highest levels of the organization to ensure success. Senior management must have both the authority and the responsibility for developing and maintaining customer satisfaction initiatives.

3. Establish service standards with the input of both customers and employees. Successful companies go one step beyond gathering customer and employee survey information. They "put their money where their mouth is" and produce a Customer Bill of Rights. This guarantee informs customers of the quality of service they can expect to receive and tells employees about the level of service they are expected to deliver. It also lets employees know the standards that management will abide by in delivering quality service to their staff.

4. Ensure that those standards are practised by employees and promoted to customers. A Customer Bill of Rights should be posted prominently throughout the organization. Customers must be made aware of it, and it should be a part of all employee training programs.

5. Encourage the service culture through training and reward programs to establish and recognize excellent service. Successful organizations understand the importance of providing motivation, positive feedback, and performance-based rewards for their employees. Effective incentives include monetary rewards such as giving employees shares in the company or linking a portion of employee commission to the performance of the business. Other less tangible, but equally important, strategies include giving trust, recognizing employee contributions, and sharing authority by involving employees in the company's strategic plan.

The first four strategies will be described in more detail in Chapter 8. In this chapter, however, we will deal primarily with issues that affect the organization's service culture.

Case Study: Bank of Montreal/Harris Bankcorp: How They Defined "What Customers Value Most"

Although reward programs are important motivators for staff, they should not be developed without customer input regarding their respective needs. The following example highlights an organization that created a measurement and reward system with such flexibility that it could be altered annually and/or between operating departments as a reflection of its stakeholders' changing needs. The organization, the Bank of Montreal/Harris Bankcorp, called this system The Figure of Merit.

The Company

Bank of Montreal is one of Canada's oldest and most respected financial institutions. As Canada's first chartered bank, established in 1918, it brings great pride and tradition to all its dealings. Globally, it has over 32,000 employees and more than US$101 billion in assets.

Through its 1,160 branches across Canada, and in collaboration with its U.S. subsidiary, Harris Bankcorp of Chicago and its investment banking arm, Nesbitt Burns, Bank of Montreal is the only bank to offer a complete range of financial services in its chosen markets in both Canada and the United States.

The Challenge—Call to Action

As a major financial institution competing in global markets, Bank of Montreal recognized the importance of client/customer satisfaction as a market differentiator. It also recognized that more than merely words or a catchy slogan were necessary to achieve this goal. Standards and measures were critical to its success and these had to be developed with its stakeholders in mind: shareholders; customers; employees; and the community.

Senior management recognized that each of these stakeholders had clearly defined goals, standards, and performance measures, which may even differ within various divisions of the bank. The challenge, therefore, was to determine how to define these standards, how to measure performance and put meaning to this process, and how to use those results to feed the Bank's recognition and reward process.

Action Taken

Following significant research assessing stakeholder needs, the Bank of Montreal created a measurement system, known as The Figure of Merit. After careful consideration and debate, each stakeholder group was assigned a weighting (as shown in the following figure). These weightings, however, were not necessarily the same for each division of the bank. (This flexibility reflected the different strategic priorities that might exist within an operating division, which reflect the needs of their various stakeholder groups).

Within each stakeholder group in each corporate division, additional subcriteria were defined—some were financially driven, some reflected internal and external research, and some were purely qualitative. Each of these subcriteria was also assigned weightings, which again varied by operating division.

Extensive customer research—in the form of syndicated and proprietary surveys—was a key element for measuring progress against these goals.

And how serious is the Bank about measurement? In

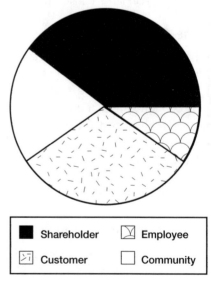

Shareholder   Employee

Customer   Community

the Corporate and Institutional Division, more than 300 customers and 1000 employees are surveyed annually. In the Personal and Commercial Division, mail panels and a national sample of over 10,000 telephone interviews/month are conducted (1,500 calls each day, six days per week). This research is used not only to drive the measurement system, but also to identify gaps in performance and thus help to set future direction for individual operating units.

For the Bank of Montreal/Harris Bank corp, the journey has just begun. And the results of their efforts are exemplary. In a continuing upward trend, earnings growth, at 16.4 per cent in 1994, ranked fourth in its Canadian peer group. The Bank ranked eleventh in earnings growth in its North American peer group. The Bank also reported its fifth consecutive year of record earnings, while sustaining its solid and consistent return on equity. Overall, its financial track record for the 1990s places it firmly among the top-performing major banks in Canada and the United States.

This success is based on a dedication to understand the needs of its customers/stakeholders and a passion to differentiate itself.

Want to Make A Change...Create a Challenge

While performance measurement is important, more is needed in order to ensure that creating "What Customers Value Most" becomes a habit rather than an isolated act that is seldom repeated. Organizations that embrace the concept of continuous improvement and implement a process to ensure that it occurs are well on their way.

Moore North America is an example of such an organization. Each year, Moore sponsors an event called Quality Forum. This event is intended to bring together three fundamental principles: education; recognition; and dedication.

At the Quality Forum, the company issues two awards: the Sam Award and the Paragon.

The SAM Award, acronym for Success At Moore, is named after its founder, Samuel (Sam) J. Moore. This award recognizes significant contributions by project teams for the following achievements:

- delivery of ever-improving value to Moore customers, and
- improvement in the company's overall operational performance.

All teams that score 70 points or more receive a recognition plaque for their entries. The highest-scoring teams are invited to attend the Quality Forum and present their award-winning projects. Winners receive the SAM Award, consisting of an individual and a team plaque, and Moore stock for each team member.

The criteria for the SAM Award serve as a planning and support guide to align team effort with the corporation's strategic direction on an ongoing basis throughout the year.

To foster healthy competition, the company also presents the Paragon Award.

The Paragon is named for one of Samuel J. Moore's first products—the Black Leaf Counter Check Book. The term, "paragon" is defined as "a peerless model of excellence," and this award reflects the excellence and rich heritage of the company.

The Paragon is awarded to the SAM team that receives the highest score from the judges' panel at the Quality Forum. This "travelling" award resides with the team until it is presented at the next year's Quality Forum.

The SAM Award and The Paragon are sponsored and administered by Moore's North American Quality Council (NAQC). The NAQC develops and administers the guidelines, criteria, scoring system, and the judging process. As such, clarification and resolution of any questions rest solely with the NAQC. The Council is chaired by the Vice President of Quality Management and comprises the chief quality officers of participating Moore North America divisions.

Let's go back to the SAM Award again. This award recognizes significant contributions by project teams (note the emphasis on teams and contribution).

All entries must adhere to the following criteria:

- Projects must be project-based. Projects must have a start date, must have concluded analysis and formulated a solution, and must have already been implemented.
- Projects must represent a team effort. For purposes of the SAM Award, a team consists of three to eight members. Projects with fewer than three or more than eight team members will not be accepted. (The North America SAM Awards make no provision for reward and recognition of more than eight members on a team.)

This award process has created exciting competition within Moore North America, which the organization takes seriously. As such, it is a strictly judged event that seeks to encourage idea generation and execution through its scoring system.

The chart below shows the SAM Award Criteria and Scoring.

Maximum Scores

Customer Focus	20
Teamwork	15
Analysis Methods	15
Actual Solutions	15
Organizational Learning	15
Results	20
Total Possible	100

The chart is the scoring template for customer focus and shows what the judges are looking for when scoring the submissions.

SAM Award Criteria and Scoring					
CRITERIA CATEGORY ADDRESS	ITEM #	CRITERIA ITEMS TO LOOK FOR?	WHAT TO DO JUDGES	POINTS POSSIBLE	POINTS ATTAINED
CUSTOMER FOCUS	1.1	Project was selected based upon specific identification of the customer	What evidence did the team give to illustrate that they know who their customer is?	5	
	1.2	Project was selected based on clear identification of customer's needs.	What evidence did team give to illustrate that they understand profoundly well what the customers requirements were?	5	

	1.3	Project was selected based upon the fact that it is a frequently recurring OR that some aspect of the company's and/or customers preformance could be markedly improved.	What evidence was presented that showed what would happen if the problem of opportunity was NOT addressed?	5	
	1.4	Project has impact on external customers.	What evidence was presented that demonstrated the impact of this project on the external customer?	5	
SUBTOTAL for CUSTOMER FOCUS				TOTAL POINTS POSSIBLE 20	

For Moore, the competition itself is not the sole objective. Its goals also include culture change and the creation of energy and momentum. For that reason, significant attention is given to acknowledge the contributions of team members and encourage future participation. Consequently, this event is promoted heavily in communication bulletins both leading up to and following the Quality Forum, which typically occurs in late September. This promotion carries on into October, which has traditionally been National Quality Month.

1. Create criteria—make sure that sufficient flexibility is built in to accommodate changes in strategic direction.
2. Publicize—ensure that all potential participants know how they will be judged.
3. Make awards meaningful.
4. Keep the vision alive—Communicate, Communicate, Communicate.

Case Study: Motorola

There are many variations on the Moore theme. This example shows how a competitive/ team-building event can be a learning situation throughout the organization—a learning situation that has continuous improvement and learning from the best practices of others as its fundamental principles. These principles again are designed to ensure that positive change and the alignment of the organization become a comfortable habit, not a forced act. The organization described in this case is Motorola—an organization more known for its quality practices than for its practices to ensure a positive internal service culture.

The Company

Ever since its "Great Quality Awakening" in 1981, Motorola has focused on Quality and Total Customer Satisfaction. To provide guidance to the Corporation, in 1982 the Motorola Corporate Quality Council began a process of biennial Quality Systems Reviews to assess the system maturity of each division or group in the company. These reviews were intended to assure that the Quality System of each business was effective in achieving Total Customer Satisfaction

The Challenge—Call to Action

Motorola recognized the importance of internal competitions as a means to support their focus on continuous improvement. Accordingly, they set five primary objectives for the team competition:

1. Renew emphasis on the participative process at all levels of the organization worldwide.

2. Recognize and reward outstanding performance at the team level.
3. Reaffirm the environment for continuous improvement.
4. Demonstrate the power of focused team effort.
5. Communicate the best team achievements throughout Motorola.

To ensure that these objectives would be achieved, Motorola also created the following design criteria to ensure that the competition would drive continuous improvement.

1. Have one competition, i.e., no differentiation throughout the organization worldwide with respect to who can participate:
   • emphasize the process;
   • avoid implications of status;
   • provide simple logistics.

2. Use universal measurements:
   • consistency of judging;
   • consistency with other national conventions in countries where Motorola operates, i.e., Japan, Malaysia, Singapore.

3. Make sure projects demonstrate significant achievements, i.e., do not accept normal departmental goals or tasks:
   • screen at the first level of competition;
   • team activities and results are to be accurately reflected.

4. Encourage the formation of cross-functional teams to enhance customer responsiveness.

Action Taken

Recognizing that this process had to be more than a competition, Motorola took the following steps:

Each team was provided with a resource handbook entitled, *Total Customer Satisfaction-TCS-Everything you wanted to know about problem solving but were afraid to ask.* This handbook covered topics that include the following:
   • forming teams
   • meeting preparation
   • problem-solving steps/methods

- problems-solving tools
- presentations
- TCS evaluation criteria and scoring

To ensure that teams were prepared for their presentations, Motorola also provided a "coach's" guide. These coaches are not members *of* the team, but coaches *to* the team—coaches that the team selects. This guide provided a set of instructions for coaches to use when evaluating a team's presentation, based on the international evaluation criteria. The summary is then used as direct feedback to the team.

Coach Evaluation Checklist

Speaker: Coach:
Title of Talk:
Date: Audience Size:
Location: Planned Length of Talk:
Type of Audio-Visual Used: Starting Time: Ending Time:

Category	Satisfactory	Needs Improvement
Presentation format Well organized opening		
Good continuity		
Clear points made		
Effective ending		
Personal dynamics Enthusiastic		
Persuasive		
Good presence		
In control		
Mannerisms Nervousness		
Distracting gestures		
Voice projection		
Modulation		
Tone		
Other		

Eyes		
Maintained		
audience contact		
Occasional sweep		
Other		
Miscellaneous		

This critique is so important because it provides a means to coach the team through its presentation.

In the following chart, "Presentation" is one of seven criteria used to evaluate the team's entry in the competition. Each criterion, as shown below, has a specific point weighting, and desired content. Refer to the Appendix for further detail. Participants/teams, coaches, and judges are each provided with these criteria and weightings. In that way, the team knows exactly what is expected and how they will be evaluated.

Following the competition, the initiative and successes are communicated extensively through newsletters and celebrations.

The following year, teams are encouraged and evaluated on the basis of their ability to incorporate improvements identified in previous years. Best practices sharing has become a habit, not an art form, and is part of the fabric of the organization.

Motorola T.C.S. Team Competition Scoring Form			
Organization: **Team Name:**			**Date:**
Key Initiative	Six Sigma Quality: Total Cycle Time:	Profit Improvement: Participative Management:	Product, Manufacturing and Environmental Leadership:

Category	Judge's Scoring Criteria	Score 0 to 10	Wgt
Project Selection (10 Points)	• Criteria and a methodology for selection evident. Project clearly defined. • Aggressive goals with linkage to key initiatives established. • Customer identified. Customer requirements and metrics defined.		30% 30% 40%
Teamwork (10 Points)	• Team participation that demonstrates commitment to the project. • Appropriate team membership evident in the improvement process. • Participative practices reinforced.		20% 30% 40%
Analysis Techniques (20 Points)	• Thorough and appropriate analysis techniques used and understood. • Benchmarking of best practices evident. • Innovative use of fundamental tools and/or progression to more advanced tools. Team growth evident.		50% 30% 20%
Remedies (20 Points)	• Alternative solutions seriously explored. • Remedies consistent with the analysis. • Implementation plans thorough and well defined. • Innovation in the remedies or implementation evident.		30% 20% 20% 30%

Results (20 Points)	• Verified improvements measured favourably against the difficulty of achievement. • Ancillary effects identified and characterized. • Customer satisfaction results evident.		40% 20% 40%
Institution-alization (15 Points)	• Improvements sustainable and permanent. • Solutions adopted by and from other groups. • Team's growth in the problem solving process is evident.		40% 40% 20%
Presentation (5 Points)	• Clear and concise. • Improvement process followed.		60% 40%
Judge:		**Total Score:**	
Comments:			

Recognition and Reward Systems

Competitions are not the only form of reward and recognition. Nor must recognition and reward systems be targeted exclusively to internal customers. There are many ways to encourage loyalty and performance improvement ideas. All it takes is a bit of creativity, just as the following examples will show. First we will discuss internal rewards and recognition, then we will examine what we could offer to customers. The final portion of this section deals with suggestion systems and how they must be encouraged and rewarded.

1. Emphasize the participative process at all levels of the organization.
2. Recognize and reward outstanding performance at the team level.
3. Reaffirm the environment for continuous improvement.
4. Demonstrate the power of a focused team effort.
5. Communicate the best team achievements throughout the organization.

Offer Employees an Incentive to Improve Customer Satisfaction

If you want employees to actively focus on providing excellent customer service, consider linking customer satisfaction ratings to their compensation. The following examples show these principles in action.

Louisville Gas & Electric Co. (LG&E)

At LG&E, a company-wide team incentive program has resulted in significant improvements in customer satisfaction as well as employee performance. The company's Team Incentive Award (TIA) was designed to emphasize the importance of the customer to all employees. According to Jon McAdams, Director of Marketing, it has been highly successful—over the last four years, overall customer satisfaction ratings have dramatically increased, moving up 15 percentage points.

A company—wide effort. LG&E surveys all of the customers in its service territory, rather than just the ones who had recent contact with the company. The company believes that it is not only responsible for customer contacts, but also for the information that it transmits in its billing channels, and how it manages its community relations—all of those things are part of its mission. (For example, whether or not customers have had direct contact with the company, perhaps they've noticed an LG&E crew working on the street. Customers might be asked the following questions: Was the crew working efficiently? Were the vehicles and equipment well maintained? According to McAdams, "Everyone in the company is responsible for the ratings. And then everyone gets the pay-out.")

A company-wide program was instituted in order to prevent a rift between groups. LG&E did not want to compensate functional groups differently. Certain groups may do better than others, which may cause factions to form rather than to pull people together in a unified response.

Here's how the organization actually defined its program elements.

Employees must manage the company's assets. The Team Incentive Award (TIA) is based on customer satisfaction surveys as well as expense control—each is weighted 50 per cent. "You can do a lot to please customers if the sky is the limit on expenses, but you need to control both," McAdams says.

Rather than using a broad corporate financial performance goal, the expense control measure is more fair to employees. "Employees have more influence on direct expense control than on overall profitability. We're a weather—sensitive business. We could have a very good year, and then be impacted by, for example, low temperatures during the summer. That would affect revenues—and it isn't anything the employees are responsible for."

Hitting customer satisfaction targets for pay-out. Daily customer interviews are conducted by an independent research firm. The company only looks at the top two ratings from a 10-point scale—these are called the "percent-excellent responses."

The data are summarized monthly. Then targets are set based on a three-month rolling average. The team can score within the established target range, below the target range, or above it. If their scores hit within the target, the team earns one point; above the target, two points; and if they're below the target, no points are scored.

"Our commitment is to make at least 12 points, which is scoring within the target range every month," McAdams explains. "If we miss a month, we can make it up by doing even better on another month, so we never get to a point where we say: 'This is the best we can do.' It generates a lot of interest among the team to keep up to date on our performance."

At every level, he adds, there's a certain amount of salary that is considered either as a bonus or as a salary-at-risk. But employees can go beyond their comparable marketplace salary if the team exceeds the targets. "The maximum targets would be two bonus points each month," he says. "That's capped at 150 per cent pay-out of the amount of salary-at-risk at that particular level."

If the team hits the target less than six times per year—or less than 50 per cent of the months—then there is no pay-out on the customer satisfaction portion of the team award.

Targets are adjusted yearly, yet customer satisfaction ratings have continued to increase on a year-by-year basis.

Spreading the word. As I've discussed before, how news about the plan is communicated is just as important as the measurement method. You have to tell employees how they can affect the measure. And point out how teams can help the groups that have direct customer contact; sometimes that's not immediately clear to them.

LG&E does this through group meetings, company publications, a computer bulletin board that all employees can access, and detailed monthly reports to managers with information they can share with employees. In fact, the company even has a communications campaign—similar to a marketing campaign—in which information is targeted to specific groups.

"An incentive award program is not something you can implement and just let run," he says. "You have to continually look for new ways to communicate information and make sure that employees understand what it's about."

Davidson Plyforms

The following example shows how and why you should try, whenever possible, to make the rewards and recognition process a team approach. Davidson Plyforms, believes in team incentives and has put an interesting twist on it. Twelve teams work towards benchmarks in productivity, quality, and profitability for incentive bonuses ranging from 5 cents to $1.35 for every work hour. Furthermore, teams can also receive a portion of division and company profits. Even if the company is not profitable, it is still possible to qualify for productivity and quality bonuses. The company president maintains that if the team does what it has been asked to do and achieves results, it deserves the bonus.

Even if hourly employees aren't on teams, they can still earn monthly bonuses pegged to the average bonus size of the 12 teams. The company believes that by doing this, it shows them that their support is critical for the other areas to achieve their goals.

As far as results are concerned, the company has seen big increases in productivity and innovation.

Low-Cost Employee Rewards

Acknowledging employees doesn't have to cost much—but it can achieve benefits worth many times the cost. A Half International survey reported that when 150 executives were asked to name the most common reason employees leave a company, 34 per cent replied "limited recognition and praise." The second most common reason—at 29 per cent of the executives—was compensation.

One of the biggest myths surrounding employee recognition awards is that only high-priced trips or lavish gifts can effectively communicate gratitude. However, most experts say that the act of recognizing and expressing thanks for an employee's accomplishments is what counts.

One company that knows the value of a strong recognition program is AT&T Universal Card Services (UCS) of Jacksonville, Florida, winner of the 1992 Baldrige Award. This company has more than 40 reward and recognition programs, such as the Best Call Award, which is given to a customer service representative for a particularly well-handled call. Once associates accumulate a certain number of Best Call certificates, their names are entered in a draw for weekend getaways.

UCS is so committed to recognizing employee achievements as often as possible that all managers are given a budget to finance their own acts of recognition such as rewarding meal tickets to the company cafeteria.

Silicon Graphics in Mountain View, California, brings a more quirky approach to its employee recognition awards. The most effective recognition programs are the most creative ones. The Red Badge of Courage Award encourages employees to challenge the system and to speak up for process improvements—large or small. The memento—literally a red badge—reinforces the Silicon ethos, as stated by the director of compensation and benefits: "We encourage the sort of person who thinks outside the lines and finds solutions to things that other people didn't even know were broken."

Silicon also offers an Off-the-Wall Award. The winner receives a T-shirt that shows a flock of birds flying in a formation one way, while another bird with a propeller on its head flies in the opposite direction. The award was developed to recognize an employee who shows a unique capacity for fun and spirit.

Maritz, another company deeply involved in award and reward practices, runs a "Thanks a Bunch" program. Workers send each other thank-you cards for special favours or jobs well done. At regular intervals, the cards are entered into a draw for awards such as binoculars or jackets with the company's logo.

Motorola also gives out rewards with a sense of humour. The Pig Pen Award serves as a gentle reminder to workers who leave their desks in a state of disarray that they may be compromising company security. (Motorola has a strict policy of clearing desks and locking away confidential materials at the end of every day.)

The overall message that these companies are sending out is worth paying attention to. As Maritz's Jerry McAdams notes, "You're going to get more value by getting people to work together than by inciting them to compete."

Creating Long-Term External Customer Loyalty Programs

Here's an example that demonstrates external customer rewards and recognition—frequent flyer programs.

In the early 1980s, frequent flyer programs began as a short-term promotion because airlines had a number of excess seats they wanted to give away as rewards or incentives to their most frequent customers. Today, these programs have blossomed. At United Airlines, more than 20 million people have enrolled in the program since it started, and approximately 7 million customers are still active in the program.

In these types of reward programs, the bigger the program, the better it is in the customer's eyes. Therefore, in a frequent flyer program, the more ways that customers can earn miles, the quicker they can earn their reward. And if they have more ways to use the rewards, the better the program is.

Now airlines are forming partnerships with banks and long-distance companies to extend and enhance the frequent flyer program and offer value-added benefits to customers. Airlines have a twofold agenda: to build a better, more rewarding relationship with frequent fliers; and to generate additional transportation revenue.

These types of programs have a very targeted audience and they don't appeal to everyone. Some customers just apply for the card because they want to be preferred customers, and have more ways to earn more miles.

> Team rewards are more appropriate than individual rewards, but don't ignore individual involvement.
>
> Better ideas or performance are not driven by large dollar pay-outs, they just have to be meaningful.
>
> Remember to include both internal and external customers.

The Role of Suggestion Systems

Suggestion systems are important, but unfortunately, they are not always given the thought and attention that they deserve. That's why IBM discarded its old system and replaced it with a system that was more streamlined and allowed any employee to participate.

On January 1, 1991, IBM Canada withdrew its previous Suggestion Plan. It then formed a cross-functional team to design a replacement. Their objective was to find a way to encourage all employees to develop and implement not more ideas but more solutions to business problems.

Nine months later, they announced their new plan, called Unlimited Solutions. What was especially innovative about this plan was that employees were not only encouraged to originate an idea/solution, but they were also required to be part of the implementation effort. In this way they would share recognition with all others in making the solution work! Here are IBM's eligibility criteria:

- ALL employee-initiated and -implemented improvements, job-related and non-job-related, are eligible for recognition.
- ALL IBM Canada regular and non-regular employees including managers and retirees are eligible to participate. (Vendors and contractors are excluded.); and
- ALL solutions that improve IBM's business are eligible for recognition, with the following exceptions:
  - ideas relating to computer programs released for customer use (for example: program product); and
  - ideas that are trivial in relation to job responsibilities.

The application process itself was thoroughly documented and communicated to the entire employee base. Here are some excerpts:

Employee Responsibility

- *Originate idea/solution.*
  Review with manager for guidance re: implementation.
  Consultation with and approval of all other areas affected by
  the idea must precede implementation.

Note: Appropriate staff work should be completed before consultation with areas affected by the idea.

- *Network.*
  If appropriate, formulate a team to assist with implementation.
  Teams could include employees from other functions or countries.
- *Document the implemented solution.*
  Following the submission, copies are sent to the originator of
  the idea and in the case of a team, to all members' managers
  signifying agreement that the solution is implemented and
  eligible for recognition.

With respect to recognition for an implemented solution, it can be given to an individual or team members once formally submitted and accepted by their manager. (Team members are defined as the individual who originates an idea and those who improve/assist with the idea/solution/implementation.)

The levels of recognition are:

- immediate informal recognition, as determined by the employee's
  manager for each accepted implemented solution.
- participation memento for the 1st, 10th, 25th, 40th, and 50th
  accepted implemented solution in a calendar year.
- quarterly draws for participation (administered by the
  Unlimited Solutions Department)
  - 10 per cent of participants up to a maximum of 200 will be
    recognized with a cash award of $250 less regular payroll
    deductions.
  - each employee named on the accepted submission form is
    submitted individually for the draw.
  - no maximum on number of entries or times recognized per
    individual.
- yearly recognition for the ideas considered the most "Significant."

For immediate recognition, it is up to the manager to be creative, ensure peers are involved, and ensure that the recognition is appropriate in view of the implemented solution.

Ideas that are considered the most significant are assessed for yearly recognition. The manager determines the significance at the time of submission, based on the following criteria:
- Impact on Customer Satisfaction
- Impact on Quality/Reliability of our Products/Services/Processes
- Estimated net savings or revenue
- Innovation (Creativity/Originality)

IBM employs the following roles and responsibilities:

Employees

- Review with manager and obtain approvals from all other areas affected by idea prior to implementation.
- Form team if required.
- Implement solution.
- Complete on-line submission.

Managers:

- Receive and review submission and accept the recommendation, if appropriate.
- Ensure immediate appropriate recognition.

Unlimited Solutions Department's Responsibility

- Records participation.
- Sends out mementos.
- Enters names of submitters separately in Quarterly Draw.

Function's Responsibility

- Determines which implemented solutions will receive yearly awards at year-end.

Another Approach Where Teams and Rewards Play an Important Role

Van Kampen American Capital has over 200 teams in operation, involving almost 90 per cent of its employee base over the past four years.

Structure has played a key role in their approach. The two other important factors have been the simplicity of procedure to identify and implement the ideas, and a well-thought-out recognition and rewards system.

Points are assigned for the identification, implementation, and benefits achieved from the implementation of an idea. These points can be accumulated and when certain levels are achieved, rewards are provided.

LEVEL	ACHIEVEMENT
BRONZE	15 Points = Certified & Implemented Points + Cost Savings
SILVER	25 Points = Certified & Implemented Points + Cost Savings
GOLD	50 Points = Certified & Implemented Points + Cost Savings
DIAMOND	100 Points = Certified & Implemented Points + Cost Savings
CLUB LEVELS	150, 200,... (50 point increments beyond Diamond) Points = Certified & Implemented Points + Cost Savings

The following is its simplified three-step structure to its program.

Step 1—Preparing a Recommendation

The team identifies an idea it would like to implement and fills out the Certification Form on the following page. One copy is kept by the team leader and one is sent to the Quality Council.

Step 2—Certifying an Idea

Once the action steps are planned, the team discusses the idea and intended results with the appropriate level manager or management team. If the manager deems the idea valid and feasible, he or she signs the form and the team can plan implementation. A copy is kept

CERTIFICATION FORM						
(1) Rec. #	(3) Status (Circle One)	Status Date	Team Name	Team Leader	Approvals	
	P Preparing Recommendation					
(2) Subject (Circle One)	C Certified				Manager	
System Policy	I Implemented				Manager	
Procedure Other	T Tabled				Manager	

(4) Quality Measurement (Circle One):
Accuracy Efficiency Customer Input Timeliness Effectiveness Other

(5) SUBJECT DESCRIPTION (limited to 30 characters):

(6) IDENTIFIED PROBLEM:

(7) RECOMMENDATION:

(8) BENEFITS:

(9a) FIRST YEAR   (9b) FIRST YEAR   (9c) FIRST YEAR
       GROSS   IMPLEMENTATION   NET SAVINGS
       SAVINGS   EXPENSE   (9a-9b)

(10) RISKS: (11) CONTROLS:

(12) WHAT CUSTOMER IS IMPACTED?

(13) (Utilize ONE as applicable)
       REASON TABLED:

       REASON NOT COMPLETED:

       IMPLEMENTATION ISSUES:

by the team leader and one copy is sent to the Quality Council for data entry. Once the certified idea is entered into the tracking system, the team receives 1/2 point.

If the idea to be certified requires another department's aid in implementation or the idea affects that department's procedures, then the team that generated the idea must first meet and discuss the idea with that department and gain approval for certification. Once the idea has been deemed feasible by both parties, it can be certified.

Step 3—Implementing an Idea

When the idea is implemented, the manager signs the form. The original copy is kept by the team leader and a second copy is sent to the Quality Council. Upon entry into the tracking system, the team receives another 1/2 point for implementation.

Additional points can be awarded based on the expected benefits and cost savings that are expected to be achieved.

After an idea has been implemented for one year, the implementing team is required to perform an assessment to evaluate the degree to which the implemented idea meets customer requirements as originally identified on the certification form under "benefits." The team is expected to assess the impact of the idea on the customer. Using a scale from (1) Does not meet requirements to (5) Greatly exceeds requirements, the team's perception serves as a tool to monitor quality results.

Customers Can be a Tremendous Source of Ideas for Improvement

As we highlighted in the introduction to this chapter, your best source of new product ideas is often your most overlooked source— your customers. At PaperDirect, executives don't worry much about where the next product idea will come from. The New Jersey-based business, which sells computer paper via catalogues, depends on its customers for great ideas.

The company holds quarterly "Show Us Your Stuff" contests that each yield up to 500 new product suggestions, five to 10 of which typically lead to new developments.

For example, one customer matched PaperDirect papers, envelopes, brochures, labels, and cards in a similarly coloured arrangement that became the model for a line of matching stationery sets. Another suggestion led PaperDirect into a new niche;

the company launched *Technique*, a how-to magazine for desk-top publishers.

Customers were constantly sending in unsolicited product ideas, says president Warren Struhl, "so we thought we'd reward them for their efforts." The top entries win money—first prize is $500 in company credit, and runners-up receive $50—and recognition in the quarterly catalogue's "Great Ideas from Our Customers" column. Struhl says that over three years, these ideas have helped increase sales from $1.1 million in 1990 to about $70 million last year.

Many organizations can "talk the talk" but few can "walk the talk." That is, senior management must visibly and meaningfully support an initiative of becoming an organization that customers value most. Take the following test and see how your organization rates as one that supports a customer-focused environment.

— CHECKLIST —

Are you Supporting a Customer-Focused Philosophy?

1. Do you collect feedback from the front line about the needs and wants of your internal customer?
   a. Yes, on a regular basis. It's then communicated back to all staff for discussion and action planning.
   b. Yes, periodically.
   c. No, but we talk about it on an informal basis.
   d. No, not at all.

2. Do you communicate the results of your suggestion system regularly throughout the entire company?
   a. Yes, at least monthly through newsletters and posters.
   b. Yes, occasionally, but not as often as we should.
   c. No, but the information is available if anyone wants to know.
   d. No, not at all.

3. Do you actively seek out customer comments and complaints?
   a. Yes, with several methods: formal surveys, customer panels, 1-800 #'s.
   b. Yes, occasionally, but not as often as we should.
   c. No, but we respond if there are complaints.
   d. No, not at all.

4. Do you know what kind of internal support your employees want and expect?
   a. Yes, we communicate in several ways with our employees to learn more about them.
   b. Yes, but we could do a better job of it. We keep records of suggestions and so forth.
   c. No, not enough. We could do better.
   d. No, but I'm sure they are few and far between.

— CHECKLIST —

5. Do front-line people receive direct feedback from customers?
   a. Yes, they actively encourage feedback, comments and complaints.
   b. Yes, I think so.
   c. Sometimes, but the feedback is complaints for the most part and it is not systematically tracked.
   d. No, and they don't care to.

6. Are there any incentives for giving good service?
   a. Yes, write-ups in newsletters, published praise letters, employee-of-the-month awards, and other recognition from management.
   b. Some recognition, yes, but we have no systems for it.
   c. There is not much recognition or incentive to do well.
   d. No recognition.

7. How customer-focused are your delivery systems?
   a. Very. We collect feedback constantly from both internal and external customers and change things if necessary.
   b. Fairly good, though it's been awhile since we've thoroughly looked them over.
   c. I don't know. I haven't given it any thought.
   d. Rather poor. They are bureaucratic and complex .

8. Are your people equipped to give good service?
   a. Yes. They get extensive training, information, and freedom to act as professional service-givers.
   b. As well as you can expect.
   c. Not very well.
   d. No. They get no training.

9. Is there a commitment from top management to support the customer-focused service concept?
   a. Yes, and management is good at communicating service goals.
   b. There is commitment but it doesn't really show.
   c. Management says they believe in it, but acts in opposition.
   d. Management doesn't seem to care about service.

—— CHECKLIST ——

10. Does your company have a spelled-out, easily communicated reward & recognition system?
    a. Yes, and all the staff are aware of it.
    b. Yes, but most front-line employees don't know it.
    c. No, but a system is under development.
    d. No, I'm not aware of one.

11. Do you have a concept of "internal service"?
    a. Yes. We all realize that we must serve one another as well as the customer.
    b. Yes. Most of us think about it at least sometimes.
    c. No. We have a lot of "silos" in the company.
    d. No. Some people would rather fight than cooperate.

12. Is management's position on customer-focused process improvement visible in the organization?
    a. Yes. Management visits all departments regularly and constantly communicates the message.
    b. Yes, fairly visible. Everyone knows what management's position is.
    c. Not very visible.
    d. No, not at all.

Now give yourself points as follows:
a. = 4 points   b. = 3 points   c. = 2 points   d. = 1 point

40-48 points Excellent!
Your organization is truly one that customers should value most.

30-39 points Good!
You have a high dedication to the customer (internal and external) and are most likely looked upon as dependable by your customers, but you need some fine tuning.

20-29 points Watch out!
Before you know it, your customers will leave you if they have somewhere else to go.

Below 20 points
Serious trouble is brewing which will impact future revenue and profitability.

8

The Tools that Will Help You Continue to Offer "What Customers Value Most"

T his is a chapter about best practices and how they can be used to achieve "What Customers Value Most." We will examine the tools that organizations use to achieve performance improvement and the roles played by benchmarking, complaint systems, and technology. These are enablers—the processes, practices, or methods that make "best practice" performance possible.

> Performance improvement is never an accident; it is always the result of high intention, sincere effort, intelligent direction, and skilful execution; it represents the wise choice of many alternatives.

Benchmarking can be viewed from two perspectives: first, as a tool to help redesign customer-focused processes; and second, as a means of monitoring how you compare to your competition and the best-in-class organizations. This chapter will guide you through the steps involved in conducting a successful best practices benchmarking initiative.

Another tool that organizations can use to tap into their customer base and identify opportunities for improvement is complaint systems. What better way to offer "What Customers Value Most" than by listening to what they are dissatisfied with? More and more executives have made this a cornerstone of their performance improvement efforts, recognizing that it costs five times more to get a new customer than it does to keep an existing one.

Finally, we will discuss the role of technology and how organizations have used it as an enabler and not as a solution in itself. Much can be learned from the successes and failures of others.

Benchmarking—Where it Fits, How it Fits

Benchmarking certainly seems to be the current buzzword and is gaining momentum at alarming speed. Every major organization, including such well-known companies as IBM, AT&T, DuPont, Ford, Eastman Kodak, Milliken, Motorola, and Xerox have numerous benchmarking studies in progress.

There are two major forms of benchmarking: process/best practices and competitive. We will first look at best practices benchmarking, followed by competitive benchmarking. Since many books address this topic in detail, I will provide only a general overview in this section.

Process Benchmarking—The Myths and the Facts

The following common questions usually arise during my client assignments, workshops, and seminars regarding the concept of process/best practices benchmarking and what you should know about its use.

What is Process/Best Practices Benchmarking?

Benchmarking is not industrial espionage. Rather, it is the art of legitimately finding out how others do something better than you do. Your ultimate goal, of course, is to imitate, or even improve upon, their techniques. The American Productivity and Quality Center (APQC), a non-profit group in Houston, which established the International Benchmarking Clearinghouse provides this definition:

> The process of continuously comparing and measuring an organization against business leaders anywhere in the world to gain information which will help the organization take action to improve its performance.

Is There a Common Methodology to Process Benchmarking?

A significant amount of literature has been written on the various process benchmarking methodologies. IBM has developed a four-phase system, AT&T has a nine-step approach, Xerox has a 10-step methodology, and DuPont has a nine-step system. However, my experience has shown that the four-phase methodology of the APQC (Plan and Design, Collect, Analyze and Adapt, and Improve/Implement) is the easiest to explain and utilize.

Each phase involves clearly defined steps, goals, and objectives. More importantly, however, are the questions that must be posed during each phase. The following list is a modified version of these questions as originally developed by the APQC. After each, I have provided a brief example of what a major property developer, Company X, discovered during this stage. The four stages are as follows:

i) **Plan and Design**—key processes for review are defined, mapped, and information needs identified, data collection tools are created, and internal information is gathered.

"Plan and Design" Questions:

What process should we benchmark?

What is our process?

How well is it performing today?

Who are the customers of our process?

What products and/or services do we deliver?

What do our customers expect from our process?

What are the critical success factors for this process?

What is our process performance goal?

What data should we collect for comparisons?

The organization identified two processes that required immediate attention: the lease issuance process and the budgeting process. The organization selected these two processes because they both had an impact on the organization's bottom-line profitability as well as on internal and external customer satisfaction. The lease process had an extended time frame (more than nine months), was burdened with excessive paperwork, and had an effect on when lease payments would commence—causing a major impact on cash flow. The budgeting process was an overly complicated process that affected almost every person in the organization, both at the corporate office as well as at the property sites. Two cross-functional teams were selected, trained, and given the tasks of mapping the existing processes and identifying inefficiencies. The process maps were reviewed with its customers (in the case of the budgeting process, internal customers) to verify the process steps and identify initial areas where improvements were needed. Once completed, each team identified performance goals for the process to be improved. In the case of the lease process, the organization set the following goals:

Desired Deliverables:

The process should have the following characteristics:

- Efficient—A streamlined process (reduce time by 30 per cent), involving the fewest number of employees, documents, and approvals.
- Responsive to internal and external customers.
  Immediate tracking capabilities and availability of information to respond to enquiries.
- Measurable—Existence of standards of performance and a system for continuous measurement throughout the lease development process.

The organization then established a set of characteristics for its potential benchmark partners. In the case of the budgeting process, these characteristics included:

Benchmark Partner Characteristics:

The benchmark partner should:

- have multiple reporting relationships
- have relatively stable revenues and operating expenses
- have operating partners (a syndicated partnership or be part of a larger corporate entity)
- be a service organization with field operations
- have top-down-driven process guidelines and approvals

Note that being in the business of property development was not a criterion. The organization realized that much could be learned from outside of its industry segment. They were then ready to advance to the next stage—collect.

ii) **Collect**—in which secondary data are collected, field visits are conducted, and information is assembled.

"Collect" Questions:

What companies perform this process?

Which company is best at it?

What can we learn from that company?

What is their process?

What is their performance goal and how was it set?

What business practices, methods, or processes contribute to the performance level of that process?

What factors could inhibit the adaption of their process into our company?

The organization then embarked on an extensive two-staged research effort. First, the organization developed a benchmarking questionnaire. The questionnaire was based on the process map developed earlier, identifying both deficiencies and also improvement opportunities. The questionnaire was designed to be used as a guide during a face-to-face interview with a potential benchmark partner. Then benchmark partners that exhibited best practices in this process were identified. The teams shared these duties and secondary source research (publications, talking with customers and suppliers, and using its own industry connections) to identify six organizations per process that warranted a best practices visit.

In the case of the lease process, these organizations included organizations in the computer segment, a major fast-food franchised organization with significant property holdings, a financial institution with a large mortgage/leasing portfolio, and a large retail department store chain with a high lease requirement (a customer of this organization).

Each company was approached, asked to participate, and offered the opportunity to share the information at the end of the process. Prior to the visit, the benchmark partner was sent a letter confirming the date and time of the meeting, and was provided with an information package about the organization and questions that would be asked. Two-member teams, together with an external consultant, visited each site, and shared interviewing and note-taking responsibilities. At the end of the two- to three-hour visit, the benchmark partner was given a token of appreciation (ensure that it has perceived value otherwise it will not be appreciated), and later a thank-you note from the participants.

The team's next task was to summarize the information in a consistent manner. Each team was given the following template to complete and asked to circulate this to the rest of the team within three days.

BEST PRACTICES BENCHMARKING
Visit Report Template

Date:

Process Benchmarked:

Define the boundaries of the process and note similarities and differences:

Company Visited:

Contact Information:	Name of Host	Benchmark Team
	Title	(Name and Title)
	Address	
	Telephone	
	Others in attendance	
	(Name and Title)	

Description of Best Practices

Highlight those practices that are most relevant to the process being benchmarked. Describe each best practice in detail.

Key Performance Measures Used

Identify which metrics are being used to measure the performance of the process and to monitor requirements for changing standards over time.

Critical Success Factors

Highlight information that is particularly relevant and is noted as having been critical to ensuring a successful outcome during the design, implementation and ongoing performance of the process.

Key Issues (Barriers, Enablers, etc.)

Evaluate the key barriers and enablers that existed and how they were addressed. Also identify key barriers (similar or different) which may exist within your organization and must be addressed.

Additional Details on Implementation

Report any relevant details on how the process was implemented, and what resources were needed.

Other Process-Specific Information

Describe any other information which may be of interest to benchmark partners and other process teams.

A more detailed briefing followed upon completion of all of the benchmarking visits... the analyze stage

iii) **Analyze**—in which internal and external data are compared, gaps identified, breakthrough improvements prioritized, short- and long-term goals established.

"Analyze" Questions:

What is the basis for comparing our process measurements?

What is the magnitude of the performance gap?

What is the nature or root cause of the performance gap?

How much will their process continue to improve?

What characteristics distinguish their process as superior?

Upon completion of the benchmark visits, the team reassembled and reviewed the interview notes. In this day long review, the focus was on three items... the "as-is" process maps, the performance goals established earlier, and the interview summary. In the case of the lease process, the key learnings/best practices encouraged the organization to redesign its process to include:

- the establishment of one multipurpose form to replace three forms used at different stages of its current process
- the development of an on-line integrated database to track the status of lease negotiations (the multipurpose form would eventually be part of this on-line system)
- increased decision-making authority for regional field sales staff to negotiate leases
- increased standardization of operating procedures
- a set of performance measurement practices that could be driven from the statistics gathered by its previously mentioned integrated database

Few of these recommendations involved major financial investment; rather they were common-sense solutions that became common sense once they were observed in practice in other organizations.

iv) **Adapt and Improve/Implement**—this is the final stage in which progress is tracked, benchmarks reviewed, and new processes identified.

"Adapt and Improve" Questions:

How does our knowledge of their process help us to improve our process?

What activities within their process would need to be modified to adapt it to our environment?

What have we learned during this study that will allow us to improve upon the "best" practices?

What goals should we set for process improvement?

How will other companies continue to improve this process?

For Company X, the process has just begun. A three-month time frame was established for implementation, and a process owner was assigned. The process owner assumed permanent responsibility for both the process and its implementation. Best practices benchmarking is now being established for other processes by the lease process team, which has not been disbanded. Every three months the team reassembles to review implementation progress. A plan has been established to prepare a second round of best practices interviews at the one-year mark. Company X has committed to this practice as part of the fabric of its organization for future years to come.

What is My First Step?

The first step is the Plan and Design stage. The first decision that must be made is, which process is to be benchmarked. A decision to choose a particular process should be based on the following criteria:

1. Does it have a reasonable chance of success? This is particularly important for those organizations that are initiating their first benchmarking exercise. A successful initiative will generate excitement and interest.

2. Will it have an impact on the organization, if successful? People need hard numbers that show them that the benchmark team has made measurable change. Teams need to know that the time and effort that they have expended on this benchmarking initiative have had a beneficial impact on the organization. A defined goal or objective will be extremely useful and act as a guide to the team to measure its progress.

3. Can it be implemented within a reasonably short time frame— one year or less, preferably six months for your first initiative? Try the invoicing process (issuing an invoice once an order has been shipped) or possibly the customer order entry process (entering a customer order received by fax, phone or in the mail). These processes

can be improved within a short time frame. Tackling the telephone system (which may involve new technology and rapidly changing customer needs) may be too difficult as a starting point. Getting consensus or agreement is a long term proposition, with little appreciable quantifiable gains. And once you have received consensus, customer needs and technology change.

Be careful. Do not start off analyzing too many processes in the beginning. Pick two or three, get some successes and then work on two or three new ones.

For each process under review, form a benchmark team. As discussed earlier, restrict it to teams of 6 to 8 members (remember the criteria established in Chapter 5). Each team must map their respective process, addressing the following additional questions:

i)   What is the deliverable of this process?
ii)   What are the apparent impediments to the achievement of this deliverable?
iii) What are the current measures of performance within the process and how do they compare with other comparable organizations (competitive benchmarking)?
iv)   What do our customers want our performance to be? (See Chapter 5).
v)   Where, within this process, do we receive customer comments/complaints? (More on this later in this chapter).
vi)   What are the obvious areas for improvement?
vii) Where are our information gaps?
viii) What are the characteristics of an organization outside of our industry segment that we would like to emulate?

Once you have this information, you are then ready to move to the next phase. But one word of caution is necessary. Some needed changes may become obvious but do not make the change yet. It is quite possible that a better solution will be found during the site visits with benchmark partners. It will reflect negatively on this initiative if you make a change, only to change it one more time three months later. The cynics will have a field day with that.

How Do I Conduct a Site Visit With a Benchmark Partner?

There is a protocol associated with conducting a successful benchmark site visit. Here are some pre- and post-visit points to remember.

Before the site visit:

Once the visit is confirmed verbally, send a confirmation letter with a brief summary of the questions to be addressed to the benchmark organization. Make the questions broad in nature (i.e., Can you explain what technology you have used to enhance customer satisfaction?) and be prepared to probe in more detail at the site visit (i.e., What software are you using, what were the implementation costs, what vendors did you consider?). As quickly as possible, inform your team of the meeting date and arrange a pre-visit briefing session.

Pre-Visit Team Briefing Session:

The following should be discussed at this meeting:
- Purpose of visit
- Objectives of visit set and agreed to by visit team
- Team roles and responsibilities of visit assigned (Facilitator, Recorder, etc.)
- Your own responses to these "Plan and Design" questions for the process you will be benchmarking (you must be able to answer these questions about your organization, after all, if you cannot, how can you expect your benchmarking partner to answer them).

During the site interview:

The following should be your protocol at the visit.
- Introduce all team members. Exchange business cards early.
- Clearly state your objectives and expectations for the visit.
- Mention that you have selected your hosts because they are recognized as having best practices within this process.
- Begin questioning with general areas of interest and confirmation of organization/process boundaries. Follow with specific topical questions in order of importance to your benchmark

After the visit is completed:

At the conclusion of the visit, follow this protocol:
- Thank your hosts for their time and willingness to share information and provide a token of appreciation.
- Reiterate your offer to share your general findings.
- Be a "Relationship" Manager; set the stage for further information sharing in the future.
- Hold a formal team debriefing session within 24 hours of the visit.

Send letter of thanks on company letterhead within 10 working days.

Your post-visit debriefing should follow the following steps:
- Debrief thoroughly, as a complete team, immediately after visit.
- Draft a trip report (brief summary of your meeting, a complete template is shown below) immediately, finalize within 10 days.
- Determine need for future information.
- Complete gap analysis.
- Incorporate results with other visits.

BEST PRACTICES BENCHMARKING
Visit Report Template

Date: xxxxxxxxxx
Process Benchmarked:
Marketing Planning -
Company Visited: XYZ Company

Contact Information:	Name of Host	Benchmark Team
	Title	(Name and Title)
	Address	
	Telephone	
	Others in attendance	
	(Name and Title)	

Description of Best Practices
- Use of data warehouse to assist in developing customer segmentation strategy.
- Widespread use of customer comment cards that are fed into the database on a weekly basis.
- Never copy competitors' products/services—always offer something different to differentiate themselves.
- Discontinued image advertising, use only direct response advertising.

Key Performance Measures Used

- Percentage redemption from direct response advertising.
- Customer comment ratings—Customer Satisfaction Index (CSI).
- Measurement against standards in Customer Bill of Rights.
- Customer retention and market growth.

Critical Success Factors

- Obtaining and using customer feedback to create marketing programs and improve services.
- Created marketing alliances with major suppliers to reduce marketing costs.
- Monitor external environment.
- Developed tactical promotion campaigns as incentives for consumers.

Key Issues—Enablers

- Marketing and Sales work as one team.
- Ongoing customer research to measure customer expectations and dissatisfiers.
- Established customer advisory panels as an ongoing part of the planning process.

How Can I Ensure That Our Benchmarking Initiative Will Be Successful?

There are no guarantees. However, if you use the following guidelines your process will have a greater likelihood for success. They are laid out in a code developed by the Boston-based Strategic Planning Institute Council on Benchmarking and in various other books and references. A modified version of these guidelines follows:

> Don't go on a fishing expedition. Pick a specific area you want to improve, like customer service or customer order fulfilment, and do your homework. Study your own process thoroughly, investigate potential benchmark candidates diligently and, obviously, choose a company or companies to benchmark that handle the process well.

> Send out the people who will have to make the changes. They need to see for themselves. It won't help if senior executives or consultants do the benchmarking, then come back and tell the

"owners" of a process what to do. Teams that go on site visits to benchmark partners should be limited to two or three members of the team only. But spread the load. Try to get as many team members as possible on site visits. Keep the visits short and keep the door open to go back and ask further questions if required.

Be prepared to exchange information. Offer all benchmark partners the opportunity to recieve a summary of your visits to other benchmark partners. Let them review your summary of your visit to them to ensure that you have summarized their information properly and not included proprietary information. As well, as a matter of protocol, you should be ready to answer any question you ask another company.

Avoid legal problems. Discussions that might imply price fixing, market allocations, or other illegal activities will lead to trouble. Don't expect to learn much about new products. Most benchmarking missions focus on existing products, business practices, human resources, and customer satisfaction.

Respect the confidentiality of the data you obtain. Companies that do not mind sharing with you may not want proprietary information going to a competitor.

Since I'm in a Unique Sector Which Organizations Can I Benchmark Against?

Although your organization may be in a unique or highly competitive sector, your processes are not.

Consider the following examples. While on a trip to the United States, a Toyota executive got his best idea for process improvement from American supermarkets and their ability to replenish foods rapidly in response to sales. Thus, the concept of just-in-time (JIT) inventory replacement was born. Similarly, Xerox improved its distribution practices by studying L.L. Bean, the catalogue distribution firm that sells outdoor wear. Mellon Bank, in an effort to improve upon its performance in handling credit-card billing disputes, benchmarked itself against an airline, a competing bank, and the credit-card operations of a number of non-competing organizations.

Furthermore, don't rule out talking to competing organizations, particularly if you do not have to address proprietary information. For example, Ford achieved breakthrough improvements in its accounts payable departments through extensive discussions with Mazda.

How Do I Ensure That My Employees Buy Into This Process?

Your employees must be involved in the process itself. One team should be formed for each process to be reviewed. Team composition is critical. Typically, teams are composed of six to eight individuals from different levels in the organization. Team members should include customers (internal) and suppliers to the process as well as individuals actively involved in the process itself. Each team should also have a "process owner," a senior executive who will benefit most from the process improvements that will result from the benchmarking exercise.

What Do Benchmarking and Reengineering Have in Common?

Reengineering focuses on eliminating non-value-added activities. Value-adding activities are defined as what the customer wants and is willing to pay for. Reengineering identifies, evaluates, and utilizes world-class concepts and principles to raise performance to a new plateau, while also establishing the capabilities required for continuous improvement. Reengineering assumes that nothing is sacred—everything is subject to review and change in the search for improved performance. Reengineering requires an open mind, a capacity to learn, a willingness to change, and an ability to envision radical alternatives to existing processes.

Benchmarking is similar in intent and practice to reengineering, although it is best described as a tool to assist in the reengineering process. Benchmarking allows an organization to review the processes being considered for reengineering, before introducing changes and improvements. This allows them to assess not only whether they meet world-class standards, but also whether they are worth performing in the first place.

What Results Have Other Organizations Achieved?

Some organizations have achieved spectacular results through benchmarking. Let's look at a few examples. Although these organizations learned lessons that are proprietary in nature, suffice it to say that they found either new tools, technology, or practices that enabled them to improve. We call these items "enablers," which are something to focus on in your site visits. (See template on page 210.)

Ford	- reduced accounts payable department from 400 to 200 employees and improved speed of payment to suppliers through electronic funds transfer.
Hewlett Packard	- 150 per cent improvement in on-time delivery - 50 per cent reduction in lead times to deliver completed orders to customers
General Electric	- 50 per cent time savings in processing customer orders - $4 million drop in inventory

Most organizations have found significant savings just by mapping their processes and by eliminating waste, old practices, and redundancies. Sometimes this involves objectively assessing your existing processes and, with the aid of field visits, challenging the way in which you currently do business.

What Costs Might I Incur?

Your major costs will be the time of your staff involved in the benchmarking initiative. The time involved will vary depending on the number of processes under review and the immediacy of your needs. You may also want to send some of the team members out on a course, or alternatively have an in-house seminar. Coaching and facilitation training may also be required, and for which you may need outside assistance.

Alternatively, some organizations choose to bring in an external consultant to coach them through the various stages of the benchmarking initiative and to set up the initial set of benchmark visits.

If you have never done this before, an external consultant may offer greater credibility with your potential benchmark partners and demonstrates your commitment to this activity. The consultant can also assist in critiquing the existing processes. Just like benchmarking, much can be learned from consultants who have been through the process with other organizations.

Where Will I Find These Organizations and Why Would They Talk to Me?

You will need to conduct research to find potential benchmark candidates (refer to the following section for more information). The most common sources are literature searches and relevant association lists. In some cases, a frank discussion with your suppliers may prove to be quite effective. Suppliers are exposed to many organizations and it is in their best interests to help you improve.

Unless the benchmarking visit is mutually beneficial, you will not secure the organization's co-operation. The organizations that you will want to visit are likely inundated with requests from other organizations, which is another reason why you may need an external consultant with established credentials to make the initial approach. If the benchmark partner perceives value in the interchange, then you will be successful.

One of the most effective ways to overcome resistance to participation is to offer these organizations similar access to your organization. You could also offer to share the results of your visits to other benchmark partners, but make sure that these organizations would not object.

These are the basic elements of your benchmark process. But benchmarking should not be a one-time effort. The process should be institutionalized within your organization as a tool for continuous improvement.

To achieve this, you must create and maintain a database of best-practices and potential best-practices benchmark partners. This database may also prove to be helpful in monitoring competitive activity.

The following will give you some guidance on how to establish this database.

Establishing a Benchmarking Database

In today's highly competitive global market, timely and accurate information is essential, yet it is not being gathered for two main reasons. First, many people and organizations view competitive intelligence as a sinister or surreptitious act and consequently avoid this practice. To the progressive business executive, however, it is simply regarded as a good benchmarking practice. Second, the perceived cost of data-gathering is grossly exaggerated. Competitive intelligence and the establishment of a best practices database is not the exclusive right of companies with unlimited research budgets and human resources. The costs associated with establishing this form of intelligence are dedication, resourcefulness, and perseverance.

Here are some of the most commonly used information sources for establishing a benchmark database, which should include both names of potential benchmark partners as well as competitive benchmark data. Many of these involve little or no cost, but remember, this is only a starting point. Detailed investigations of the best practices that created these benchmarks are still needed.

Annual Reports

Public companies must publish annual reports, which are available in most reference libraries. These reports will highlight corporate philosophy and mission statements, major strategic directions (both long- and short-term) and selected historical financial results. Some will also highlight recent awards or expected investments in new technology and the expected customer benefits from these investments.

Newspaper and Business Magazines

Several databases will provide you with access to the most current reported information on competitive companies, senior officers of these companies, sales (current and projected), and even new product launches. General market information might also be provided in this reference material.

In addition to the above, government agencies occasionally prepare industry profiles or collect statistical information on an industry/business segment. In foreign countries, trade embassies have detailed files on key market segments, major suppliers, and customers.

Suppliers

Not surprisingly, you may share some of the same suppliers as your competitors. They may be able to provide you with some general information on your competitors' sales growth, financial strength, possibly salesforce structure, degree of outsourcing of products or services, and systems and processes.

Government

Another effective source of information is government files. Information about organizations that have made submissions to government for special licensing or taxation considerations, are accessible under Freedom of Information Acts. These documents contain details about company philosophy, sales and gross margin information, profiles on key executives, new acquisitions and investments, corporate strategy, and other strategic, competitive information. Although it may take more time and be more costly to obtain, the results can be quite rewarding.

Customers

Primary research, either in the form of focus groups or telephone surveys, will help to identify your strengths and weaknesses relative to your competition.

You may wish to interview only those customers that use your competition exclusively and test their receptivity to your product, service, or process variation.

Your Salesforce and Customer Service Staff

These employees should be your eyes and ears on the front line. They should be able to provide you with information on competitive packaging, pricing, promotion, activity, and changes in salesforce or distribution structure. In some cases you may have to provide employees with a script to ensure that they use a common set of questions.

Industry Activities

Trade shows and memberships in trade associations play an important role in gathering competitive intelligence. Promotional and product literature as well as price lists are usually available at these shows and exhibits.

Community Activities

Membership lists at local chambers of commerce, boards of trade, and community service groups will occasionally reflect additions or departures of key executives. A review of new building permits may also alert you to your competitors' expansion plans.

Conferences, Seminars, and Even Business Books

Don't be surprised to find your competition speaking about their best practices, systems, or processes at a conference or seminar. They may even be written up in a business book (such as this one), which you will find in your local library or bookstore.

Professional Market Researchers

Consultants with direct market experience in either this or related markets can be invaluable. They can assemble the required information in a short period as well as objectively interpret the strategic implications of this information.

Existing Benchmarking Databases

Another inexpensive option is to purchase information on industry norms or best practices. The following would be a good first step:

The International Customer Services Association (ICSA) Benchmarking Study Report—This biennial report features the results of over 400 ICSA member companies and their practices in terms of order-processing, service levels, invoicing, material return, complaint-handling, and more.

International Benchmarking Clearinghouse (IBC)—The Clearinghouse provides library services, data analysis, newsletters, case studies, videos, networks, research, etc. for those looking for benchmarking information. The mission of the IBC is to facilitate the growth of benchmarking networks and information exchanges among its member organizations.

Although information alone is not the final solution nor is it a complete benchmarking process, it is the first step along the journey.

And remember, this information must be as current as possible, which means you may have to dedicate resources to that task.

Customer Satisfaction Indices

If you have not yet heard about the American Customer Satisfaction Index (ACSI), you probably will hear quite a bit about it over the next several years. The ACSI was developed by Claes Fornell and his colleagues at the National Quality Research Center (NQRC) at the University of Michigan. It is based on a tested and proven Swedish Customer Satisfaction Barometer (SCSB), which was also created by

Fornell (1989). Soon after this, Germany created an index with other European countries, and Japan and Singapore are currently in the development stage of creating a similar index.

The ACSI is purported to be a new economic indicator that measures the satisfaction of U.S. household consumers with the quality of the goods and services available to them (both domestic and imported). The American Customer Satisfaction Index has been designed to quantify both quality and customer satisfaction, through the use of a specially designed questionnaire, and relate them to the firm's financial performance. (Seven industry SIC codes representing 40 industries were chosen for measurement on the basis of having reachable household, not business-to-business, customers.) In total, 203 companies, including seven government agencies, which sell nationally to household consumers, are represented in this study. (Sweden's SCSB is much broader—it not only measures more than 30 industry sectors, but also estimates the relationship of customer satisfaction to customer loyalty, product performance, and profitability.)

The National ACSI for 1994 was 74.5. As shown in the following figure, this index varies by sector from a high of 81.6 in Manufacturing/Nondurables to a low of 64.3 for Public Administration/Government.

ACSI's for Industry Sectors - 1994	
Sector	ACSI Score
National ACSI	74.5
Manufacturing/Nondurables (SIC 2)	81.6
Manufacturing/Durables (SIC 3)	79.2
Transportation/Communications/Utilities (SIC 4)	75.4
Retail (SIC 5)	75.7
Finance/Insurance (SIC 6)	75.4
Services (SIC's 7, 8)	74.4
Public Administration/Government (SIC 9)	64.3

Source: 1994 American Customer Satisfaction Index, ASQC and NQRC Report.

These scores are further subdivided into four-digit SIC codes, which are not provided here.

Although the potential for a satisfaction index similar to the ACSI is great, the potential for abuse may be even greater.

I would like to describe the use of Customer Satisfaction Indices (CSIs) by drawing an analogy with the Chinese symbol for crisis. As shown this symbol has two parts: opportunity and danger.

Crisis

Danger

Opportunity

Let's first examine the opportunity component.

The publication of the American Customer Satisfaction Index (ACSI) in 1994, jointly sponsored by the American Society for Quality Control and the National Quality Research Center may be appropriately classified under this symbol.

There are high hopes for this index, which is intended to be published quarterly. According to Jack West, Chairman of the Board of the ASQC, "The index has the potential to raise the public's perception and understanding of quality in much the same way as the public has become aware of the meaning of the U.S. Consumer Price Index and other macroeconomic indicators....I believe that companies whose customer satisfaction ratings are above their industry averages will see gains similar to those of Baldrige-Award winners."

Now let's turn to the danger component. It's not the index itself, but how it can be used.

First, unlike Sweden's SCSB, the American index is based on only one year of data. It is much too early to use it for its intended primary purpose: that is, to establish a linkage between this index and trends in the economic viability of businesses that serve the customer (both households and business-to-business). According to an interview with Fornell in *Quality Progress Magazine,* at least five years of trend data are necessary before any directional information is meaningful. In the case of Sweden's SCSB, Fornell believes that it is only now possible "to trend the rise and fall of this index and compare it with the profitability of companies, gross domestic product, productivity and employment."

It is very important to mention that in the limited amount of time that this index has been available, organizations and consultants alike have been using it for the wrong purposes. Without considering the questionnaire design or the sample selection used for this survey, organizations are now using this index to compare their own

Customer Satisfaction Index (CSI) measurements. This is an invalid comparison and may lead to some inappropriate actions, all in the name of exceeding this ACSI and improving customer satisfaction. To reiterate, the original purpose of this study was to quantify quality and customer satisfaction. Both quality and customer satisfaction have very broad meanings that vary by industry segment and by customer needs. Point-to-point comparisons may be difficult, if not impossible.

Finally, progressive organizations are moving away from a single CSI (or measure of customer satisfaction) to multiple CSIs. Consider the following. Can one measure truly tell you how satisfied your customers are? Think back to Chapter 5 when we talked about Maslow and the stages of customer need. We have many customer segments and not all of them have similar customer "touch" points.

Although a single measure may be desirable from senior management's perspective—being able to measure progress against a single goal, customer satisfaction—it cannot identify the drivers of customer satisfaction and dissatisfaction, nor can they be tied directly to the processes within the organization that affect customer satisfaction. Consequently, I have seen clients increasingly moving away from this single measure to a more focused and tailored series of measures that can pinpoint opportunity areas. Because of this approach, comparisons to industry or National CSIs are inappropriate.

The ACSI is an important measure and a necessary first step. However, it must be used with caution and sensitivity otherwise it can lead an organization down the wrong path. How it will be used by organizations in the future will determine the degree of crisis associated with this measure.

> A single CSI is too limiting for an organization. Multiple measures are required to reflect the perceptions of different customer segments.

Using Complaints as a Benchmark

Although you may be familiar with the following information, it bears repeating. A study examining why customers leave a company revealed the following:

- 3 per cent of customers move away;
- 5 per cent develop relationships with other companies;
- 9 per cent leave for competitive reasons;
- 14 per cent of customers are dissatisfied with the product;
- 68 per cent quit because of an attitude of indifference by the owner, manager, or some employee.

(For those of you who were counting, 1 per cent died.)

Most customers would rather walk than complain. Their reasons are quite simple:

- Often they don't know who to speak to. The clerk? The supervisor? A senior manager?
- They feel that complaining won't do them any good. They perceive that dealing with complaints is a low priority for the company.
- They think their complaint will end up at the bottom of some one's in-basket and never be seen again.
- They hear the line, "It's company policy."

So the customer thinks, "The company doesn't really care. They have my money and that's the end of it." Rather than do anything about the complaint, the customer decides that it's just as easy to walk out and take his or her business elsewhere.

Organizations incur costs by not encouraging complaints. A recent study conducted on behalf of British Airways revealed that the number of complaints that reach the top of the organization represents only a small percentage of customers who have a negative experience. As shown in the figure on the following page, the potential lost revenue can be quite significant.

The importance of having a customer complaint process and a mechanism for service recovery is based on the fact that customers do not complain—they just walk away. Consider the following facts:

- Only 4 per cent of dissatisfied customers complain.
- 96 per cent of dissatisfied customers just leave.
- 91 per cent of dissatisfied customers will never come back.
- Dissatisfied customers will tell eight to 10 people about the problem.
- 95 per cent of these dissatisfied customers may come back if the problem is resolved properly.

These facts have been a call to action for progressive North American firms.

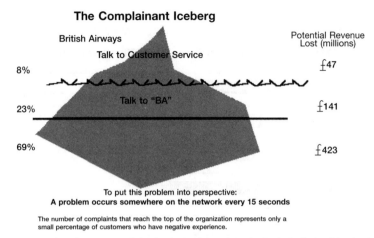

The Complainant Iceberg

To put this problem into perspective:
A problem occurs somewhere on the network every 15 seconds

The number of complaints that reach the top of the organization represents only a
small percentage of customers who have negative experience.

Source: Coopers & Lybrand seminar entitled *Achieving Breakthrough Service for the Professional Service Firm*

According to the 1994 Customer Service Benchmarking Study of the International Customer Service Associations (ICSA), more companies are now tracking customer complaints than ever before. In 1993, 70 per cent of manufacturing companies tracked complaints compared with 59 per cent in 1991; 68 per cent of services companies tracked complaints in 1993 compared with 54 per cent in 1991. Why is this trend important? Because by encouraging complaints you are sending a message to your customers that you are concerned and are prepared to make changes. If you do not show this willingness, your customers may be tempted to walk away and not return. But remember, it's not the sheer number of complaints that indicates good or bad business, but rather how many are resolved in the eyes of your customers.

Perhaps as a result of increased attention to the complaint process, as well as action taken to improve activities that affect customer dissatisfaction, the average number of complaints was down for both sectors. In 1992, the average manufacturer logged 1,290 customer complaints compared with 1,707 in 1990; the average service company received 1,582 in 1992 versus 2,117 in 1990.

According to the study, customers complained for the following reasons: product quality, 26.3 per cent; shipping errors, 19.3 per cent; order-entry mistake, 13.9 per cent; early/late delivery, 12.2 per cent; packaging error, 5.1 per cent; other, 21.9 per cent.

Does senior management really study customer complaints? About 35 per cent of executives say they reviewed detailed information on customer complaints weekly or more frequently; 43 per cent say they do so on a monthly basis; and 9 per cent do so quarterly. Here's the breakdown of those executives who review complaints:

Does Senior Management Really Study Customer Complaints?

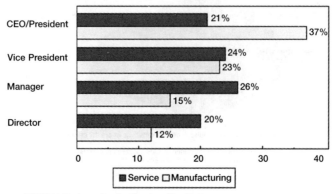

Source: *1994 ICSA Customer Service Benchmarking Study.*

What is disturbing, however, is that only 10 per cent of manufacturerers had a formal customer retention program while 30 per cent of service companies did. Although some executives have received the message, they are the minority—and the customer continues to suffer and to leave.

More and more research confirms the importance of measuring and monitoring customer satisfaction. Consider this information reported by customer satisfaction expert Joan Knob Cannie in *The Marketing Report:*
The good news—

- 80 per cent of companies had a formal system in place to contact customers on a regular basis.
- 90 per cent indicated they had a system for finding out why a customer left.
- 40 per cent said that they contact lost customers once or twice, and an additional 20 per cent said they make contact three or more times.

The bad news—

- 78 per cent of executives surveyed said they don't know the lifetime value of their customers.
- 90 per cent indicated they didn't have a system in place to tell them when a customer was about to stop doing business with their company.
- 60 per cent said they didn't know how many customers they lost each year.

And there is more. According to the Coopers & Lybrand IDEAS study, organizations that achieve high levels of customer satisfaction take the complaint process seriously. They measure not only the number of complaints received and resolved, but also the speed with which they are resolved. The IDEAS study found that among organizations that achieved improved customer service in the past year, 57 per cent resolved customer complaints within 24 hours, 22 per cent within 48 hours. Furthermore, successful organizations circulate customer complaint information not only to senior management but also to all employees.

What can we learn from these statistics? In my view, one of the most important lessons is that customer complaints are a powerful indicator of current problems and the processes that affect customer satisfaction. Use this information wisely. Focus your best practices benchmarking effort at those processes identified as most troublesome by your complaint process. Monitor your progress by monitoring your complaints. If the complaints persist, the source of your problems may be another process that feeds the one identified earlier. Take heart...once corrected, your improved process will lead to enhanced customer satisfaction and positive word-of-mouth.

How Customer Complaints Led to Customer Satisfaction: The IBM Perspective

IBM Rochester interviewed 2,400 customers to better understand the value of customer satisfaction. The research was so revealing that the organization created a new process to ensure and improve customer satisfaction.

These are some of the key findings of their research:
- a one percentage point increase in customer satisfaction (i.e., an increase from 95 to 96 per cent satisfaction) would result in a net revenue improvement of $257 million over a five year period;
- to regain a lost customer would cost 12 times the original investment made to attract that customer;
- a customer's experience during a complaint process had a marked impact on the chance of repurchase and positive word-of-mouth.

Degree of Satisfaction With Help Process (%)		Predisposition to Purchase Again (%)	Predisposition to Favourably Recommend IBM to Others (%)
Completely Satisfied	46	92	94
Moderately Satisfied	44	78	81
Dissatisfied	10	46	48

From this research, IBM learned a very important principle that few companies recognize: the value of acquiring and maintaining a "customer-for-life." A satisfied customer is a valuable asset that must not only be cherished but also constantly nurtured. To achieve this, IBM set up a process that almost any organization—large or small—could easily implement.

The first step in the process was to establish and promote a customer complaint/comments line. The line was staffed by highly qualified individuals with a passion for resolving customer complaints and issues. Each customer complaint was logged, including relevant information on the issue and how the issue was resolved (for example, was the complaint resolved immediately or was follow-up action or intervention from another department or division required?). Most organizations would have stopped at this point. But IBM took the process a step further.

The organization created a "double-loop" process for its customer complaint system. When the staff on the customer complaints line had resolved an issue, a follow-up notice was sent to the department or regional office that was responsible for the customer. A sales representative was then required to follow up directly with the customer to determine whether the customer was satisfied not only with the complaint resolution, but also with the manner in which they had been treated. The customer's response was treated as an evaluation of the customer service department itself and if further action was required, the customer's concern was again logged onto the system for further resolution.

The company exhibited an unrelenting focus on the customer and a passion for customer retention. Think of the value of that customer measured against the cost of a lost customer and the potential negative word-of-mouth.

What is the value of a customer-for-life? What are you willing to do to ensure that your customers only speak positively about the service you provide? A double-loop customer service response system may be the key.

Remember, customer satisfaction requires a process to support it.

A Closed-Loop Complaint System: Vistakon

Another variation on a corrective action system was developed by a contact lens manufacturer, Vistakon, also known as Johnson & Johnson Vision Products, Inc. Vistakon revolutionized the contact lens industry by introducing ACUVUE Disposable Contact Lenses. But the company realized that it could not maintain its success without ensuring a high level of customer satisfaction.

Recognizing this need, Vistakon developed C²LASS, or Customer Closed Loop Action and Satisfaction System—a process designed to proactively collect, evaluate, and respond to every customer interaction, with the goal of "closing the loop" within 48 hours. The system is available to customers in both Canada and the United States and integrates an automatic number identification system, to first identify and then direct the call to the appropriate group. The system identifies the customer by virtue of its telephone number, which then provides the customer service representative with information on the customer's order history and whether the customer had a recent inquiry or problem. Consequently the representative has a clear profile of the customer on the computer screen in front of him or her and can focus on providing quality personal service even before the conversation begins.

The system also generates a customer relations monthly report. This report is distributed to management board members and department heads. This report provides a breakdown of all customer complaints, inquiries, and compliments, and provides specific analysis of customer needs and concerns. Armed with this information, the organization can strategically plan not only to meet, but also to exceed customer needs and concerns.

Vistakon's distribution department is also using C²LASS to improve its order-processing accuracy. By monitoring the system, Distribution can track the number of customers who receive their orders incorrectly. C²LASS provides the distribution department with a detailed explanation of what was wrong with a customer's order. This detailed information allows the department to identify error types and then prioritize and address them, either with system enhancements or new processes and procedures.

ISO Requirements for Corrective Action

In Chapter 9, we will discuss in detail the ISO quality standard and its relevance to customer satisfaction. Regardless of whether you are considering certification under ISO, you should consider a number of elements within these quality standards.

One of these elements is the need for a corrective action procedure. The ISO standard clearly states what an organization needs to document and the guidelines it needs to follow to ensure that it addresses customer concerns and corrects problems. To evaluate your organization's current procedural documentation, conduct the following self-assessment. You may find this exercise to be quite enlightening. Beside each point, score yourself as follows: AD—Adequate; NI—Needs Improvement; UN—Unacceptable.

ISO 9002	STATUS		
	A **D**	**N** **I**	**U** **N**
Corrective Action The organization/supplier shall establish, document, and maintain procedures for: a) investigating the cause of non-conforming products and the corrective actions needed to prevent recurrence; b) analyzing all processes, work operations, concessions, quality records, service reports, and customer complaints to detect and eliminate potential causes of non-conforming products;			

c) initiating preventive actions to deal with problems at a level corresponding to the risks encountered;			
d) applying controls to ensure that corrective actions are taken and that they are effective;			
e) implementing and recording changes in procedures resulting from corrective action.			

The Role of Technology in Capturing Customer Comments

Technology can and does help businesses to meet the challenges of competition—globally and locally. If businesses harness technology to get to know customers and prospects better, and then use this information to be more responsive to customers, they will gain and maintain a competitive advantage. It is important to remember, however, that technology is only an enabler and not the solution itself. For most organizations, customer research or customer complaints typically identify that a change is necessary. Through competitive or best practices benchmarking, the process solution becomes clear. Although technology enhancements are not required in some cases, they are an important component in many instances. Best practices benchmarking is an important practice when technology may be part of the solution. The following highlights where technology may be a helpful process improvement enabler.

Using Technology as an Enabler

According to AT&T Global Information Solutions, technology is currently underused by organizations as a tool to help build stronger customer relationships. In a recent presentation addressing the role of technology to enhance customer satisfaction, three primary areas where technology has played a significant role were identified. These include strategic leverage of information, empowerment, and reengineering. Let's look at an example of how technology has played a role in each area.

Strategic Leverage of Information

A major retailer links its stores and suppliers into a computer network. The retailer can collect and process daily sales data; identify and monitor customer buying patterns; coordinate product mix, display and pricing strategies; and have its suppliers participate in inventory management. The resulting effect is quite significant. The retailer benefits from reduced inventory and distribution costs. The customer benefits from aggressively competitive pricing, improved product availability that is tailored to regional needs, and fewer out-of-stocks.

Empower the Enterprise

A Midwestern bank builds an integrated banking delivery system so that customer-service representatives at all branches can access a common customer information file; gain up-to-the-minute financial information; leverage the knowledge of the bank's experts; and service specific needs of the customer immediately.

Reengineer the Business

A major insurance company replaces outdated "assembly-line" processes with workflow automation processes, sharing customer data throughout the organization to empower underwriters, raters, and managers while enhancing their productivity and ability to provide top-notch customer service. Sales personnel are equipped with laptop computers, proposal, and decision-making software and linked access to head office databases. The salesperson can prepare all calculations, in the customer's office and even print out the forms. If a customer wants to know the status of a claim, he or she can dial into head office and look it up immediately.

Building customer-focused solutions requires a structured approach that ensures that technology is not simply developed for technology's sake, but rather to address specific business objectives. (Critical success factors must be identified for the business, which drive information technology (IT) principles, strategies, and architectures. The IT systems developed support critical business processes as a business enabler.)

Here are some examples of how technology is being harnessed to address customer satisfaction, revenue enhancement, and improved profitability. When reviewing these examples, it is important to remember that the need for the IT solution was first identified through customer research, repeated customer complaints, or a best practices benchmarking initiative as part of the organization's reengineering efforts.

The Call Center Environment

The future call center environment will have not only automatic call distributors (devices that automatically route calls to appropriate personnel) and interactive voice response systems (where customers can receive information such as a product catalogue or statement information without human intervention) but also integrated computing and telephone applications to provide the following services:

- Automatically pre-identify callers and their needs, to allow businesses to improve their personal attention to customers.
- Provide information and notes pertinent to the customer, which allows call takers to resolve all of the customer's needs in each call.
- Match callers' needs with agents' skills to provide expert assistance.
- Automate the exchange of routine information to maximize the time spent with customers.
- Use the information learned from customers in these calls to better anticipate requests.

Let's look at an example that has the call center as its foundation. A financial services organization recognized that it was creating customer dissatisfaction because it was unable to respond promptly to customer requests. The solution involved providing the customer service representative with instantaneous access to all relevant information that would affect the customer's investment decision. By consolidating customer information from various resources, such as the customer information file, account statement balance, and mortgage loan balance, customer service representatives could provide one-stop expert advice about mutual funds investment. Customer satisfaction improved dramatically—as did the organization's revenue.

Another application, this time in retail catalogue sales, has created systems that allow knowledge workers to serve customers more fully by having the right information at the right time. Now, instead of just processing an order from a customer over the phone, the system can analyze the customer's buying patterns while he or she is on the phone with the customer service representative. The system can then advise the customer service representative to cross-sell a certain product or to advise the customer of a current sale on items that he or she has purchased before. A more advance application might even allow for special pricing on products in order to increase the revenue generated per call.

One of the most innovative uses of technology is used by Prudential's call center. We all know that great ideas can come from just talking to the customer. However, often the biggest problem is finding the time to write down those good ideas. To solve that problem, Prudential equipped all call center personnel with headsets that have tape-recording devices within them. Then, when a representative hears a good idea, he or she simply pushes a button on the side of the headset and speaks into the receiver. The idea can be transcribed at a later time and become yet another opportunity for performance improvement.

These examples are just a few samples of the unharnessed potential that exists if we are innovative in our approach. Many more exist, but only a focused best practices benchmarking initiative will help to uncover them. Once they have been implemented, it is time to research new enablers and process improvements.

How Technology is Being Used to Drive Customer Satisfaction

The following are other examples of best practices in the use of technology that enhance customer satisfaction. The approaches are quite different, and some are more advanced than others. After reading each brief summary, consider how this approach could be applied to your environment.

PPG Industries, Inc.

PPG Industries, Inc. recognized that there were not enough hours in the workday to accomplish everything. That's why it created a system called GlasTrac VIP. The system was designed with its customers in mind. The company recognized that their customers had customers too, and that in order for PPG to be the preferred supplier, it had to address both their needs. Its product literature describes its technology solution, GlasTrac VIP, this way:

> With GlasTrac VIP, you can cater to your customers' (the car or truck owner with a broken windshield) needs during the workday,

then connect with us before or after hours, as well as during the work day.
The GlasTrac VIP System empowers you to cruise through our inventory at your leisure. Place an order. Specify delivery preference. Or simply take the time to explore all the selections.

PPG's customers can place their own orders without human intervention (that is, without talking to a customer-service representative, at any time of the day, and receive a confirmation date instantaneously). The system is detailed, flexible, easy to use, and current. Order and inventory status is continually updated from all of its factories on a real-time basis. In order to be as customer friendly as possible, the company provides all software, a reference guide, and knowledgable PPG representatives for personal assistance.

Ross Systems

No doubt you are familiar with the expression, "letting the left hand know what the right hand is doing!" Consider the following situation. A customer phones into your customer service center and voices a complaint. The customer service representative quickly resolves the problem. The customer is so pleased with the result that it would like to go on record as saying your company has exceeded its expectations. The salespeople should be made aware of this endorsement, which they may be able to use for future sales presentations. Testimonials and referrals from satisfied customers speak volumes to prospective customers.

Or consider the salesperson who is about to make a routine call on his or her account. Before the call, the salesperson reviews the customer file. In doing this, the salesperson notes a disturbing trend. He or she does an instantaneous search to see if this problem existed with any other customers and how it was resolved with other clients. Armed with this information, the salesperson can perform the routine call with the customer's interest in mind and an ability to add value. In the meeting, he or she can open up the laptop computer and hook into the Internet. Together with the client, they can review the file history and print out the suggested solution. The result—customer delight.

Are these the solutions of the twenty-first century? Absolutely not. This is the call-tracking database system of Ross Systems. Its Electronic Bulletin Board (EBB) service includes product release information, reported software issues, product requests, troubleshooting/log history database, and articles and tips accessible to the customer, salesperson, and customer support representative.

Ross Systems' call-tracking database allows its client support group to place customer requests solutions, phone contacts (not just with the client, but messages posted to the assigned salesperson), literature requests and more—directly onto the database.

Here's how their Electronic Bulletin Board (EBB) works. EBB is an on-line menu-driven database accessible by modem at home or the office. By dialling into the EBB, the customer can research information to solve problems 24 hours a day, seven days a week. They have access to known software problems and their workarounds. They can also read expert advice written by Ross employees and other clients in their industry. And if they cannot find the answer they are looking for, they can simply log their question in the on-line log entry screen and a Ross Systems' client support analyst will respond by phone to the inquiry.

EBB provides customers with data in the format they need, regardless of whether their need is to quickly look up when the next release of software is scheduled, or to use inquiry screens. The system even allows the customer to enter articles, tips, and inquiries on-line so that Ross can share them with other clients in that industry.

Ritz Carlton

The Ritz Carlton hotel chain takes its customer database seriously. The company provides every staff member (whom it calls "associates"), from the front-of-house staff to maintenance and housekeeping with a "guest preference pad." Each associate, from any of the 28 Ritz Carlton hotels worldwide, is responsible for noting the special needs or concerns of their guests. Every day, the company enters these special comments into a chain-wide database that contains data on over half a million guests.

Having that wealth of information on file has allowed the company to change a number of its practices that have directly affected customer satisfaction. Employees at any of the 28 worldwide hotels can gain access to those profiles through the Covia travel reservation system.

Let's consider an example of this system in use. Suppose that you prefer your coffee with milk rather than cream. The last time you stayed at the hotel, you ordered it that way from room service.

A month later, you stay at a Ritz Carlton hotel on the other side of the continent. You phone down for room service and order coffee, but forget to ask for milk. Imagine how surprised and thrilled you will be to receive the milk when room service delivers your coffee. An accident—hardly. Ritz Carlton hotels make it a point to know their customers' preferences.

By retaining such information, a company becomes better equipped to respond to suggestions and preferences that personalize the guest's stay. They remain abreast of customer's changing needs. Many companies err by treating their customers as if they were static entities rather than people whose lifestyles, preferences, and circumstances are constantly changing.

Organizations that are not prepared to take this focus seriously are living dangerously.

USAA

One of the best examples of a company that has used its customer profile information to provide more for its customers is United Services Automobile Association (USAA). From its inception over 70 years ago as a provider of automobile insurance to military officers, USAA has maintained an unrelenting focus on exceptional service delivery. The strength of this organization has been its customer database, its commitment to its customers, and a single-minded focus on providing value to its customer base.

USAA is currently a worldwide insurance and diversified financial services institution, with headquarters in San Antonio, Texas. The company comprises 77 subsidiaries and affiliates and owns and manages over $34 billion in assets. It supplies its customers, which is limited to military officers and their families, with a wide range of products and services. These include a variety of insurance products, full-service banking, investment brokerage and travel services, (some of these services are provided by third-party organizations). The company also offers a buying service through which it purchases and delivers other companies' products, including automobiles, jewellery, major appliances, and consumer electronics.

If you were to phone into USAA's customer-service center, they would instantaneously know your history and buying needs. While you are on the phone renewing your car insurance, the customer-service representative might ask about your son who is entering college soon and inquire if a college loan is required. Or perhaps a timely direct-mail piece is sent to your home suggesting that you might be interested in this new product or service (USAA is the largest mail-order company in the U.S. in terms of sales volume and is the fourth-largest internationally).

Does this customer intimacy irritate the customer? Financial results and growth would suggest that this is not the case. Bothered by junk mail? No! Perhaps it is the manner in which they approach the customer. Maybe it's that the customer knows that USAA stands behind everything it sells and looks after its customers' best interests. Whatever the reason, more than nine of every 10 active-duty and former military officers, and 50 per cent of their families are members.

The customer database is rich with information and is constantly updated. By reviewing the database and monitoring trends, the company continues to add more products and services that its members willingly subscribe to.

Technology has been an important enabler for this organization and has played a key role in its growth and overall success. The company has been a pioneer in the use of computers, telecommunications, image processing, and other information management tools and is committed to maximizing the use of technology to maintain its competitive edge. Its investment in technology allows it to offer customers access through its automated voice response system, 24 hours a day, seven days a week. Ninety per cent of USAA's business transactions are conducted by telephone (over 343,000 calls a day, 86 million per year) and traditional mail service is used for the rest. USAA's corporate goal of a "paperless" environment led to the development of an Image Processing System. The technology scans and digitizes incoming mail for on-line viewing through high-resolution terminals. Another technology being studied is the "intelligent" workstation with features such as knowledge-based systems, interactive video, telephone/computer integration, office automation, and video integration.

A Modified Evaluation From Motorola

Motorola publishes *The Motorola Corporate Quality System* to assist its divisions to develop a standard approach to Total Customer Service.

In the following checklist is a modified version of sections from this document. I have only included those sections that apply to best practices benchmarking as well as corrective action.

As you review the material, score yourself using the evaluation criteria proposed. Although there is no threshold score that you must surpass, I believe that this self-evaluation may encourage you to take some specific action.

—— CHECKLIST ——

QUESTION 1: Are benchmarking and customer satisfaction studies performed to determine best-in-class for all products, services, and administrative functions? Are goals set so that quality is a competitive weapon?

Considerations

a) Competitor and best-in-class products or services are benchmarked. These benchmark studies are documented and are used to drive product, service and administrative improvements.

b) Members of the management team visit customers on a regular basis to assess customer satisfaction.

c) The organization performs customer field surveys and reports on results on a regular basis.

d) Follow-up surveys of customers are performed to assure that the organization is perceived as improving.

Scoring

Poor: There is no evidence of competitive benchmarking or customer satisfaction studies.

Weak: Some products, services, or administrative functions have been benchmarked. A few members of the management team have visited customers. Little is known about best-in-class products, services, or administrative systems.

Fair: Several customer satisfaction and benchmarking studies have been performed. The organization has determined best-in-class examples for some of their products/services. Visits are made to some top-tier customers regularly. There is evidence that customer satisfaction surveys are used or are being developed.

Marginally Qualified: Benchmarking is routinely used to drive improvements in product, service, and administrative areas. Regular visits to customers and customer field surveys are used to determine customer satisfaction levels. Many products and services have been baselined against best-in-class.

——CHECKLIST——

Qualified: There is evidence of extensive use of benchmarking to determine best-in-class products, services, and administrative functions. Customer satisfaction feedback from visits and surveys is a major component of the goal-setting process. Follow-up surveys with customers are routinely performed to assure that the organization is perceived as improving satisfactorily.

Outstanding: The benchmarking process has helped the organization to establish world-class quality leadership for all products, services, and administrative areas as well as internal and external processes. Customer satisfaction feedback and benchmark data are continuously validated and updated.

QUESTION 2: Is quantitative benchmarking used to evaluate all new products/technologies/services in comparison to best-in-class offerings?

Considerations
a) Best-in-class competitive products, technologies, and services are evaluated by comparing capabilities, functions, and features.
b) Competitive products are purchased and benchmarked where possible.
c) Administrative functions are also benchmarked.

Scoring
Poor: There is no indication of benchmarking taking place.

Weak: There is evidence of benchmarking in a few areas but it tends to be focused only on competitive products. Some managers believe that more benchmarking is needed.

Fair: The principles of benchmarking are widely understood. There are examples of benchmarking activity in some areas of the business. Although some of these areas have successfully benchmarked their products or technologies to determine best-in-class offerings, the process is inconsistent across the whole organization. Management support for benchmarking is growing, with some interest in benchmarking administrative functions.

——CHECKLIST——

Marginally Qualified: The benchmarking process is formalized in many areas of the business. Most major areas have done some benchmarking of their new products, technologies, or services against best-in-class offerings. Many functions have determined how their new products or services compare to best-in-class products or services. There is evidence that benchmarking information was used to improve some aspects of the organization's new products, technologies, or services. Some administrative areas are beginning to use benchmarking as a means of identifying ways to improve their systems and efficiencies.

Qualified: The benchmarking process is well defined, documented, and used to establish competitive advantage. Benchmarking is used across all major areas of the business. There are numerous examples of positive results from benchmarking in the product and process areas as well as administrative areas. Management is active in promoting and rewarding benchmarking activities.

Outstanding: Benchmarking is routinely used for all products and services throughout the organization. Some key customers recognize the organization's extensive use of benchmarking as a means of improving their products and services. The organization is recognized within the company and external to the company for having a model benchmarking process for others to follow. Benchmarking has resulted in the organization offering many best-in-class products and services to its customers.

QUESTION 3: Does a roadmap exist to ensure continued development of leading-edge, best-in-class products/technology/services?

Considerations
a) A five-year development road map exists and shows a clear vision of how the organization expects to become or remain best-in-class in the areas of products, technology, and service.
b) There are road maps, Motorola's quality standard (or equivalent for non-Motorola companies) for product, technologies, services, and administrative functions. Reviews of progress to these road maps are held regularly.

——CHECKLIST——

c) Road maps are consistent and complementary across functional boundaries.

Scoring

Poor: There is no evidence that road maps exist for the development of leading-edge products, technology, or services.

Weak: A few road maps are being defined in some functions. There are a few cases where the road-mapping process has aided groups to remain on track in developing best-in-class products. Management is beginning to see the value in the process. In general, however, the effort is fragmented and inadequate.

Fair: Road maps for development of best-in-class products and technologies are part of the organization's five-year plan. Six Sigma road maps are evident in some major business areas; however, there are still some disconnects in road maps across organization and functional boundaries.

Marginally Qualified: Good road maps exist in most areas of the business, including administrative areas. Development road maps show evidence of links to benchmarking and provide insight into how and when best-in-class status will be achieved or maintained. Efforts are being made to remove disconnects (where linkages do not exist or where process breakdowns exist) in road maps that cross functional boundaries.

Qualified: Well-defined road maps are evident for development projects in most of the major areas of the business. Milestones are being met and are on schedule for all road maps. The organization can demonstrate positive results from this road-mapping discipline. Management is fully supportive of the process. Road maps clearly take into consideration benchmarking results, customer expectations, and future needs in order to achieve or retain best-in-class, leading-edge products, technologies, and services. There are no disconnects in road maps across functional boundaries. Management reviews road map progress regularly.

—CHECKLIST—

Outstanding: The road-mapping process is a key element in the organization's pursuit of leading-edge, best-in-class products and services. They are "living documents" that all levels use to drive daily activities. Progress to development and road maps are the major focus of regular management reviews. Road maps are often shared with key customers. Everyone in the organization is aware of the key development strategies and plans and their role in helping the business achieve best-in-class products, technologies, and services.

QUESTION 4: Are all findings of customer dissatisfaction reported back to the proper organization for analysis and corrective action?

Considerations
a) There is an effective, documented reporting system to ensure that a designated person within each organization has correctly been notified of specific customer dissatisfaction issues. Analysis of customer complaints performed is timely and responsive, with a closed-loop corrective action system and responsible parties identified.
b) There is timely follow-up with a designated person to confirm that an appropriate corrective action has been implemented, verified, and communicated back to the customer.
c) This applies to non-manufacturing- as well as manufacturing-related customer dissatisfaction.

Scoring
Poor: There is no system for reporting and responding to incidents of customer dissatisfaction.

Weak: There is a sensitivity to customer dissatisfaction incidents in a few areas; however, results are spotty and follow-up tends to be disconnected. Only "major disasters" seem to get attention.

Fair: Some key people and departments are beginning to address specific customer issues but response is still slow and inconsistent. A system of commitment is beginning to emerge with management involvement seen beyond just "disasters."

——CHECKLIST——

Marginally Qualified: An increased sensitivity to customer dissatisfaction issues is evident in most major business areas. An adequate system for handling such issues and incidents has been defined and continues to be refined. There are some examples of timely root-cause analysis and corrective action responses.

Qualified: There is an effective system for reporting, tracking, assigning responsibility, and responding to customer dissatisfaction issues. Cycle time goals are established for root-cause analysis and corrective action responses. Most such goals are being met. The customer dissatisfaction response system applies to non-manufacturing as well as manufacturing areas of the organization.

Outstanding: The organization's customer complaint response system is very effective and timely. The system is so effective in responding with timely root-cause identification and permanent corrective action that few customer complaints are received. The organization is focused on anticipating customer problems and preventing them from occurring. This organization is a reputable leader in customer responsiveness.

How did you score?

9

How to Ensure That You Do Not Lose Focus

Earlier in this book, I suggested a new definition for innovation— "stealing." Some of the best ideas that organizations should use or consider, are already in place within other organizations. As outlined in the previous chapter, learning from these organizations should be a practice that is built into your continuous improvement efforts. But we can also learn much from the practices of other countries, most notably the ISO Series of quality standards, which was established first in the European community, and the European Quality Award.

This chapter is dedicated to organizations that are willing to "steal shamelessly." But a word of caution—in most cases, these concepts and ideas cannot be brought into your organization without modifying them to your unique culture and resources.

This chapter deals with three major topic areas: the ISO 9000 Series for quality assurance; the Baldrige Award; and the European Quality Award (EQA). For many best practices organizations, these award criteria or quality assurance guidelines have been used as benchmarks against which they can measure their ability to provide "What Customer Value Most,"—an organization that is easy to do business with. For some organizations, only one of these three benchmarks may apply, but they should have some applicability nonetheless.

As you read through this information, consider the following. All three quality assurance guidelines have significant application in both the service and manufacturing industry segments. In fact, many tend to overlap each other. The Baldrige Award is heavily concerned with the provision of quality goods and services and its integration with customer satisfaction, whereas the ISO 9000 Series is highly focused on consistency of practice. Customer satisfaction is achieved by delivering in a predictably consistent manner. According to my previous definition, the EQA is probably the most innovative as it was most recently created in the design of the Baldrige but also considers various elements of ISO. All three will give you some guidelines on which to model the practices that your organization should follow. By following and institutionalizing these practices, you will be able to ensure that you do not lose focus on your road to "What Customers Value Most."

ISO 9000—Its Role in Achieving Customer Satisfaction and Performance Improvement

In Europe, Asia, and North America, companies are not gaining competitive advantage by applying to the various quality awards, but rather by registering their quality assurance programs in the ISO 9000 series of quality standards. In fact, an ISO 9000 registration certificate has quickly become a key requirement for doing business with major customers worldwide.

Companies as diverse as C.I.L., Northern Telecom, Exxon, and Digital Equipment Corporation have all applied for ISO registration. Customer service departments within Kodak, AMP, and Occidental Petroleum have also received certification. The reason for this groundswell of interest is quite simple—it makes sense and can provide a competitive advantage.

Yet despite all the compelling reasons why you should be involved, a tremendous amount of disinformation remains. Although we do not have the space to provide detailed explanations, we will look at some of the more common myths as well as the actual facts.

Myth 1: ISO is just a "flavour-of-the-month." It will fade by next year only to be replaced by a new acronym.

To understand why this is unlikely to happen, we must look at the origins of the ISO Series and the motivations behind it.

ISO 9000 provides a uniform framework for quality assurance that can be used worldwide. Developed by the International Organization for Standardization, it was adopted first by the European Community as part of its drive towards unification by providing a means for cross-border quality among its original 12 members. To qualify for ISO certification, a company must document its quality procedures and, where necessary, upgrade them. Then a registered third-party audits the procedure. If the audit meets the standard, the organization's quality system is "certified," the organization itself is "registered" and can advertise this designation.

> ISO Series certification requires an organization to document the processes that touch the customer and to rigorously follow them. Internal processes, such as financial processes or human resources processes, do not fall into the basic requirement unless the organization chooses to include them.
>
> The process orientation is consistent with the customer-focused process orientation described in previous chapters. As will be described, it has found application in both the manufacturing and service industry as it fundamentally relates to the customer order fulfilment process in its broadest sense.

It is unlikely that ISO will be the "flavour-of-the-month" for three fundamental reasons. First, some governments have either already committed or announced that ISO certification will be a necessary prerequisite to be on their approved bidders' lists, either domestically or internationally. Second, many companies that purchase goods and services from other countries, particularly the European Common Market, are demanding that their suppliers be ISO 9000-certified. Third, both manufacturers and service industries alike are discovering that implementing ISO 9000 standards makes good sense. It enables organizations to institute, monitor, and improve the quality of their business.

Furthermore, ISO certification has already gained widespread approval in its brief existence. It has been estimated that more than 45,000 certificates have been issued worldwide. Most of these have been issued in the European Union, where markets have dictated that companies have ISO certification to sell to other countries. In North America, approximately 5000 certificates had been issued by the end of 1994, and growing at a rate of approximately 200 per month.

But there are further reasons why ISO is a long-term endeavour, and these deal with the fundamental principles behind the ISO Series of quality standards. The ISO 9000 series standards have two primary roles:

Quality Management

The ISO 9000 series standards provide guidance to suppliers of all types of products that want to implement effective quality systems in their organizations or to improve their existing quality systems.

Quality Assurance

The standards also provide generic requirements against which a customer can evaluate the adequacy of a supplier's quality system.

Legal concerns are also driving registration. Some companies register a quality system, at least in part, for the role that an ISO 9000 registration may play in a product liability defence. Companies that sell regulated products in Western Europe may be subject to increasingly stringent product liability and safety requirements similar to the strict liability concepts prevalent in the United States.

Companies are also being asked by purchasers of their products and services to register in the ISO 9000 Series as a precondition to placing a contractual purchase order. In many cases, suppliers have multiple sites making the same product. When only some of the sites are registered, the customer may require the supplier to ship only from the registered site(s).

The certification process requires that a Supplier Quality Requirement manual must be written and used. Vendors are evaluated through a survey, history, and audit. A supplier that has an approved quality system (for example, ISO registration) is preferred since this is one way of ensuring that only high-quality goods and services are brought in to start the process. For most organizations, this means reducing the number of their suppliers to only those with proven quality systems, thereby ensuring less checking of incoming orders for conformance. For the approved suppliers, this means larger orders, better pricing, and fewer inspections by their customers. Even Motorola—one of the first companies to win a Baldrige Award—is pursuing ISO 9000 registration for many of its plants around the world. Why? Because its customers are asking for it.

Finally, the ISO standards also require the supplier to ensure that materials purchased from subcontractors conform to specified requirements. Consequently, an increasing number of companies are requiring that their subcontractors become registered, even though the ISO 9000 Series standards do not specifically require them to. This feature alone has had a most dramatic impact on the service segment and has forced companies to become concerned about ISO 9000 certification.

Myth 2: There is no evidence to suggest that ISO has quantifiable benefits to an organization nor does it have any impact on customer satisfaction.

In fact, there is significant documented evidence to the contrary. The British Standards Institution estimates that by implementing ISO 9000, registered firms reduce operating costs by an average of 10 per cent. The savings have resulted not from documenting their processes, but rather from adopting a new discipline and, in many cases, improved processes that are focused on providing what customers value most.

Let's look at two such examples. Eastman Teleco, a manufacturer of oil and gas exploration equipment, found that since certifying its quality assurance system, its annual scrap and rework costs were reduced by 34 per cent. Similarly, for Clark-Reliance Corp., a manufacturer of liquid processing equipment, ISO helped to improve their on-time delivery rate. As part of their implementation process, they brought together their sales and production department to review their process—the result: on-time delivery rose from 30 to 90 per cent.

Need more proof? In a recent article in *The Globe & Mail,* Toronto Plastics Operations manager, David McQueen, stated that through their involvement in ISO and improved attention to quality, the number of defects was reduced significantly. How significantly? "The reduction in defects and improved machine monitoring have pared $100,000 to $150,000 out of the cost base." With production workers more involved in quality, he has reassigned one of the six quality-control personnel to other tasks.

According to a *Quality Systems Update* survey, U.S. and Canadian companies that have achieved registration under the ISO 9000 Series

standards report an average annual savings of $179,000 as a conse-
quence. This survey, conducted in July 1993, canvassed companies in the
United States and Canada that had one or more registration certificates.
Here are some additional findings of that research.

Reasons to Pursue Registration

Only nine per cent of all respondents said that their principal reason
for pursuing registration was to comply with European Community
(EC) requirements. However, nearly 28 per cent cited meeting customer demands and expectations and almost 22 per cent cited the
quality benefits. (See the following table.) Companies in all industries
are feeling customer pressures to seek registration. Two-thirds of all
respondents ranked it among their top three reasons, along with
quality benefits (at 62 per cent) and market advantage (60 per cent).

Reasons to Attain ISO 9000 Registration	
Customer Demands/Expectations	27.4%
Quality Benefits	21.8%
Market Advantage	15.6%
Requirements of EC Regulations	9.0%
Corporate Mandate	8.9%
Part of Larger Strategy	8.9%
Competitive Pressures	2.4%
Reduced Costs of Production	1.5%
Non-EC Government Requirements	0.8%
Other	1.0%
No Answer	2.7%

Benefits

In terms of defining the top three internal benefits of registration,
approximately 75 per cent of respondents noted greater quality
awareness; 73 per cent pointed to improved documentation; 48 per cent

listed positive cultural change; and 39 per cent pointed to enhanced intercompany communications.

As for external benefits, nearly 34 per cent of respondents cited higher perceived quality; 27 per cent ranked improved customer satisfaction on top, and 22 per cent identified gaining a competitive edge.

External Benefits of Registration		
Higher Perceived Quality	208	33.5%
Improved Customer Satisfaction	165	26.6%
Competitive Edge	133	21.5%
Reduced Customer Quality Audits	53	8.5%
Increased Market Share	28	4.5%
Quicker Time to Market	4	0.6%
Other	6	1.0%
No Answer	23	3.7%

Savings

Although most companies registered under the ISO 9000 Series standards report significant annual savings, not all companies experienced the same return on their investments. Some 26 per cent of survey respondents estimated their domestic annual savings to be $10,000 or less. The average annual savings, however, was nearly $179,000.

Myth 3: Once you have an ISO registration, you are there.

Not quite. Your quality system will then be evaluated against a specific standard (9001, 9002, or 9003) by a third-party organization called registrars. Once the registrar is satisfied that your system is adequately documented, implemented, and conforms to defined requirements, a certificate of registration will be issued. However, this is not a "permanent" registration. Following registration, the registrar is responsible for continuing to assess your quality system. The frequency of this assessment depends on the registrar, but a full audit usually occurs every three years, and partial audits once or twice a year. Any deficiencies that are discovered by a registrar must be addressed quickly. Failure to do so could result in registration being withdrawn.

As changes to your system are implemented, your policies, procedures, and instructions must also be revised. Copies of the revisions must be sent to everyone who has quality manuals, including the registrar. Then individuals involved in these revisions must be retrained and their compliance to these updated standards monitored.

Myth 4: ISO has application only in the manufacturing segment; it has no relevance in the service sector.

Although ISO registration has its roots in the manufacturing segment, this is only part of the story. ISO registration has a domino effect on the suppliers/vendors for the approved organization. To understand why, we have to look again to the fundamental objective of ISO: to ensure that the customer receives what was asked for—the right quantity, to the agreed quality, when specified, and at the price agreed. In order to deliver on this commitment, an organization must in turn ensure that its suppliers can also deliver on these same principles. An organization has two options. First, it can rigorously review and inspect all inputs into its organization, which is traditionally very costly. The second option is to insist that all of its suppliers also conform to the ISO 9000 Series—a less costly and equally acceptable alternative. For example, General Electric's plastics division has instructed its 340 vendors to meet ISO 9000 Series standards. The general manager of global sourcing explains, "There is absolutely no negotiation. If you want to work with us, you have to have it." This applies to both product and service suppliers.

Hospitals, hotels, banks, and even some government agencies in a number of countries have embraced the ISO 9000 Series. Companies like AMP, Oxychem, and Kelly Services, discussed earlier, are no longer exceptions to the rule, but rather the mainstream today. By some estimates, although manufacturing organizations still form the majority of certified organizations, growth within the business services is greater than all other segments. The ISO governing body, recognizing the importance of ISO for the service industry, has modified the ISO 9000 Series to accommodate this change. Guideline 9004.2 has been written for the service industry in particular. Your registrar can help you to define how this can be integrated with the 9000 Series standard.

Myth 5: ISO registration will ensure that your product meets customer needs.

ISO 9000 makes no demands or assurances about the quality of a company's products or services; it only ensures that the procedures are followed consistently. The organization itself must define the standards of quality it wishes to follow. It is assumed that if the organization wishes to remain in business, it will have standards that meet customer needs. Nor does it acknowledge the need for continuous improvement.

Organizations applying for ISO registration do not have to show that they know how to reduce cycle time, cut inventories, or speed up delivery. Nor do they have to demonstrate that their customers are either happier than they used to be or happy at all. As stated by Motorola, "With ISO 9000 you can still have terrible processes and products. You can certify a manufacturer that makes life jackets from concrete, as long as those jackets are made according to the documented procedures and the company provides the next of kin with instructions on how to complain about defects." In fact, this may be one of the major drawbacks to this standard as it currently exists. That is, certification can be received for a flawed process, as long as it is performed in a consistent manner and follows your documented procedures.

The ISO standard, however, provides a road map. If followed consistently, and developed with customer needs, it will help to ensure that your product consistently meets customer needs. Thus the importance of listening to the voice of the customer (Chapter 5).

Myth 6: The responsibility for quality and ISO registration rests with the quality manager.

Everyone in the organization must be responsible for quality. Quality personnel can only verify product or service compliance. You can't improve quality by increasing the level of inspection along the line. The entire organization must be willing to identify non-conformance and opportunities for improvement. The quality department can be responsible for taking corrective action. Lastly, a selected group of individuals, such as an inspection panel must be given authority. This allows you to avoid delivering unacceptable products or services to your customers and to prevent further processing of non-conforming items.

Implementing ISO 9000 is an extremely difficult task, which cannot rest with a handful of individuals or a quality "champion." It is a painstaking, tiring period of change within the organization, focusing on business process improvements, documentation, defining responsibility, training, and attitudinal changes.

Of prime importance is the need to generate awareness, by forming and using working groups to develop the documentation and improve processes, performing internal audits and doing further fine-tuning. Do not underestimate the scope of work that needs to be done. The time required for implementation depends on senior management's commitment to the program, the understanding or capability of the project manager, and resource allocation.

Myth 7: It should not take too long to satisfy the documentation requirements, since it should just be my policy and procedures manual.

Research has shown that almost 60 per cent of companies seeking ISO 9000 fail to be immediately recommended for registration. Of this number, more than half require at least six months of corrective action and reassessment before they are ultimately registered. This rejection usually relates to documentation deficiencies, in particular, documentation control and process control. You must describe in sufficient detail what you are doing to ensure that customers get what they ordered, on time, and at the specified price. Not only that, but all employees in the organization must know their role in the service delivery chain.

Typically, three levels of documentation are required:

Level 1 - Quality Policy Manual
Level 2 - Departmental/Business Procedures Manual
Level 3 - Work Instructions

The Quality Policy Manual states, in simple terms, how your company meets the requirements of ISO 9000 (whether it be 9001, 9002, or 9003) and directs the reader to the departmental procedures.

The Departmental/Business Procedures Manual describes how jobs are done. It is typically an easy-to-read document that can be used for training purposes.

The Work Instructions contain all detailed information that is likely to change as policies and procedures are modified. It is similar to the procedures manual, but provides a more detailed sequence of activities.

The ISO standard defines what must be contained within the documentation and refers to the need for information and documentation control, as well as a management structure to monitor issues such as conformance, corrective action, process description, and quality audits, to name a few.

Although it can be a very onerous exercise, it is time well spent since it requires you to review all of your practices to ensure that they are being followed and that all staff are dedicated to providing quality assurance.

Survey respondents reported that the most time-consuming aspects of registration involved preparing documentation and developing procedures. Thirty-five per cent listed documentation as the single most time-consuming activity, while 28 per cent identified procedure development as taking the most time.

Evidently, the greatest challenge in attaining ISO 9000 Series registration is creating procedures and developing the necessary documentation. Companies overwhelmingly cited both factors as the greatest barriers from a list of 16 choices. Fewer companies, but still a substantial number, also cited lack of management commitment and not following set procedures high on their list.

Barriers to Registration		
Procedure Creation	122	19.7%
Document Development	116	18.7%
Lack of Management Commitment	59	9.5%
Not Following Set Procedures	50	8.1%
Employee Resistance	49	7.9%
Conflicting Interpretations	46	7.4%
Training Requirements	27	4.4%
Mandated Time Frame	23	3.7%

Policies or Procedures "Inherited" from Other Divisions/Locations	22	3.5%
Implementation of Corrective Action	21	3.4%
Lack of Information	21	3.4%
Calibration of Instruments/Equipment	20	3.2%
Document Approval Process	10	1.6%
High Preparation Cost	5	0.8%
Registrar Selection	2	0.3%
Other	17	2.7%
No Answer	10	1.6%

Source: *Quality Systems Update Survey*

ISO is not a fad. Rather, it is a practice that every business organization must be aware of and embrace. Despite this, however, ISO may not be applicable for every size of business, as the cost may be prohibitive. But the principles behind ISO— "to ensure that the customer receives what it ordered"—is a practice that all organizations can and should follow.

The registration process takes time, company commitment, and discipline to adopt a new method for doing business. Moreover, it is not a one-time effort since organizations will be re-audited at least every three years in order to maintain registration.

As a first step, regardless of whether you are a manufacturing or service organization, you should be actively asking your customers to identify which ISO standard will meet their quality needs. Then you can begin direct contact with a registration organization. Throughout these efforts, external consulting assistance may be required to review existing systems and to assist in the streamlining and documentation of a quality assurance system.

ISO certification involves several rigorous and detailed steps. In the not-too-distant future, your customers will be dealing with fewer suppliers of products and services. The ones they select for a long-term, profitable relationship will be those organizations that provide consistent quality. The mark of excellence will be ISO 9000 certification.

The Baldrige Award

The most widely accepted formal definition of a total quality management company exists in the criteria for the Malcolm Baldrige National Quality Award. This annual award, given by the U.S. Commerce Department since 1988, recognizes U.S. companies that excel in quality achievement.

The General Accounting Office (GAO) of the U.S. Government was asked to examine the impact of formal total quality management performance on selected U.S. companies. GAO's review of 20 companies that were among the highest-scoring applicants in 1988 and 1989 for the Malcolm Baldrige National Quality Award indicated the following:

- Companies that adopted quality management practices experienced an overall improvement in corporate performance.
  In nearly all cases, companies that used total quality management practices achieved better employee relations, higher productivity, greater customer satisfaction, increased market share, and improved profitability.

- Each of the companies studied developed its practices in a unique environment with its own opportunities and problems. However, there were common features in their quality management systems that were major contributing factors to improved performance.

- Many different kinds of companies benefitted from putting specific total quality management practices in place. However, none of these companies reaped those benefits immediately. Allowing sufficient time for results to be achieved was as important as initiating a quality management program.

GAO analyzed data in four key areas of corporate operations and found the following:

- Somewhat better employee relations were realized
- Improved quality and lower cost were attained
- Greater customer satisfaction was accomplished
- Improved market share and profitability were attained

Although the Baldrige application process may apply to all organizations, it is unlikely that more than a handful have an opportunity to win the award. However, some key practices, categorizations, and performance measurement principles can be followed by any organization, regardless of its industry designation. This process is viewed as having three important roles in strengthening organizational competitiveness:

1. by helping to improve performance practices and capabilities;
2. by facilitating communication and sharing of best practices information; and
3. by serving as a working tool for managing performance, planning, training and assessment.

The award criteria are based on a set of 11 values and concepts that should be viewed as the foundation for integrating customer and company performance requirements.

These core values and concepts are as follows:

- Customer-Driven Quality
- Leadership
- Continuous Improvement and Learning
- Employee Participation and Development
- Fast Response
- Design Quality and Prevention
- Long-Range View of the Future
- Management by Fact
- Partnership Development
- Corporate Responsibility and Citizenship
- Results Orientation

These core values and concepts are embodied in the following seven categories. Note the heavy emphasis on customer satisfaction and customer value. In fact, one-quarter of the points to be awarded deal with customer focus and satisfaction.

1.0 Leadership
2.0 Information and Analysis
3.0 Strategic Planning
4.0 Human Resource Development and Management
5.0 Process Management
6.0 Business Results
7.0 Customer Focus and Satisfaction

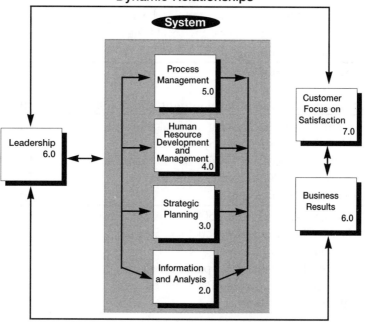

BALDRIGE AWARD CRITERIA FRAMEWORK
Dynamic Relationships

Goal
- Customer Satisfaction
- Customer Satisfaction Relative to Competitors
- Customer Retention
- Market Share Gain

Measures of Progress
- Product & Service Quality
- Productivity Improvement
- Waste Reduction/Elimination
- Supplier Performance
- Financial Results

The chart below describes these seven categories and the point value associated with each.

1995 Examination Categories/Items	Point Values
1.0 Leadership	**90**
1.1 Senior Executive Leadership	45
1.2 Leadership System and Organization	45
1.3 Public Responsibility and Corporate Citizenship	20
2.0 Information and Analysis	**75**
2.1 Management of Information and Data	20
2.2 Competitive Comparisons and Benchmarking	15
2.3 Analysis and Use of Company-Level Data	40
3.0 Strategic Planning	**55**
3.1 Strategy Development	35
3.2 Strategy Deployment	20
4.0 Human Resource Development and Management	**140**
4.1 Human Resource Planning and Evaluation	20
4.2 High Performance Work Systems	45
4.3 Employee Education, Training, and Development	50
4.4 Employee Well-Being and Satisfaction	25
5.0 Process Management	**140**
5.1 Design and Introduction of Products and Services	40
5.2 Process Management: Product and Service Production and Delivery	40
5.3 Process Management: Support Services	30
5.4 Management of Supplier Performance	30
6.0 Business Results	**250**
6.1 Product and Service Quality Results	75
6.2 Company Operational and Financial Results	130
6.3 Supplier Performance Results	45
7.0 Customer Focus and Satisfaction	**250**
7.1 Customer and Market Knowledge	30
7.2 Customer Relationship Management	30
7.3 Customer Satisfaction Determination	30
7.4 Customer Satisfaction Results	100
7.5 Customer Satisfaction Comparison	60
TOTAL POINTS	**1000**

Key Differences Between the Baldrige Award and ISO 9000

According to *ASTM Standardization News,* the Baldrige Award and ISO 9000 standards differ significantly in focus, purpose, and content. For instance, the Baldrige Award is more focused on ensuring market competitiveness and embracing customer-driven quality, whereas ISO places greater emphasis on conformity to practices and quality assurance on behalf of the customer. Baldrige depends heavily on results, while ISO does not assess outcome-oriented results.

Despite their major differences, the two standards are often confused and depicted as equivalent. This occurs for two reasons: 1) there is a misconception that they cover the same requirements; and 2) there is a perception that they both recognize high quality. This comparison assists companies that have launched ISO 9000 efforts to integrate these efforts with improving competitiveness.

In highlighting the differences between the Baldrige Award and ISO 9000 registration, however, we do not intend to portray these instruments as mutually exclusive. In fact, an increasing number of excellent companies are using the Baldrige Award and ISO 9000 compatibly—either simultaneously or sequentially. Either approach, however, requires an understanding of their important differences.

	Baldrige Award Program	ISO 9000 Registration
Focus	Competitiveness—criteria reflect two key competitiveness thrusts: 1) delivery of ever-improving value to customers, and 2) improvement of overall company operational performance.	Conformity to practices specified in the registrant's own quality system.
Purpose	Educational—to encourage sharing of competitiveness learning and to "drive" this learning nationally. It fulfils this purpose by: 1) promoting awareness of quality as an important element in competitiveness,	To provide a common basis for assuring buyers that specific practices, including documentation, are in conformance with the providers' stated quality systems. Some organizations use

Purpose cont'd	2) recognizing companies for successful quality strategies, an 3) fostering information sharing of lessons learned.	the ISO 9000 standards to bring basic process discipline to their operations.
Meaning of Quality	Customer-drive quality— concerned with all factors that matter to customers. Conformity issues are included in criteria under Process Management, which addresses other key operational requirements.	Conformity of specified operations to documented requirements.
Improvement /Results	Depends heavily on results—"Results" are a composite of competitiveness factors: customer-related, employee-related, product and service quality, and overall productivity. "Management by fact," tied to results, is a core value. Trends (improvement) and levels (comparisons to competitors and best performance) are taken into account. Results play a dual role, 1) representing business improvement indicators needed to demostrate a successful quality strategy, and 2) representing indicators that drive improvement.	Does not assess outcome-oriented results or improvement trends. Does not require demonstration of high quality, improving quality, efficient operations or similar levels of quality among registered companies.
Role in the Marketplace	A form of recognition. Despite its heavy reliance on results, it is not intended to be a product endorsement, registration or certification.	Provides customers with assurances that a registered supplier has a documented quality system and follows it (in some case, registration will reduce

Role in the Marketplace cont'd	Award winners may publicize and advertise their recognition and must share quality strategies with other U.S. organizations. The winners' role is public education and inducement for others to improve. Award winners adhere to a voluntary advertising guideline that prohibits attributing their awards to their products.	the number of independent audits otherwise conducted by customer.) While some registrars encourage advertising registration as a market advantage, some also prohibit advertising that registration signifies a product evaluation or high quality. ISO 9000 registration does not translate meaningfully into a Baldrige Award assessment score.
Nature of the Assessment	Involves a four-stage review conducted by a volunteer private-sector Board of Examiners. Applications are reviewed by five to 15 board members, depending on application progress. Final contenders receive site visits (two to five days) by a team of six to eight examiners. Focus is the customer and the market-place. Evidence of pervasive improvement, backed by results, must be in place. Improvement includes customer-related and operations-related factors. It may include relevant financial indicators. Conformity and documentation are addressed as part of process management. Assessment is not an audit or conformity assessment.	Evaluates organization's quality manual and working documents; a site audit to ensure conformance to stated practices and periodic re-audits after registration. Focus is on documentation of a quality system and on conformity to that documentation.

Feedback	Applicants receive feedback covering 28 items in seven categories. Feedback is diagnostic, highlighting strengths and areas for improvement in overall competitiveness management system. Three scoring dimensions: approach, deployment, and results.	Audit feedback covers discrepancies and findings related to practices and documentation. Feedback takes the form of major and minor nonconformities. Organization's documented quality system requirements and deployment of these requirements are assessed.
Criteria Improvement	The criteria booklet is revised annually to capture lessons learned from each cycle. Since 1988, the document has undergone six cycles of improvement, becoming more focused on business management. Major changes include greater results orientation; more emphasis on speed, competitiveness, productivity, improved integration of quality and other business management requirements; greater emphasis on human resource development; and better accommodation to service organizations' requirements.	Revisions of ISO 9001, 9002 and 9003 have been issued in 1994, with a focus on clarification of the 1987 documents, themselves based on the first commercial quality system standard in 1979 (Sawin and Hutchens, 1991). The roots of BS 5750 trace to MIL-Q-9858A established by the U.S. Department of Defense in 1959. Since 1987, additional guidance documents have been and are being developed.
Responsibility for Information Sharing	Award winners are required to share nonproprietary information on their successful quality strategies with other U.S. organizations.	Registrants have no obligation to share information with others.

Service Quality	A principal concern in guiding the criteria evolution has been compatibility with service excellence. Criteria and supporting information are evaluated to improve compatibility with requirements for service excellence. Criteria are relevant to service organization. The most important "process" time (Customer Relationship Management) is a principal concern of service organizations, but also a major concern for manufacturers that seek competitive advantage via service.	ISO 9000 standards are directed towards the demonstration of a supplier's capability to control the processess that determine the acceptability of their product or service, including design processess in ISO 9001. ISO 9000 standards are more oriented toward repetitive processess, without an equivalent focus on critical service quality issues such as relationship management and human resource developement.
Scope of Coverage	Criteria addresses all operations and processes of all work units to improve overall company productivity, responsiveness, effectiveness, and quality. Approach offers wide latitude in developing customer-focused cost reduction strategies, such as re-engineering of business processess. Due to broader nature of the Baldrige criteria and assessment, a rigorous audit of a printed quality manual and compliance with its procedure do not occur during an assessment.	ISO 9001 registration covers only design/development, production, installation and servicing. Registration covers parts of several items in the Baldrige Award criteria (primarily, parts of Management of Process Quality). ISO 9001 requirements address less than 10 per cent of the scope of the Baldrige criteria, and do not fully address any of the 28 criteria items. All ISO 9001 requirements are within the scope of the Baldrige Award.

Document-ation Requirement	Criteria does not spell out ongoing documentation requirement. Criteria implies that documentation should be tailored to fit requirements and circumstances, including internal, contractual or reg-ulatory requirements. Some analysts confuse the appli-cation report with an ongoing documentation requirement. Assessment relies on evidence and data, but this does not define or prescribe a docu-mentation system.	Documentation is a central audit requirement. Documentation require-ments are ongoing, mean-ing that documents are a permanent part of the qualtiy system needed to maintain registration.
Self-Assessment	Principal use of criteria is in self-assessment of improvement practices. Inclusion of a scoring system and evaluation factors allows companies to chart their own progress. Some compa-nies correlate their progress in Baldrige cri-teria self-assessment with changes in financial indi-cators.	ISO 9000 standards are used primarily in "contractual situa-tions" or other external audits. Additional registrar-developed audit checklists define actual cri-teria/requirements for registra-tion. Registration by external assessor is needed to fulfil most contractual requirements (i.e., self-assessment is generally not accepted). Aside from benefits of self-assessment while pursu-ing registration, it is not clear that ISO 9000 self-assessment after registration leads to oper-ational improvement because standards do not address con-tinuous improvement or com-petitiveness factors.

Having read the above, you might be asking, "Which one do I use?" Unfortunately, there is no one easy answer. You may be forced to consider ISO because of pressures from your customers. Organizations with as few as 10 employees, in both manufacturing and service industries, have received certification and found it to be cost-justifiable. ISO provides you with a documentation protocol and a discipline that, if followed, will ensure that your customers receive products and services from a company that is easy to do business with. After all, isn't that what customers value most?

The Baldrige, however, is an award that few companies will ever apply to, and even fewer will win. But we have not discussed it here to encourage you to apply. Rather, it has been included to identify best practices in quality/customer satisfaction. These are benchmarks against which you must compare your practices. That is, the message is if you aspire to be among the best-of-the-best, you must embrace the following practices:

a) a focus on processes and a dedication to continuous improvement (Chapter 6);

b) an active customer research program in order to continuously tap into the voice of the customer (Chapter 5);

c) a passion for performance measurement (Chapter 7); and

d) a dedication to continuously improve, assisted in part by an active benchmarking program (Chapter 8).

Which one should you use? As I mentioned at the beginning of this chapter, take the components that apply to your organization, steal shamelessly from the best practices of others, and adapt it to the culture of your operating environment.

The European Quality Award—The New Kid on the Block

The Baldrige Award, Canadian Award for Business Excellence (CABE), Juran Award, Federal Quality Award, and ICSA Award of Excellence, are perhaps some of the most widely recognized quality/service awards in North America. But, most organizations can benefit from a new international award, even though you probably will never apply for it. It's called the European Quality Award and is awarded annually to the most successful exponent of Total Quality Management in Western Europe.

In 1988, in recognition of the potential for competitive advantage through the application of Total Quality, 14 of the leading

Western European businesses formed the European Foundation for Quality Management (EFQM). By October 1992, membership had grown to over 230 members from most Western European countries and most business sectors.

Since that time, the EFQM has played an important role in enhancing the position of Western European businesses in the world market in two ways:

- by accelerating the acceptance of quality as a strategy for global competitive advantage; and
- by stimulating and assisting the deployment of quality improvement activities.

One of the enablers was the establishment of the European Quality Award. In 1991, with the support of the European Organization for Quality and the European Commission, the Award was established, and was presented for the first time in 1992. As you will note later in this section, the Award criteria can best be described as a mixture of both the ISO and Baldrige. The criteria are somewhat less restrictive in that they primarily comprise a self-evaluation. Companies apply for the Award by submitting self-appraisal information using a guideline provided by the EFQM.

The self-appraisal involves regular and systematic review of the organization's activities and results. This process allows the organization to clearly identify its strengths as well as the areas in which improvements can be made. The aim of this appraisal was to encourage, facilitate, and optimize self-appraisal, by providing guidelines on the following:

- the organizational activities, processes, resources, and results that should be appraised;
- the process for self-appraisal; and
- the area, within those organizational aspects, that could be addressed.

Despite the fact that every organization is unique, the following model was prepared as a framework for self-appraisal that would apply to almost any business organization.

The European TQM Model

As highlighted below, processes are the means by which the organization harnesses and releases the talents of its people to produce results. In other words, the processes and the people are the enablers that provide the results.

Expressed graphically, the principle looks like this:

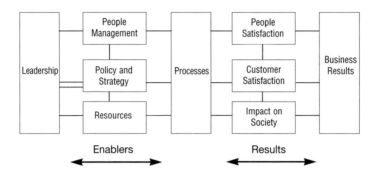

Essentially the model tells us that: customer satisfaction, people (employee) satisfaction, and impact on society are achieved through leadership driving policy and strategy, people management, resources and processes, leading ultimately to excellence in business results.

Each of the nine elements in the model is a criterion that can be used to appraise the organization's progress towards Total Quality Management.

The Results section is concerned with what the organization has achieved and is achieving.

For scoring purposes in both the "Results" and "Scope" segments, the Assessor may choose one of the five levels 0 per cent, 25 per cent, 50 per cent, 75 per cent, or 100 per cent as presented in the chart below, or interpolate between these values.

How The Award Is Scored

The Assessor scores each part of the Results criteria on the basis of a combination of two factors.

1. The degree of excellence of your results.
2. The scope of your results.

RESULTS	SCORE	SCOPE
Only anecdotal comments provided.	0%	Results address few relevant areas and activities.
Some results show positive trends. Some favourable comparisons with own targets.	25%	Results address some relevant areas and activities.
Many results show positive trends over at least three years. Favourable comparisons with own targets in many areas. Some comparisons with external organizations. Some results are caused by approach.	50%	Results address many relevant areas and activities.
Most results show strongly positive trends over at least three years. Favourable comparisons with own targets in most areas. Favourable comparisons with external organizations in many areas. Many results are caused by approach.	75%	Results address most relevant areas and activities.
Strongly positive trends in all areas over at least five years. Excellent comparisons with own targets and external organizations in most areas. "Best in Class" in many areas of activity. Results are clearly caused by approach. Positive indication that leading position will be maintained.	100%	Results address all relevant areas and facets of the organization.

The Enablers section of the evaluation is concerned with how results are being achieved.

In evaluating the "Approach" and "Deployment" section, the Assessor may choose one of the five levels 0 per cent, 25 per cent, 50 per cent, 75 per cent, or 100 per cent as presented in the chart below, or interpolate between these values.

The Enablers

The Assessor scores each part of the Enablers criteria on the basis of a combination of two factors.

1. The degree of excellence of your approach.
2. The degree of deployment of your approach.

APPROACH	SCORE	DEPLOYMENT
Anecdotal or non-value-adding.	0%	Little effective usage.
Some evidence of soundly based approaches and prevention based systems. Subject to occasional review. Some areas of integration into normal operations.	25%	Applied to one-quarter of the potential when considering all relevant areas and activities.
Evidence of soundly based systematic approaches and prevention-based systems. Subject to regular review with respect to business effectiveness. Integration into normal operations and planning well established.	50%	Applied to about half the potential when considering all relevant areas and activities.
Clear evidence of soundly based systematic approaches and prevention-based systems. Clear evidence of refinement and improved business effectiveness through review cycles. Good integration of approach into normal operations and planning.	75%	Applied to about three-quarters of the potential when considering all relevant areas and activities.
Clear evidence of soundly based systematic approach and prevention-based systems. Clear evidence of refinement	100%	Applied to full potential in all relevant areas and activities.

and improved business effectiveness through review cycles. Approach has become totally integrated into normal working patterns. Could be used as a role model for other organizations.

The objective of a comprehensive self-appraisal and self-improvement program is to regularly review each of these nine criteria identified in the model, with either an internal or external assessor, and, therefore, to adopt relevant improvement strategies.

In the self-appraisal document, specific areas could be addressed for each of the criteria in the model. The documentation as shown below and in the checklist that follows gives you some guidance on what could be included. The Award judges are looking primarily at the narrative provided on your organizational practices and at the scores that you have provided relative to that narrative. The choice of the areas to address lies with the organization; however, the areas chosen should have particular relevance to their organizational culture.

Here's an example of what is contained within the self-appraisal document.

Visible involvement in leading Total Quality. Areas to address could include how managers take positive steps to:

- communicate with staff
- act as role models by leading by example
- make themselves accessible and listen to staff
- give and receive training
- demonstrate commitment to Total Quality.

Although many lessons can be learned from these tools, perhaps the greatest lesson may be what not to do. The ISO, Baldrige Award, and European Quality Award are all models, which as explained earlier, can be used for self-evaluation. Compare your practices to those required to satisfy the components of the award criteria or standard, and identify what changes are required. Do a cost-benefit analysis to identify if it is worth the effort. Check with your customers to determine whether introducing this practice will bring you closer to "What Customers Value Most." Don't make your goal winning an award or achieving certification—that will not help you keep customers-for-life. If you do this, you will only be investing time and human resources to achieve self-gratification instead of true customer satisfaction.

A Self-Evaluation: The Results Segment of the EQA

How would you score in the results segment of the European Quality Award?

The results segment is a true test of what the organization has achieved and will be able to achieve in the near future. Here's the scoring template for two areas in that segment: Customer Satisfaction and People Satisfaction. Be objective and realistic and this may lead to a focus in new, yet uncharted areas.

The following is a suggestion of how to use this template.

Using the results scoring format starting on page 267 (i.e., 25%, 50%, 75%, 100%), score your organization on each of the items listed below. Next, give the template without your scores to a selected group of internal customers (who should only respond to the people satisfaction section) and a selected group of external customers (who should respond to the customer satisfaction section only). Plot your scores against the average scores of the internal and external customer groups. Subtract the internal customer scores from those of the average external customer scores. That will provide you with a GAP analysis of your respective perceptions. The areas with the largest negative gaps are the priority issues that must be addressed first.

In the narrative of your analysis, you should describe:

a) your company's actual performance
b) your company's own targets and wherever possible describe them in relation to:
c) the performance of competitors
d) the performance of "best-in-class" organizations.

The self-appraisal should indicate the extent to which the organization's activities are covered by the evaluation and the relative importance of the parameters chosen to measure results.

RESULTS

Customer Satisfaction: (External Customer)

This segment addresses external customers' perception of the organization and of its products and services.

Areas to address could include customers' perceptions of the organization in the following areas:

Product and service quality:
- capability of meeting specifications
- defect, error, rejection rates
- consistency, reproducibility
- maintainability
- durability
- reliability
- on-time delivery
- in-full delivery
- logistics information
- delivery frequency
- responsiveness and flexibility
- product availability
- accessibility of key staff
- product training
- sales support
- product literature
- simplicity, convenience, and accuracy of documentation
- awareness of customer problems
- complaint handling
- warranty and guarantee provisions
- spare part availability
- innovation in service quality
- product development
- payment terms and financing.

Additional indications of customer satisfaction could include:
- complaint levels
- customer returns (by value and quantity)
- warranty payments
- re-work levels
- accolades and awards received.

People Satisfaction: (Internal Customer)

This segment deals with internal customers' feelings about their organization.

Areas to address could include people's perceptions of their organization in the following areas:

- working environment; location, space, amenities
- health and safety provisions
- communication at local and organizational levels
- appraisal, target-setting, and career-planning
- training, development, and retraining
- awareness of requirements of job
- awareness of organization values, vision, and strategy
- awareness of Total Quality process
- involvement in Total Quality process
- recognition schemes
- reward schemes
- organization (line management)
- organization for Total Quality
- management style
- job security

Additional indications of people satisfaction could include:
- absenteeism and sickness
- staff turnover
- ease of recruitment
- grievances
- use of company-provided facilities

There are no right or wrong answers here. Your self-evaluation and scoring should indicate where specific attention should be paid.

10

A Methodology to Help You Deliver "What Customers Value Most"

W hat is the best way to end a book? Perhaps with a review—from a somewhat different perspective—and a reference—a pointer back to previous chapters that describe various tools and techniques that are required to ensure success. In this case, the review is of our four-phase model—the best practices model born from the IDEAS study described in previous chapters: align, explore, focus, and commit/support. Whether your organization is about to embark on a new initiative to deliver "What Customers Value Most" or your organization requires a bit of fine-tuning, the following model will be an effective guide.

The Best Practices Model

First, let's review why we need a model to guide us in becoming *what customers value most.*

Whether they are located in Vancouver or Bangkok, Amsterdam or Sydney, companies around the globe face the same challenge: competition is more aggressive and differentiation is more difficult to achieve. The Free Trade Agreement and NAFTA have forced companies that were once concerned only with national competition to face new market concerns that extend far beyond their country's borders. In fact, today's market extends beyond continental boundaries as well. Competition has reached global proportions, and businesses are realizing that winning strategies depend on more than lowering prices. As markets become increasingly commodity-based, succeeding in the global game requires a strategy that will set companies apart from their competition.

Reduced prices will not achieve this goal—they will drive down profit margins. Product differentiation is becoming more difficult to achieve, and advertising without a unique selling proposition just sounds the same.

Only one strategic opportunity remains: differentiation through improved customer satisfaction.

Through my work with various organizations, I have recognized that some companies were having tremendous success in improving customer satisfaction, while others seemed to be losing market share by neglecting the customer service edge. The reasons for the companies' varying success rates were not always obvious, which is why the IDEAS (Innovative approaches to Deliver Excellence through improved customer practices And total quality Service) study was initiated.

The study's findings revealed some fundamental differences between companies that have achieved improved customer satisfaction and those that have been less than successful in satisfying their customers. Many of these differences have been described in various chapters throughout this book.

But there is more.

An analysis of the research results and subsequent interviews with a wide variety of organizations, revealed four key practices followed by companies that have been successful in improving customer satisfaction. These four practices are actually the following four process phases:

ALIGN: aligning senior management in the commitment to excellence,

EXPLORE: listening to the voice of the customer,

FOCUS: focusing on customer-related processes, and

COMMIT/SUPPORT: supporting a culture of continuous improvement.

Although these practices are not new, the manner in which they are implemented is critical. Thus the purpose of the model and the tools and techniques described in the previous chapters.

The following summary is designed to bring together the contents of these chapters, organized under these four key headings. **This model can be compared to building a house.** The first step, aligning senior management, is the foundation; it must be firm and secure before you proceed any further. The second step, listening to the voice of the customer, is the design, which provides the basic outer shell. The third step, focusing on customer-related processes, is analogous to the process of adding the essential fixtures to the house—when and where each fixture is added is crucial if all systems are to work together. The fourth and final step, supporting a culture of continuous improvement, is the maintenance and upkeep of the house.

All of these practices must be timed correctly if they are to be effective. If they are, these four steps will help you to build a solid "house" of quality service and customer satisfaction. To assist you in this process, I have provided a summary of the key points related to each phase.

MODEL STEP	Activity Required	Key Enablers/Tools	Chapter Reference

The first reference column, "Activity Required" refers to the general activities that must be completed within this step. The column entitled "Key Enablers/Tools" lists those practices that are essential if an organization wishes to effectively implement that step of my model. The next column identifies the chapters in which there are key discussions of that practice.

The Steps of the Best Practices Model

ALIGN: Align Senior Management in a Commitment to Excellence

The first step in improving customer satisfaction requires an alignment of attitudes within the company. One of the first parties that must be aligned is senior management. To do this, attention must initially be focused on the area of language. Every executive has preconceptions of the meaning of various terms or how to conduct benchmarking, reengineering, or customer satisfaction surveys. Thus you must bring together all managers to review and standardize methodology and terminology.

Another area that requires attention is a review of appropriate definitions for "innovation" and "customer value." The IDEAS survey results show major differences in the philosophies of companies with satisfied customers and companies that are not meeting all of their customers' needs, in terms of definitions for innovation and customer value.

Successful companies differentiated themselves in their willingness to define innovation as "the successful adaptation of innovations produced elsewhere," while less successful companies tended to define it as "the creative development of new products, services or internal process improvements."

In fact, adopting "tried and true" methods has been a practice of Japanese organizations for years and has played an important role in Japan's success in the global marketplace. Successful organizations have adopted a more "Japanese approach" to customer satisfaction, but most businesses lagging in the service game have not yet embraced outside ideas—even though learning from others has proven to be one of the most effective tools for improving performance.

The IDEAS survey results indicated another key difference between successful companies and their less successful counterparts—the way they define customer value. Respondents were asked to choose from a list of definitions of "customer value." Successful organizations were more likely to define it as "exceeding customer expectations," while less successful businesses were satisfied with "meeting customer expectations." Clearly, it's the businesses willing to "go the extra mile" that are rewarded with satisfied, loyal customers—

and it's the loyal customers who keep coming back.

Changing the way a company defines innovation and customer value requires nothing less than realigning the entire philosophy of the organization. That, of course, is an incredible undertaking, which is precisely why there has to be a firm commitment to the process at the executive level. That commitment includes an investment of dollars and people. In less successful organizations, management often pays lip service to improving customer satisfaction, but does not support its statements with a substantial budget. A meaningful budget, however, must be allocated to enable the organization to achieve its customer satisfaction objectives. There must also be visible executive involvement in customer satisfaction initiatives as well as a reasonable time line and measurable goals for improving customer satisfaction and their payoffs, so that staff throughout the organization have something tangible to work for and can see the benefits of their efforts.

Part of a management commitment to improving customer satisfaction also includes a focused reward program designed to recognize excellence-in-service within the organization. Successful organizations know the power of incentives and performance-based reward systems for employees. Less successful organizations recognize the error of their ways: when asked to identify those factors that limited their potential to succeed, they resoundingly stated insufficient budget, lack of management support, and inadequate rewards and recognition.

Having definitions and gaining commitment are obviously important elements, but not more important than having a purpose and goals. Seeking awards such as the Malcolm Baldrige Award, or pursuing ISO 9000 Series certification may be the answer for some organizations. Regardless, as part of the alignment stage, the organization must establish its common goal against which it will measure its progress.

MODEL STEP	Activity Required	Key Enablers/Tools	Chapter Reference
ALIGN	Direction	Mission/Vision/Values	4
	Leadership		4
	Goal		4
	Budgets		2
	Structure	Team	6
		Roles and responsibilities	6
	Common Language	Glossary	
	Goals	Malcolm Baldrige Award ISO 9000 Series Standards European Quality Award	9

EXPLORE/LISTEN: Listen to the Voice of the Customer

Successful organizations survey their customers extensively and regularly to determine their needs and the extent to which the company is meeting—or exceeding—these needs. Successful companies are more likely to survey customers on a variety of areas, including the effectiveness of complaint handling, customer satisfaction, conformance to standards, customer needs, and new product ideas.

But successful companies don't stop there. Not only do they measure their actual performance against the standards they have established for themselves, but they also research and compare themselves against their competition to see how they measure up. In short, the companies that satisfy their customers are the companies that do their homework. They know that a commitment to customer satisfaction must be reinforced by a complete understanding of the customer, the competition, and the marketplace, as well as an ability to identify and respond to areas where change is needed.

MODEL STEP	Activity Required	Key Enablers/Tools	Chapter Reference
EXPLORE /LISTEN	Internal Research	Cycle of Service Workshop	4
		Focus Groups	4
		Surveys	4
	External Research	Competitive Benchmarking	8
		Surveys	4
		Customer Segmentation	4
	Gap Analysis		4

FOCUS: Focus On Customer-Related Processes

In addition to constantly surveying customer needs, companies that have improved their customers' satisfaction levels are more likely to have initially examined their customer-related processes and, in many cases, to have reengineered them. These processes, as outlined in earlier chapters, include customer order fulfilment, billing, complaint systems, account management, salesforce management, and other processes that deal directly with customers. Successful companies, which focus on these systems, see positive effects on both revenue and customer satisfaction, while less successful companies tend to focus on systems that drive cost improvements and reduce labour—strategies that bring only temporary advantage in the marketplace.

Another important area in which successful companies have focused their energies is tracking customer complaints. These companies practise the philosophy that "what gets measured gets done" and they actively encourage customer feedback. Management is apprised of the types and amounts of customer complaints being received in all departments as well as the general trends in the quantity of complaints being received by the company and the corrective action being taken. In many companies, this tracking information is not just for management—the entire organization is made aware of complaint trends.

Knowing where to begin a process improvement initiative requires an understanding of the company's options. This is where differences in company philosophy become readily apparent. Companies that are achieving improved customer satisfaction know that a good rating from customers must be measured against their competitors' ratings. If, for example, Company A is seen as an "excellent" service provider, then Company B's "good" rating obviously isn't good enough. Company B must understand why Company A is viewed as excellent and look at a variety of ways to make improvements, by researching direct competitors as well as other industry segments. That's where process benchmarking comes in—and where less successful companies are often dropping the ball.

Change cannot be made in a vacuum; it requires teamwork, knowledge of the current and future needs of customers, and an appreciation of the best practices of others. And it should be given high priority.

MODEL STEP	Activity Required	Key Enablers/ Tools	Chapter Reference
FOCUS	Methodology	Business Process Reengineering	6
		TQM	6
		Process Benchmarking	8
	Training/ Education	Coaching	6

COMMIT/SUPPORT: Support a Culture of Continuous Improvement

Successful companies state the importance of understanding that improving customer satisfaction is an ongoing process—one that must be constantly nurtured with attention to the "human" side of the organization. It has to become part of the day-to-day operation of the organization, which means creating an internal service culture throughout the company.

As highlighted earlier in this book, companies with improved customer satisfaction use five key strategies to create an Internal Service Culture.

1. **Communicate with employees to determine their needs and level of job satisfaction.** Successful companies follow the Golden Rule of Service: "Do unto your internal customers—your employees—as you would have them do unto your external customers." Why? Because satisfied employees create satisfied customers. And satisfied customers (internal and external) create momentum. They help the company innovate, by giving it ideas on how it can improve. As these ideas are implemented, improved customer satisfaction results, which, in turn, stimulates new ideas and keeps the process alive.

2. **Empower senior management with the responsibility for developing and maintaining the service culture.** The commitment to improve customer satisfaction has to begin at the highest levels of the organization to ensure success. Senior management must have both the authority and the responsibility for developing and maintaining customer satisfaction initiatives.

3. **Establish service standards through the input of both customers and employees.** Successful companies go one step beyond gathering customer and employee survey information. They "put their money where their mouth is" and produce a Customer Bill of Rights. A Bill of Rights informs customers of the quality of service they can expect to receive and tells employees about the service they are expected to deliver. It also lets employees know the standards that management will abide by in delivering quality service to its staff.

4. Ensure that those standards are practised by employees and promoted to customers. A Customer Bill of Rights should be proudly and prominently posted throughout the organization. Customers must be made aware of it, and it should be incorporated into all employee training programs.

5. Encourage the service culture through training and reward programs to establish and recognize excellence-in-service. Successful organizations understand the importance of providing motivation, positive feedback, and performance-based rewards for their employees. Effective incentives include such monetary rewards as giving employees shares in the company and linking a portion of employee commission to the organization's performance. Other less tangible but equally important strategies include giving trust, recognizing employee contributions, and sharing authority by involving employees in the company's strategic plan.

MODEL STEP	Activity Required	Key Enablers/ Tools	Chapter Reference
COMMIT/ SUPPORT	Incentive to Change	Awards	7
		Rewards	7
		Suggestion Systems	7
		Performance Measurement	8
	Feedback Mechanism	Complaint/ comment process	8

Summary

The IDEAS survey results outline some important strategies for companies dedicated to improving customer service. Perhaps the most important strategy is that customer satisfaction starts with an analysis of both internal and external needs and practices.

On an external level, successful organizations understand that innovation comes from what works for others. Accordingly, these companies constantly review the best practices of others and adopt the practices that suit their needs. On an internal level, successful companies know that although ideas may come from external sources, change must start within the organization. Establishing an internal service culture must combine a commitment from management with the input of employees and customers. Although the initial investment is sizeable, developing a service culture ultimately results in revenue enhancement (increased sales) and improved profitability (decreased internal costs) without requiring cutbacks.

The benefits of improving both internal and external customer satisfaction are best reinforced by the Customer Satisfaction/Revenue Enhancement Model.

Customer Satisfaction/Revenue Enhancement Model

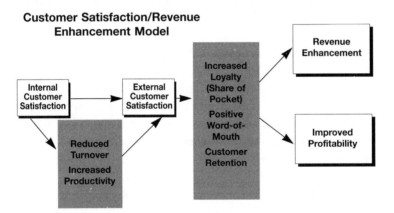

For successful organizations, improved customer satisfaction leads to revenue enhancement and improved profitability. First, as the IDEAS study and a wealth of research reveal, improved internal customer satisfaction leads to increased employee productivity and reduced staff turnover.

Satisfied employees are infectious—their satisfaction encourages confident, happy customers that are more loyal, which increases customer retention and the company's share of pocket. That is, satisfied customers will purchase more from the company they are happy with, rather than going to the competition. In addition to bringing in repeat business, satisfied customers also generate positive word-of-mouth for the company. These three elements—positive word-of-mouth, increased loyalty, and customer retention—lead to revenue

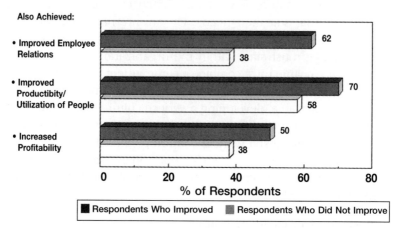

Organizations that Have Been Successful in Achieving Improved Customer Satisfaction are more Likely to Achieve Significant Side-Benefits

Also Achieved:

- Improved Employee Relations — 62 / 38
- Improved Productibity/ Utilization of People — 70 / 58
- Increased Profitability — 50 / 38

% of Respondents

■ Respondents Who Improved   ■ Respondents Who Did Not Improve

Source: *1994 C&L I.D.E.A.S. Study*

enhancement through increased sales and improved profitability.

The cost of poor customer service can be high. Sales lost through dissatisfied customers can be as high as 10 per cent, in addition to the hiring, firing, and retraining costs associated with unhappy employees. Conversely, companies offering good service achieve a 12 per cent return on sales, a higher market share, lower employee turnover, improved products and productivity, and a solid, loyal customer base—definitely goals worth striving for.

As we move toward the twenty-first century, success will be more difficult to achieve. Organizations that will be most successful will be fast, flexible, and obsessed with continuous improvement.

And, not unlike the tortoise we discussed in Chapter 1, these organizations will stick their necks out. And, not unlike successful organizations, they will listen to the voice of the customer.

May your house be one that will stand the test of time.

Glossary

Affinity diagram: A group process that takes large amounts of information, which indicate the drivers of satisfaction and dissatisfaction within a process, and divides them into categories.

Belief: An acceptance of something as true.

Benchmarking: The process of continuously comparing and measuring an organization against business leaders around the world to gain information that will help the organization take action to improve its performance.

Brainstorming: A group process for generating creative and diverse ideas.

Business Strategy: A set of decisions and activities that describes the approach the organization will take to accomplish long-term business goals. A strategy defines the way goals will be accomplished. Using a well-defined strategy provides management with a thought pattern that helps it to better utilize equipment and direct resources towards achieving specific goals.

Celebration: An activity in which a team's success is communicated to the entire organization and praised by management. This may include tangible rewards and award certificates.

Check Sheet: A data collection tool, perhaps a form, in which one tallies, or checks off, the number of occurrences of a particular event.

Commitment: A pledge to customers to produce products and services that meet their requirements and add substantial value in comparison to competition. (See also Customer Bill of Rights.) Commitment occurs when management realizes the importance of an activity or subject and provides the required resources to improve all affected functions within the organization.

Competitive Benchmarking: A process of comparing, through quantitative measurement, the performance of your organization relative to competitors, primarily within your own industry segment. This form of benchmarking seeks strictly to identify performance measures or critical success factors/ratios. This activity is designed to identify the measurable gap between the organization and its competitors.

Continuous Improvement Process: The concept that improvement is a constant and necessary set of activities to ensure ongoing customer satisfaction and improved efficiency, effectiveness, adaptability, and control (*Kaizen*).

Control Tools: A group of measurement methods that allow you to statistically assess, track, and monitor processes to determine if they are producing output that meets requirements.

Council Charter: A formal agreement between the council and senior management that defines some special agreement, privilege, concession, mandate, and/or activity.

Critical Success Factors: Those characteristics, conditions, or variables that directly affect the satisfaction of customers and, therefore, the success of an organization.

Customer: The current or potential receivers of the outputs (products, services, or information) that an organization, team, or individual supplies. This includes current customers, customers that you lost but wish to regain, new customers, internal customers, and external customers.

Customer Bill of Rights (CBR): A statement that clearly identifies the quality of service that customers can expect to receive from the organization. Such a statement would begin as follows: Our Customers have a Right to.... This statement also tells employees about the service they are expected to deliver. The Customer Bill of Rights should also exist for internal employees. In this way, employees will know the standards management will abide by in delivering quality service to their staff.

Customer, External: The ultimate purchaser of a product or service.

Customer-for-Life: The value of a customer that purchases from you exclusively for 10 to 20 years. How much profit can your organization realize from this relationship? This must be calculated in order to appreciate the importance of a "customer-for-life."

Customer Satisfaction: The state in which external customer needs, wants, and expectations throughout the product or service's life are met or exceeded, resulting in repeat purchase, loyalty, and favourable word-of-mouth.

Customer Satisfaction Index (CSI): A measure or rating that signifies a level or degree of satisfaction by an organization's customers within its market segment.

Customer vs Consumer: There is much confusion over this definition in many business sectors including packaged goods, insurance, and other financial services segments. Customers are the first line of sales; that is, in the example of Quaker Oats, the retail store. Consumers are the customers of the retail store. In the insurance sector, the agent/producer is generally regarded as the customer, with the individual policyholder considered to be the consumer.

Cycle Time: The time from the beginning to the end of a specific work process, or the amount of time it takes to complete one transaction through a work process; for example, the time it takes to process one vendor invoice, from start to finish.

Design of experiments: A systematic approach to experimentation that makes it possible to determine which factors have significant (real) effects on the outputs of a process after determining the random (natural) variation of the process. This method permits determination of a mathematical relationship between process variables and measures responses.

Disconnects: A disconnect exists when a process does not function smoothly and is prone to break down. Operational silos are typically causes of this type of failure, as are poor training and role definition.

Enablers: Giving people the knowledge, skills, and means to act.

Entitlement: The best that can be achieved using current resources to eliminate waste and improve cycle time.

Errors: Any output that does not meet individual or customer expectations. The result of failing to correctly perform an action. Errors result in non-conforming outputs if left uncorrected.

External Customer: The person or group to whom the term "customer" has been applied traditionally. This is the person or group who buys or receives what an organization produces.

Focus Group: A research tool to gather directional, qualitative comments from a group of customers.

Gap Analysis: A methodology to highlight differences in perspective between customer groups and the organization. Typical gaps may include:
- The gap between what the customer expects and what the organization is prepared to deliver.
- The gap between what the customer believes to be a priority or value and what the organization believes the customer wants or needs.

Goals: A goal is a desired, measurable result that the organization wants to accomplish in a set period to support its business objectives. Goals should be hard (quantifiable) rather than soft (qualitative), so there is no ambiguity.

Histogram: A graphical description of individual measured values in a data set that is organized according to the frequency or relative frequency of occurrence. A histogram illustrates the shape of the distribution of individual values in a data set along with information regarding the average and variation.

Improvement Process: Activities aimed at continuously improving the reliability, efficiency, effectiveness, and capability of processes, products, and services.

Innovation: The process of looking beyond the organization to identify standards, best practices, and processes that can be adapted and modified within the culture and entitlements of the organization.

Internal Customers: A person or group who receives work in progress from another person or group within the same organization. The internal customer has requirements for the work in progress that must be satisfied by the supplier, however, these requirements should ultimately be based on the external customer's requirements.

Just-in-Time Training: Training provided only to those who require this level of training and only immediately before it will be put to active use.

Key Improvement Opportunities: Key customer-focused processes that are in greatest need of process improvement and that, when improved, will better enable the organization/division to provide its customers with superior value.

Leadership: The ability to lead, including inspiring others in a shared vision of what can be, taking risks, serving as a role model, reinforcing and rewarding the accomplishments of others, and helping others to act.

Management Buy-in: Management buy-in occurs when management generates its own vision of the company's future status and is self-motivated to make the changes necessary to it and the organization.

Mission: A customer-oriented statement of purpose for a unit, team, or the organization as a whole. Its basic purpose is to guide the organization's directions by identifying what the organization does and whom it serves. The mission is broad enough to have a direct relationship to all activities that go on within the organization. It provides the overall boundaries that objectives, goals, and strategies provide for the organization.

Moment of Truth: Any moment in time when your customer interacts with your product or service that influences his or her level of satisfaction, or dissatisfaction, with the total experience.

Objectives/Deliverable: An objective communicates the direction or intention that an individual or organization has for the future. It is the end product of a process or a series of processes and may be the material or information provided to customers, internal and external.

Paradigm Shift Question: "What today is impossible to do, but if it could be done, would fundamentally change our approach to doing business."

Pareto Chart: A bar chart that illustrates causes of problems in order of severity by frequency (percent) of occurrence, by cost, or by performance.

Performance Measures: Indicators of the work performed and the results achieved in an activity, process, or organizational unit—can be financial or non-financial, qualitative, or quantitative.

Plan: A plan is defined as the process of using related facts and future assumptions to arrive at a course of action to be followed in seeking specific goals and objectives. It is a systematic method for defining, developing, and outlining possible courses of action to meet existing and/or future needs, interests, or problems.

Practice: A frequent or usual action or method used to effect a particular change.

Problem-Solving Methodology: A process of established criteria to determine the one solution that best meets the criteria to relieve the problem. Steps may include first defining the problem, then establishing the criteria for the best solution given your resources and objectives, and finally evaluating all possible solutions against the established criteria.

Process: A series of interrelated transactions that converts inputs into results (outputs). Processes consume resources and require standards and documentation for repeatable performance.

Process Benchmarking: The benchmarking of discrete process performance and functionality against organizations that lead in those processes. Best practices benchmarking seeks to answer the question: what is the measurable gap between our organization and the "world-class" performers...competitors or those outside your industry? It also addresses the question, what are the key enablers that must be considered to allow me to close that gap?

Process Control: The process of regulating and guiding operations to detect, avoid, or prevent defects and taking corrective action when a defect occurs.

Process Improvement: Activities aimed at improving the reliability, effectiveness, efficiency, or capability of a process. The focus is on the redesign or restructuring of work processes, and results tend to be revolutionary.

Process Management: The process of ensuring that processes are documented, controlled, compliant with standards, and continually improved. (Also refer to ISO.)

Process Map: A diagram that shows the sequential steps of a process or work flow around a product or service.

Process Mapping: A diagram technique that shows the sequential steps of a process or work flow around a product or service.

Process Owners: The designated person who is ultimately responsible for delivering the process. The "owner" is responsible for process documentation, clarity of roles within the process, updating, administration, and process integrity. Process owners must also assume responsibility for leadership, support, direction, and measurement to the process. They are accountable for customer satisfaction, and they have the authority to change the process when it no longer meets requirements.

Process Specifications: Customer and competitive requirements are translated into specifications for process capability.

Quality: For many organizations, it is restricted to only conformance to requirements. In a highly competitive commodity environment, it is the totality of features and characteristics of a product or service that bear on its ability to satisfy stated or implied needs.

Quality Function Deployment: A systematic matrix method used to translate customer wants or needs into product or service characteristics that will have a significant positive impact on meeting customer demands.

Quality Service Audit: A systematic and independent examination and evaluation to determine whether customer satisfaction-related activities and results comply with planned arrangements and whether these arrangements are implemented effectively and are suitable to achieve customer objectives.

Recognition: Recognition is having someone acknowledge either individual or group worth.

Rewards: A positive reinforcement of a desired behaviour.

Run Chart: A graph of data point in chronological order used to illustrate trends or cycles of the characteristic being measured for the purpose of suggesting an assignable cause rather than random variation.

Service Culture: An attitude within the organization best described through the Golden Rule of Service: do unto your internal customers as you would have them do unto your external customers.

Service Delivery Chain: A chain of activities that describes the interaction between functional groups within an organization in delivering a service to a customer. The sequence must include the initiation, processing, execution, and follow-up to the external customer and would describe the internal and external standards of performance required to meet or exceed customer expectations.

Service Guarantee: A meaningful customer statement that represents an investment in customer satisfaction and loyalty. To be effective, the guarantee must be unconditional, meaningful, and easy to invoke, collect on, understand, and communicate.

Services: Activities provided to customers.

Share of Pocket: The proportion of the consumers'/customers' potential and current buying power that you currently own.

Silos: Artificial barriers put up between departments to avoid interaction and divert responsibility.

Statistical Process Control (SPC): The application of statistical techniques for measuring and analyzing the variation in processes. It includes four of the basic statistical quality tools: design of experiments, control charts, characterization, and sampling.

Strategic Alliance/Partnership: A term used to describe how a supplier and a customer work together to establish agreement on input and desired output/deliverable.

Supplier: An individual or organization that supplies inputs needed to generate a product, service, or information to a customer.

System Audit: A documented activity performed to verify, by examination and evaluation of objective evidence, that applicable elements of the system are suitable and have been developed, documented, and effectively implemented in accordance with specified requirements.

Total Quality Management: The integration of quality and management methods, practices, concepts, and beliefs into the culture of the organization to bring about continuous improvement.

TQM: A structured approach for managing a business to achieve the best results. A management approach by which, at every level and in every department every day, a culture of continuous improvement exists to meet or exceed customer expectations by establishing systems that suggest a continuous improvement culture.

Value: The worth or usefulness to customers of a product or service.

Value-Added: A task or activity whose output a customer is willing to purchase.

Values: The understanding and expectations that describe how the company's people behave and upon which all business relationships are based (e.g., trust, support, and truth).

Vision; Depicts how the organization will look after the change process is complete. It provides a picture of the results of successful change. Typically includes performance measures and targets that can be used to determine whether the vision has been achieved.

Visioning Workshop: A work method in which a group of people is facilitated in using brainstorming techniques to envision a changed organization.

Workflow: A group of tasks linked by matching inputs with outputs. A process can be made up of one or several workflows.

World Class: The best in the world in a particular category, activity, or process.

Appendix

MOTOROLA'S T.C.S. TEAM COMPETITION CRITERIA

Project Selection   10 Points

This project must be clearly tied to Motorola's key initiatives and should deal with specific customer input, including customer metrics.

Projects should be within the span of control and capability of the team. To enhance the sense of achievement, projects should be of 3 to 13 months duration, or a discrete phase of a larger project, carried out primarily in the current year.

Group interaction in the project selection must be demonstrated, with emphasis on the methodology and criteria used.

Presentations should provide evidence of:

- The criteria and methodology used in arriving at the selection;
- Identification of the customer and a clear understanding of their needs;
- The project's linkage to the customer needs and its linkage to the key initiatives;

- Specific and aggressive goals including expected results and timetables and taking into account customer-generated metrics, commensurate with the team's capability;
- Group interactions used in the project selection.
- Customer, as used throughout this document can mean the external customer who buys Motorola products or the internal Motorola customer to whom you provide product or service.

Teamwork   10 Points

Teamwork, cooperation, and assuming ownership drives the improvement process. The team should be capable of handling the total project, from selection and analysis, all the way through implementation of the remedy. This includes taking the initiative to form teams and a willingness to seek and adapt expertise from outside the team when needed.

Teams may be functional or cross-functional and permanent or ad hoc, as appropriate for the project. Participation of customers and/or suppliers on the team is encouraged. All members are expected to contribute to all phases of the project.

Presentations should provide evidence of:

- The process of team formation and a team structure that recognizes the scope of the project;
- Team skills and experience that support the goals of the project;
- Team participation that demonstrates commitment to the project;
- Significant contribution to the project by all the team members;
- Timely and effective search and adaptation of expertise from outside the team if needed;
- An understanding of team dynamics that demonstrates mutual respect, good communication and methodology for achieving consensus and resolving conflict.

Analysis Techniques   20 Points

The team's selection of analytical techniques will vary with its range of experience and the nature of the project. The techniques selected should support an analytical process appropriate for the project, should lead to the root cause, should identify alternative solutions, and should reflect innovation in the use of analytical tools, and/or new analytical tools and methodologies.

Presentations should provide evidence of:

- Benchmarking of best practices to give scope to the project;
- Mapping of the "as is" and "should be" processes, if applicable;
- The use of fundamental analytical tools such as brainstorming, cause-and-effect diagrams, and pareto charts;
- The use of more specific quantitative tools where applicable, e.g., histograms, scatter diagrams, control charts, design of experiments;
- Innovation in the use of analytical tools (quality function deployment, total cycle time management, design of experiments, product development assessment, or others) commensurate with the team's capabilities;
- Growth of the team's knowledge and skill with the analysis tools.

Remedies   20 Points

The team should substantiate its choice of remedies from among the alternative solutions examined. The team should demonstrate a clear understanding of the difference between remedy and containment in its use of these approaches.

Remedies should demonstrate enhancements or improvements to the project. Creative and innovative solutions that advance the "state of the art" of the project should be especially noted.

Remedies should be consistent with the analysis. Implementation should be complete, including all necessary training and documentation.

Presentations should provide evidence of:

- The pros and cons of alternative solutions examined;
- Containment, if used, as a temporary solution only. A permanent solution should include prevention;
- Thoroughness of implementation;
- Innovation in the remedies of their implementation.

Results   20 Points

Teams should report results compared to the original goals and customer requirements. Significant ancillary effects may result from the solutions as well and should be noted.

The degree of achievement of the goals compared to the amount of "reach out" aggressiveness in the original goals will be considered by the judges.

Presentations should provide evidence of:

- Results that reflect the project goals, including the customer's expectations and metrics;
- Identification of ancillary effects resulting from the solution;
- Verified and documented results, accurately reflected.

Institutionalization 15 *Points*

Institutionalization requires that improvement is maintainable over time. This may have elements of organization change, written process changes, equipment improvements, material changes, etc. Training alone does not generally institutionalize a process. Institutionalization of improvement beyond the original work group is important. Teams should adapt solutions from other teams and actively spread their success story across Motorola. As a result of completing the project, the team should have advanced in understanding and application of the problem solving and continuous improvement processes. Teams should emerge as leaders in their own right and be willing to offer consulting assistance.

Presentations should provide evidence of:

- Actions taken to ensure the improvement is sustainable over time;
- Adaptation of solutions from other teams;
- Communications and/or adaptation of solutions in other parts of Motorola;
- The team's growth in understanding and application of the problem solving and continuous improvement growth.

Presentation 5 *Points*

Presentation can score up to 5 points on its own merit; however any number of points can be deducted from teams running over the 12-minute limit. The team will lose one point for each minute or fraction of a minute they run over the 12-minute limit.

Presentations should be clean and concise, using the 12-minute time limit skilfully. It is important to clearly communicate the data requested in the first six competition criteria. Listeners should be able to easily follow the team's thinking through the entire process.

Overhead graphs and charts used in the presentation should be clear and easy to read and should highlight the key information the team wishes to convey.

It is recognized that presentation styles will vary according to country and custom. Presentations should be made in the style most comfortable for the team. Judging is based on the content of the presentation, not showpersonship.

Presentations should provide evidence of:

- Careful preparation of the presentation material to provide maximum impact within the time and the visual aids allowed;
- The absence of spurious information that consumes time and does not add to the content;
- Use of props, skits, costumes, etc., may be used by the team if desired. If used, they should enhance the presentation, but not detract from the content itself.

Bibliography/ Footnote

Chapter 3
Page 40: David Carr and Henry Johansson. *Best Practices in Reengineering.*
Page 41: Coopers & Lybrand. *TQM Quarterly* (Winter/Spring 1993).
Page 45: Coopers & Lybrand. *TQM Quarterly* (Winter/Spring 1992).
Page 51: John C. Kenny. *Executive Report On Customer Satisfaction* (May 10, 1994).
Page 56: John C. Kenny. *Executive Report On Customer Satisfaction* (May 30, 1994).

Chapter 4
Page 82: *Executive Report On Customer Satisfaction* (Sept 30, 1994).

Chapter 5
Page 119: Christina Luik. Coopers & Lybrand Centre for Excellence in Customer Satisfaction.
Page 121: Scott Stratman. *Executive Report On Customer Satisfaction* (Nov. 1994).

Chapter 6
Page 141: Glenn Parker. "Cross-Functional Teams," *Executive Report On Customer Satisfaction* (Aug.15, 1994).
Page 143: Trine Aanensen Lyman. *Executive Report On Customer Satisfaction* (Aug. 15, 1994).

Page 151: Barry Wittacker. *CMA Magazine* (April 1993).
Page 153: Lou Holtz. "The Importance of Taking a Coaching Perspective - Success" (Dec. 1994).
Page 159: Ian Littman. The Centre of Excellence and Change Management. *Quality Insights,* (Arlington, VA: April 1994).

Chapter 7
Page 183: *Executive Report On Customer Satisfaction* (Aug. 15, 1994).
Page 185: *INC. Magazine* (Jan. 1995).
Page 186: Half International Survey. *Performance Magazine* (March 1995).

Chapter 8
Page 223: International Customer Association. "Customer Service Benchmarking Study" 1994.

Footnote
[1] Mike Herrington, "What Does a Customer Want?" *Across The Board* (April 1993), p. 104.

Index